The
North
Highlands
of Scotland Guide Book

by Charles Tait

*This book has been produced with help from His Royal Highness
The Prince Charles, Duke of Rothesay's North Highland Initiative.*

*Launched in 2005, the North Highland Initiative was created by
His Royal Highness to enhance and develop the economy, the environment and the culture of the North Highlands through its quality
produce, tourism and built environment.*

*This guide is associated with the environment and tourism elements
of the North Highland Initiative.*

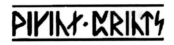

ISBN-13   978-0-9517859-6-6

"I have given you the trouble of walking to this spot, Captain Waverley, both because I thought the scenery would interest you, and because a Highland song would suffer still more from my imperfect translation, were I to introduce it without its wild and appropriate accompaniments. To speak in the poetical language of my country, the seat of the Celtic muse is in the midst of the secret and solitary hill, and her voice in the murmur of the mountain stream. He who woos her must love the barren rock more than the fertile valley, and the solitude of the desert better than the festivity of the hall."

Sir Walter Scott, *Waverley*

The North Highlands Guide Book
First Edition
copyright Charles Tait 2009
Published by Charles Tait Photographic
Kelton, St Ola, Orkney KW15 1TR
Tel 01856 873738 Fax 01856 875313
charles.tait@zetnet.co.uk
www.charles-tait.co.uk

Text, design and layout copyright Charles Tait, all photographs copyright Charles Tait unless otherwise credited, old photographs from Charles Tait collection.
OS maps reproduced from Ordnance Survey mapping with permission of the Controller of HMSO, Crown Copyright Reserved 100035677
Printing by Kina Italia/L.E.G.O.

ISBN-13   978-0-9517859-6-6

Front cover: (Clockwise from top left) Duncansby Stacks, Red Deer, Sango Sands, Houstry Standing Stone, Eilean Donan Castle, Loch Fleet from the Mound, Torridon from the south.
This page: Sunset over Loch Fleet from the Mound, Sutherland

The
North
Highlands
of Scotland Guide Book

by Charles Tait

Katanes, Gallaibh, Caithness
Sudrland, Cataibh, Sutherland
Ros, Siorrachd Rois, Ross-shire

This book is dedicated to my foster-mother, Susie Rosie and to Rob and Helen Maclennan of Ham

The North Highlands from Blau's 17th century Atlas

HOW TO USE THIS GUIDE

This book is designed to help visitors find their way around the North Highlands of Scotland. The detailed introduction covers many aspects of natural history, archaeology, history and culture of the area and is followed with a gazetteer which describes each county and district in turn.

COUNTRYSIDE CODE

We are justly proud of our historic sites, wildlife and environment. Please help ensure that future visitors may enjoy them as much as you by observing these guidelines:

1. Always use stiles and gates, and close gates after you.
2. Always ask permission before entering agricultural land.
3. Keep to paths and take care to avoid fields of grass and crops.
4. Do not disturb livestock.
5. Take your litter away with you and do not light fires.
6. Do not pollute water courses or supplies.
7. Never disturb nesting birds.
8. Do not pick wild flowers or dig up plants.
9. Drive and park with care and attention - do not obstruct or endanger others.
10. Always take care near cliffs and beaches - particularly with children and pets. Many beaches are dangerous for swimmers.
11. Walkers should take adequate clothes, wear suitable footwear and tell someone of their plans.
12. Above all please respect the life of the countryside - leave only footprints, take only photographs and pleasant memories.

Notice: Whilst most of the sites of interest in this guide are open to the public and have marked access, many are on private land. No right of access is implied in the description, and if in doubt it is always polite to ask. Also, while many roads and tracks are rights of way, not all are.

MAPS AND BOOKS NORTH HIGHLANDS

This guide book includes 1:250,000 Ordnance Survey maps covering the whole of the North Highlands. These are placed regularly throughout to help navigation. Each area also has a smaller scale map to locate and describe it.

Many sites of interest have Ordnance Survey grid reference included and it is assumed that visitors will be using the relevant 1:50,000 Landranger Series or 1:25,000 Explorer Series maps. Ordnance Survey maps of the North Highlands are listed in the Bibliography at the end of the book.

A GPS and compass are recommended, especially when heading into remote regions. The use of a GPS to geotag digital images will be found very useful later when identifying images. Even those familiar with mountains and glens can make errors!

Suggested reading is included in the Bibliography. Local bookshops, information centres and shops stock books related to the area as well as many small booklets, brochures and other publications of interest. VisitScotland produces information about accommodation providers, visitor attractions, services and activities annually.

www.visitscotland.com

CONTENTS

INTRODUCTION

Welcome to the North Highlands	6
A Tour of the Main Sites	8
Natural Environment	10
Geology	12
Climate	18
Habitats	20
Birds	28
Flora	44
Fauna	60
Archaeology, History & Culture	72
Neolithic	74
Bronze Age	78
Iron Age	80
Picts	84
Vikings	90
Early Churches	100
Castles	104
17th and 18th Centuries	106
19th Century	108
Herring Boom	112
20th Century	114
Language and Placenames	118

GAZETTEER

Caithness	122
North Coast - Reay to Thurso	124
North Coast to Duncansby	141
John o'Groats to Wick	158
Wick to The Ord	168
East Sutherland	188
Helmsdale to Golspie	190
Loch Fleet NNR	202
Rogart, Lairg & Bonar Bridge	206
Dornoch & the Dornoch Firth	216

Easter Ross	222
Struie Hill to Tain	224
Tarbat Peninsula	228
Cromarty Firth	236
Dingwall & Strathpeffer	240
Black Isle	248
South Coast	250
Cromarty	256
North Coast	260
Wester Ross	266
Kintail & Lochalsh	268
Plockton & Loch Carron	272
Applecross	278
Torridon to Ben Eighe	280
Loch Maree	286
Gairloch to Little Loch Broom	290
Loch Broom & Ullapool	300
Coigach & Achiltibuie	308
West Sutherland	316
NW Highlands Geopark	318
Assynt	320
Lochinver & Stoer Peninsula	328
Kylesku to Scourie	334
Handa to Kinlochbervie	336
North Sutherland	344
Cape Wrath & Durness	346
Eriboll to Tongue	354
Bettyhill to Melvich	362
The Flow Country	368
Reference Section	374
Travel	374
Services	378
Advertisers	382
A Trip to Orkney	384
Bibliography	392
Index	396

ACKNOWLEDGEMENTS

During the years of work on the research, photography, design and production of *The North Highlands Guide Book* many people, books, websites, publications and bodies have been consulted. The author would like to thank everyone for their assistance. In particular, thanks are due to Magnus, Thorfinn, Papa, Sandra and Muriel.

Thank you to the following people for permission to reproduce their work - Laurie Campbell, Adam Ward, Shona McMillan, Iain Sarjeant, Hugh Harrop, Richard Jones, Debby Snook and Julia Willmott.

WELCOME TO THE NORTH HIGHLANDS

Torridon in Wester Ross from the south

Welcome to the North Highlands of Scotland. This vast landscape encompasses the former shires of Caithness, Sutherland and Ross & Cromarty. It covers 5,200 miles^2 (13,500 km^2) and had a total population of just over 87,000 in 2001. The main inhabited areas are Easter Ross and Caithness, which means that the population density in much of the area is very low.

This is a region of natural contrasts, caused for the most part by its complex geology. Much of Easter Ross and the Black Isle is fertile farmland, mostly given over to cereals. To the north, Caithness is gentle, rolling, green and fertile cattle grazing country.

The north and west coasts are rugged with many inlets and are backed by high mountains. Here, crofting, forestry and fishing are predominant with small, scattered settlements. Inland the population is sparse although this was not always so. The empty glens of Kildonan, Strath Halladale and Strath Naver are testament to what we would now call economic development.

Today the whole area, together with Inverness-shire and Skye, is administered by the Highland Council. However, the former counties still very much exist in the minds of the inhabitants and are therefore referred to in this book. The gazetteer follows a sunwise trail around the North Highlands which can be joined at any point.

Access by road (A9, A96 or A82) is via (mostly) single-carriageway roads, which can be very busy and slow. There are rail links via Inverness to Wick, Thurso and Kyle of

Sango Bay, Durness in the far northwest of Sutherland

Lochalsh. A wide range of connections are available from Inverness Airport and there is also an airport at Wick.

Ptolemy's 2nd century AD map is perhaps the first written reference to the North Highlands, and names several headlands and rivers. The oldest archaeological evidence dates from 8,000 years ago, in Applecross.

Ben Loyal near Tongue in Sutherland is one of the most iconic mountains in Scotland

Although the area has many interesting archaeological sites to visit and there are several prime visitor attractions, most people come to experience the natural beauty and diversity of the landscapes. Many places of interest are described, some iconic, others less well known. It is hoped that users of this guide will enjoy their visits to the North Highlands of Scotland as much as the author does.

Portmahomack is a delightful little village in Easter Ross

Ardvreck Castle in Assynt had a turbulent history

The Old Red Sandstone Stacks of Duncansby in Caithness

A Tour of Some of the Main Sites

The North Highlands has a vast range of archaeological and historic sites to visit. The first people to arrive left scant trace, mainly mounds of shells and some flint knives and scrapers. This is enough evidence to know when they were there and what they ate, but little else.

The Neolithic Grey Cairns of Camster in Caithness

The first farmers arrived in the Neolithic Age. They built several hundred chambered cairns for their dead, mainly sited in fertile valleys where these people settled and grew grain and grass. They also kept cattle, sheep and pigs.

Achavanich Stone Setting in Caithness

There was plenty of good timber here, so houses and farm buildings were usually built of wood. They did, however, build stone circles and alignments as well as erect many solitary monoliths.

Bronze Age settlement remains, including hut circles, burial cairns and field walls are scattered on hillsides and in glens. No doubt further ruins lie hidden under the peat.

Dun Dornaigil Broch stands below Ben Hope in north Sutherland

During the Iron Age sweeping changes took place. Large round buildings which we call brochs or duns were built all over the North Highlands, especially in the fertile areas. These people were farmers and fishermen as well as expert stonemasons who used iron tools and weapons.

Varrich Castle overlooks the Kyle of Tongue

The Romans were the first people to describe the Picts.

Many Pictish symbol stones have been found, mostly in Easter Ross, East Sutherland and Caithness. Evidence of several monastic sites and ancient chapels show that Christianity came early to the North Highlands.

The *Orkneyinga Saga* and Irish Annals describe many events in medieval times. Monasteries were sacked and bishops were killed but cathedrals were also built, notably at Dornoch which has the only intact 13th century church in the North Highlands. A much larger cathedral once stood at Fortrose but it was demolished for its lead, stone and timber.

After the 1745 Jacobite rebellion and its defeat at Culloden, the Government was forced to placate and control what they saw as the lawless Highlanders. The ancient traditions of clan life were seen as anachronistic and many people either emigrated to North America voluntarily, or were cleared from their ancestral lands.

Late in the 19th century, developments in harbours and fishing technology led to the Herring Boom which ended in collapse due to overfishing. In the 20th century an experimental fast breeder reactor was built at Dounreay. The site is now being decommissioned but remains at the forefront of nuclear technology.

There are many fine Pictish symbol stones in the area

Dornoch Cathedral is the finest church in the North Highlands

Dunrobin Castle near Golspie

20th century nuclear research at Dounreay

Natural Environment

In addition to the vast range of archaeological and historic sites, the North Highlands offer a great variety of natural attractions. The complex geology makes for an interesting and beautiful landscape of mountains, lochs, rivers, moorland, bogs and fertile farmland.

Brora Beach is one of many lovely sandy shores backed by extensive sand dunes

The coast has everything from sheltered sandy coves and wonderful long sandy beaches with dunes and machair to some of the highest cliffs in Britain. Most are easily accessible, but others such as Sandwood Bay and Cape Wrath take some effort to reach. This only enhances the sense of achievement in reaching them.

Each of the mountains in the North Highlands is unique, carved from ancient rocks by erosion. Wind, ice, water, glaciers, rivers and sunshine have all played their part in breaking down the metamorphic and sedimentary rocks into the landscape of today. In addition to the elements, plants, animals and humans have contributed to the shaping of the surface scenery.

Cape Wrath is one of the most remote places in Britain

From the North Highlands, rivers flow into the North Sea and the Atlantic Ocean. In the west they are short and usually run into deep sea lochs through glacier carved valleys. Those that flow to the north and east tend to be longer and run into shallow firths. Many are famous for their Salmon and Sea Trout fisheries.

The mountain of Suilven dominates Lochinver

Waterfalls are very much a feature, from the impressive but small Falls of Shin, where Salmon may be seen leaping, to the dramatic and high Falls of Glomach. Most take

Salmon may be seen jumping at the Falls of Shin

a strenuous walk to reach, but on the right day it is worth the effort. Until medieval times, most of the Highlands were covered in forests of mature Scots Pine, while Oakwoods dominated in some areas. Many of these trees were used to make charcoal or cut down for timber. The largely bare landscape of today is maintained by grazing ungulates, mostly Sheep and Red Deer, which prevent regeneration of trees.

Stac Pollaidh in Coigach is verdant green

Another prominent feature of the North Highland landscape is the extensive bogs, marshland and moorland epitomized by the Flow Country. In these areas deep peat has built up. Lochs and pools develop in the hollows and hummocks are drier. The effect is to create a special habitat which supports a diverse range of wildlife.

Solitary Scots Pine at Loch Maree - an area once covered in Pinewood and Oakwood

In former times access to most of the North Highlands was easier by boat, which partially explains the lack of inland settlement. The building of Military Roads in the 18th century was for the purpose of control by the Government, not economic development. In the 19th century, landowners such as the Duke of Sutherland and the Caithness Sinclairs, as well as bodies such as the British Fisheries Society, invested heavily in harbours and planned settlements.

The moorland, lochs and mountains of the north are unique

Kylesku Bridge somehow merges its 20th century concrete into the ancient landscape

In the 20th century, wars and attempted industrial development brought heavy investment in services housing and infrastructure. However, the population has remained stubbornly low and, unlike in other areas, the impact of humans also remains minimal.

11

The Moine Thrust at Loch Glencoul, West Sutherland

GEOLOGY The highly varied and often spectacular scenery of the North Highlands is markedly influenced by the complex geology of the area.

Lewisian Gneiss forms the basement, but is only exposed to the west of the Moine Thrust. These ancient Precambrian rocks were formed deep in the Earth between about 2,900 and 1,700Ma (million years ago).

By about 1,000Ma, as a result of erosion and uplift, these gneisses were exposed as the land surface. Today they give a rocky, ice-smoothed landscape, studded with lochans, which is very typical of north Sutherland.

Torridonian Sandstone was laid down between 1,000 and 750Ma as beds of red sandstone, conglomerate and grey shales up to 7km deep. The

steep sided mountains of the northwest have been formed by erosion of these hard sandstone beds. Applecross, Torridon and Coigach are typical such landscapes.

Moine Succession East of the Moine Thrust another deep succession of sandstones and shales was deposited and later, about 750Ma, was metamorphosed deep within the Earth's crust. A rolling, rather featureless landscape of hills, peatbogs and lochans results. This forms most of the interior of the area.

Cambrian Quartzite, Shales and Limestones were laid down in a shallow ocean near the coast. Many of the mountains of the west are capped by Quartzite, which shine brightly in the sun. The Limestone outcrops at Elphin, Inchnadamph and Durness create havens of green grass and wild flowers.

Caledonian Orogeny In the Ordovician about 500Ma a huge continental collision resulted in the formation of a huge mountain range called the Caledonides. The rocks were deformed and some were metamorphosed deep in the Earth.

Moine Thrust During the Caledonian Orogeny Moine rocks were pushed or thrusted westwards over younger rocks to form the Moine Thrust Zone. This runs from the east of Loch Eriboll to Sleat in Skye. The North West Highlands Geopark covers the northern part of this zone.

Old Red Sandstone (Devonian) was laid down in thick beds as the Caledonides were eroded. This sandstone covers most of Caithness, the east coast of Sutherland and Easter Ross, including the Black Isle. The landscape is rolling and soils are fertile.

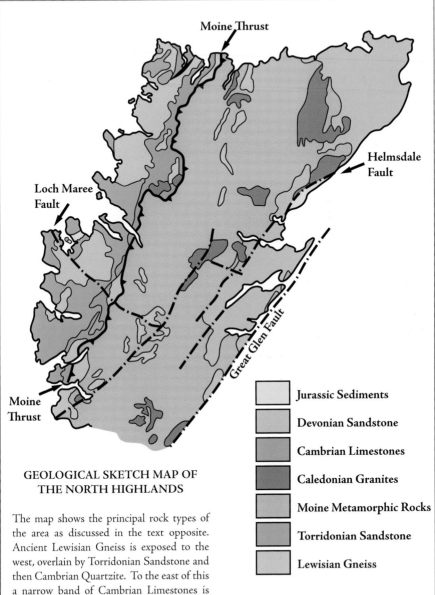

British Geological Survey

Moine Thrust

Helmsdale Fault

Loch Maree Fault

Moine Thrust

Great Glen Fault

Jurassic Sediments

Devonian Sandstone

Cambrian Limestones

Caledonian Granites

Moine Metamorphic Rocks

Torridonian Sandstone

Lewisian Gneiss

GEOLOGICAL SKETCH MAP OF THE NORTH HIGHLANDS

The map shows the principal rock types of the area as discussed in the text opposite. Ancient Lewisian Gneiss is exposed to the west, overlain by Torridonian Sandstone and then Cambrian Quartzite. To the east of this a narrow band of Cambrian Limestones is exposed.

The Moine Thrust runs from Loch Eriboll to Sleat in Skye and Moine rocks extend eastwards until met by Devonian Sandstones on the east coast, along with later Jurassic layers.

Faults include the Great Glen Fault, which forms the east coast of the Black Isle and of the Fearn Peninsula and the Helmsdale Fault, which runs inland from near Helmsdale to near Golspie. The pre-Torridonian Loch Maree Fault runs north-west along the loch.

Lewisian Gneiss and intrusions, Oldshoremore

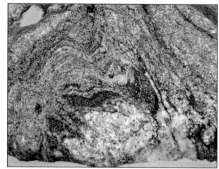

Lewisian Gneiss. Oldshoremore

Torridonian Sandstone beds, Loch Torridon

Torridonian Sandstone beds, Rubha Reidh, Gairloch

Crystallized Limestone, Durness

Limestone. Inchnadamph, Assynt

Contorted rocks, Portgower, Helmsdale, Sutherland

Red Sandstone at Tarbatness

Lewisian Gneiss and contortions

Torridonian Sandstone

Cambrian Quartzite, Beinn Eighe

Cambrian Quartzite, Ben Mor Assynt

Moine Thrust at Knockan Crag

Twisted rocks, Knockan Crag, Assynt

Jurassic rocks, Brora, Sutherland

Raised beach south of Helmsdale

Stromatolites at Balnakeil Bay, Durness, Sutherland

Fucoid Beds, Loch Assynt

Pipe Rock, Loch Assynt

Jurassic period rocks were laid down in shallow seas. Sandstone, limestone and shale beds accumulated. The Brora coal seams and offshore North Sea Oil date from this time, while the Helmsdale Boulder Bed, best seen at Portgower, is of a slightly later date.

FOSSILS can be found in several places in the North Highlands. Pipe Rock and Fucoid Beds are found in Torridonian Sandstone beds and may be seen in road cuttings beside Loch Assynt. The Old Red Sandstones and Flagstones of Caithness are famous for their abundant fish fossils. Examples may be seen in Caithness Horizons in Thurso, and quarry waste at Achanarras can be investigated for possible fossils.

Jurassic rocks on the coast at Helmsdale, Brora, below Dunrobin Castle as well as at Balintore and Eathie on the Black Isle hold many plant and animal fossils. These range from tropical plants to corals, ammonites, molluscs and other marine animals.

Queenie Scallop fossil, Brora

Ammonites, Cromarty

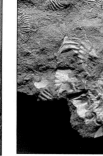

Examination of rocks on these shorelines will soon reveal examples of fossils. Perhaps one of the most interesting sites is at Balnakeil Bay, Durness below the golf course. Here some of the oldest-known living organisms have left their fossil remains. Stromatolites are formed by Cyanobacteria (Blue-green Algae) and some may date from 3Ma. These ones are perhaps only from 500Ma. Similar organisms still live in Australia.

The Orcadian Stone Company in Golspie is an essential stop for everyone interested in rocks, minerals and fossils. The collection covers 3,000Ma of the geological history of the Earth and includes large numbers of specimens from the North Highlands. The shop has minerals, fossils, books and maps as well as jewellery and Highland stone giftware.

GLACIATION The Ice Ages of the last 100,000 years are evident everywhere, from the ice-smoothed and scratched rocks of the west and north to the smooth contours of much of the area. Glacial erratics are common. These boulders have been carried often long distances by glaciers and then dumped as the ice melted.

Only a few of the higher mountain tops in the west stood out from the ice sheet. By 11,000BC most of the ice had gone, although there was

Fallen Stack of Portgower, near Helmsdale

a further advance around 9,000BC when glaciers again formed. Soon after, the climate warmed rapidly and all the ice melted.

MAJOR FAULTS The Great Glen and Helmsdale faults are very apparent in the landscape. The former created the straight coastlines of the Black Isle and the Fearn Peninsula. This fault extends south through the Great Glen and north to Shetland. The latter fault can be traced just inland from Helmsdale to the Dornoch Firth. Another interesting fault formed Loch Maree in Wester Ross. During the Ice Age it was then carved out by a large glacier.

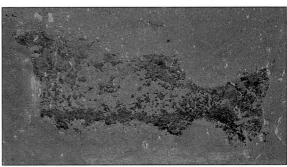

Cheirolepus trailli from Caithness

Ostreolepus Macrolepidotus from Caithness

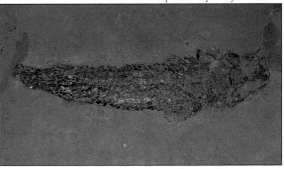

NATURAL ENVIRONMENT

Midsummer sunset over Torrisdale Bay, Bettyhill, Sutherland

Snow covering the hills at Strath More, Sutherland

have a very pleasant microclimate. However, winters can be colder with frost and snow most years.

The North Highland Watershed lies to the east of the Moine Thrust. As a result the rivers which run to the west coast are short and usually debouch into sea lochs such as Loch Broom.

In contrast, the northern and eastern rivers are nearly all much longer. In most cases they flow through systems of lochans and lochs which are navigable by Salmon and Sea Trout. In several instances they have major estuaries such as the Cromarty and Dornoch Firths.

CLIMATE The climate of the North Highlands varies greatly from west to east. The west coast with its high mountains and exposure to weather coming from the Atlantic has relatively high rainfall, but is mild all year. As a result snow lies only briefly except on the higher slopes. The success of Inverewe and other gardens

where a wide range of plants thrive despite the latitude attests to effects of the North Atlantic Slope Current.

By contrast, the east coast is much drier, but has a wider range of annual temperature. The growing season is much longer, especially in the Black Isle and Easter Ross which

Purple Saxifrage flowers in February, Sutherland

Laurie Campbell

Soft Autumn rain on a spider's web

BEST TIME TO VISIT

This depends on expectations and the purpose of the trip. July and August are peak months for visitors but not necessarily the best time to come. Out of season offers advantages but many visitor attractions and remoter hotels are shut in winter.

Broom at Loch Fleet, Sutherland in early summer

Spring arrives earlier in Ross-shire than further north, with wild flowers in the woods, clear days and quiet roads. This is a good time for birds too, as migrants prepare to head north and breeders start to return. Snow can still fall in March, creating ephemeral Narnia landscapes.

Summer mist at the Grey Cairns of Camster, Caithness

Summer In May and June many wild flowers are at their best and birds are active with breeding. These are also two of the best months for fine weather and less midgies. July can often be damp with mist and rain. During August the hills and moors glow with the purple of flowering heather.

Autumn September can be beautiful, with harvest in the east, hills still green and purple and quiet roads. Later, and into October, is the best time to see migrant birds on their way back from their breeding grounds. Autumn colours are at their best then before storms strip the trees.

Autumn colours at the Mound, Sunderland

Midwinter sunrise at Duncansby Stacks, Caithness

Winter November is perhaps best avoided but December to February can be lovely when a large high may give fine settled weather, perhaps after snow.

Torridon in early autumn

WILDLIFE The flora and fauna of the North Highlands are the result of the geology, climate and actions of people, birds, plants and animals since the end of the Ice Age over 10,000 years ago. The various soil types resulting from the underlying rocks, glacial till and blown sand would have soon received seeds carried by wind, sea and birds. As a result, when man first arrived the land was covered with a mixture of grassland, heather moorland, woodland and scrub.

With the arrival of the Neolithic farmers the vegetation on the better land was slowly altered as they planted crops and kept animals such as sheep, cattle and pigs. Seaweed and the contents of the midden were used in quantity to improve the soil on the good land which was used for crops of cereal and hay for winter keep.

Clearance of woodland and scrub for grazing would have slowly modified the vegetation on more marginal areas.

Regeneration was largely impeded by domestic animals and deer. A combination of geology, grazing and climate variation resulted in the development of many of the blanket peat bogs of today.

HABITATS The North Highlands has a diverse range of habitats for plants and animals. These include coastal, lowland, agricultural, wetlands, rivers, lochs, woodland and montane areas. Only in the east is much of the landscape agricultural. Most of

Oykel Bridge and autumn colours

Rogart autumn colours

the rest of the area remains covered by semi natural vegetation. The very long and varied coastline includes saltmarshes, intertidal zones, beaches, sand dunes, machair, sheltered bays and long sea lochs, sea blasted coastal areas and cliffs.

In the agricultural areas there are permanent pasture, cultivated fields, field edges, verges and ditches, as well as areas of waste ground and patches of scrub and woodland. The lower lying parts of Easter Ross and the Black Isle are very fertile and produce a great deal of crops, including barley, wheat and oilseed rape. Caithness and East Sutherland are less intensively farmed, with mostly grassland for cattle and sheep.

Sadly, very little remains of the ancient Caledonian oak and pine woods, which were variously cleared by farmers, used for ship building, or burnt to make charcoal for iron making. Finally they were cut down to make ammunition boxes in WW1. Attempts at regeneration are in progress in several places today.

The lower hills are dominated by heather moorland and rough heath, while herb and fern communities thrive in valleys, mires, marshes, burns, as well as on lochs and small islands. Much of the area is montane even at low altitude due to exposure and soil fertility and includes heathland, scrub and wetlands.

Loch Assynt, Sutherland, relict Sots Pines on islets

Adam Ward

Ben Mor Assynt with Quartzite scree on the summit, Assynt, Sutherland

Flow Country, Strath Halladale, Sutherland

Heather in flower, Kildonan, Sutherland

Natural Environment

The many attractive beaches are varied, with everything from tiny coves to expansive stretches of sand. In places they are backed by extensive sand dunes and machair. Oldshoremore, Sandwood Bay, Durness, Torrisdale Bay, Dunnet Sands, Sannick Bay and Brora are some of the best to visit.

Sandwood Bay, West Sutherland

There are dramatic cliffs, especially where the rocks are sandstone. Some of the most spectacular are on Handa Island, at Cape Wrath, Dunnet Head and Duncansby Head. Many seabirds breed on these cliffs in early summer, while the clifftops are a riot of colour from the wild flowers.

Duncansby Head, Caithness - winter sunrise

Sea inlets range from huge deep sea lochs in the west and north such as Loch Torridon, Loch Ewe or Loch Eriboll to the much gentler estuaries of the east including the Beauly, Cromarty and Dornoch Firths, all of which are popular with breeding and migrating waterfowl and waders. The sheltered east coast also supports a more diverse flora.

Autumn scene at Loch Fleet

Saltmarsh at Kishorn

Brackish saltmarshes often form at the head of tidal inlets. They support an interesting range of plants and can be very colourful in summer. They are also popular with waders, which come to feed on the invertebrates present in the mud. High tides during the migration periods are usually the best time to seek out birds here.

Most farming in this area is not very intensive, with the result that there remain many patches of woodland, scrub, hedges, wetland and other cover for birds. These include habitats for a diverse range of plants as well as small animals, insects and other invertebrates.

Strathconon above Maryburgh

Very little croftland is cultivated nowadays. Some cattle (often Highland) are still kept along with much fewer sheep than just a few years ago. As a result there are many lovely meadows, especially where the underlying rock is limestone. Today the chief culprit for overgrazing is the Red Deer.

Caithness flagstone dyke and spring colours

The countless lochs and lochans are home to a variety of aquatic plants as well as Red-throated and Black-throated Divers, many species of ducks and, of course, Brown Trout. The surrounding moorland supports breeding Greenshank, Redshank, Golden Plover and Dunlin. Hen Harriers and Short-eared Owls also breed in these areas.

Whins in flower at Loch Rangag, Caithness

MAIN HABITAT TYPES

Sea, Skerries and Islets
Exposed Cliffs
Low Cliffs and Banks
Beaches & Dunes
Saltmarsh
Maritime Heath
Moorland
Marshes and Bogs
Lochs, Ditches and Burns
Farmland
Roadside verges
Woodland and Gardens

Verdant green over Limestone at Elphin, West Sutherland

Buzzard in characteristic pose

CAITHNESS

Duncansby Head
Ness of Duncansby
Stroma
Dunnet Head
Dunnet Woodland
Dunnet Sands
Thurso River
Loch of Mey
St John's Loch
Loch Watten
Loch Watenan & Warehouse Hill
Freswick Beach and Dunes
Spittal
Achanarras Quarry
Flow Country
Morven
Scaraben
Lybster Harbour & Reisgill Burn
Latheronwheel Harbour & Woodland
Dunbeath Strath
Badbea

EAST SUTHERLAND

Kildonan and Loth
Helmsdale Raised Beach
Portgower Fallen Stack
Brora Coastline
Loch Brora & Carrol Rock
Big Burn, Golspie
Balblair Wood and Littleferry Dunes
Loch Fleet National Nature Reserve
Carbisdale Wood
Falls of Shin
Rogart area
Achany Wood
Ord Hill and Ferry Wood Lairg
Loch Shin
Raven's Rock Gorge
Dornoch and Embo beaches and dunes
Dornoch Firth and Kyle of Sutherland
Fairy Glen, Spinningdale

EASTER ROSS

Struie Hill
Tain Hill
Skelbo Wood
Aldie Burn
Tarbat Ness
Inver tidal mudflats
Fyrinish Woods, Evanton
Nigg Bay Nature Reserve
Tailich, Fearn peninsula
Cromarty Firth west shoreline
Brahan Estate, Maryburgh
Strathconon
Ben Wyvis

THE BLACK ISLE

Chanonry Point
Udale Bay Nature Reserve
Munlochy Bay Nature Reserve
Belmaduthy Dam, Munlochy
Eathie and Cromarty Coastlines
Fairy Glen Nature Reserve, Rosemarkie
Inner Cromarty Firth
Beauly Firth

WESTER ROSS

Knockan Crag
Applecross
Loch Maree Islands, Gairloch
Beinn Eighe NNR
Rassal Ashwood NNR
Torridon
An Teallach
Loch Broom
Beinn Dearg
Summer Isles
Coigach
Isle Ristol, Achiltibuie
Gruinard Bay and Loch Ewe
Loch Kishorn
Loch Carron
Balmacara Estate, Lochalsh
Five Sisters of Kintail
Falls of Glomach
Ratagan Forest
Glenelg

WEST SUTHERLAND

Northwest Highlands Geopark
Suilven
Elphin
Quinag
Stoer Peninsula
Ardvar Woods
Laxford Braes
Handa Island
Loch Glencoul, Kylesku
Assynt area
Ben More Assynt
Inchnadamph Limestone and caves
Inverkirkaig and Falls of Kirkaig
Culag Community Woodland, Lochinver
Loch a'Mhullin, Badcall
Oldshoremore
Sandwood Bay
Foinaven and Arkle
Ben Klibreck

NORTH SUTHERLAND

Durness, Faraid Head
Smoo Cave
Cape Wrath and Clo Mor
The Parph
Whiten Head
Loch Eriboll
Ben Hope
Strath More
Strath Naver
Torrisdale Bay & Invernaver
Ben Loyal
Kyle of Tongue
Borgie Wood
Rosal, Strathnaver
Farr Bay
Strathy Point
Strath Halladale
Melvich
Forsinard Peatlands Nature Reserve
The Flow Country - Peatbogs and lochs

Atlantic Puffins are very numerous on offshore islands

Feeding Most seabirds feed on fish, and cliff nesting species tend to breed in locations where food is plentiful. Where the warm, saline, Atlantic waters meet the colder, less saline but nutrient-laden waters of the North Sea, there are ideal conditions for plankton growth. Such conditions pertain around the Pentland Firth in particular.

SEABIRDS breed in many locations around the coast of the North Highlands. The varied habitats include high cliffs and maritime heath especially in the north, areas of sand dunes as well as inland areas of moorland and small offshore islands.

Horizontally bedded sandstone and flagstone cliffs occur at various locations around the coast. These are attractive to many species of seabirds which nest on inaccessible ledges, crevices and burrows, often on small offshore islands. They do this to escape predators, which include rats, gulls, skuas and Peregrines.

Perhaps the best place to see a variety of breeding seabirds is Handa Island, near Scourie in Sutherland which can be reached by a small ferry. There are also a number of good cliff sites in the north of Caithness and Sutherland.

Puffins Just about everyone wants to see Puffins. These entertaining and colourful auks can be seen best on Handa Island, where there are no rats. They also breed on several other islands. Small numbers can be seen on the cliffs to the east of Melvich Bay, at Dunnet Head and at Duncansby Head as well as a number of other locations on the coast.

Many species forage far and wide in search of prey. Gannets breed on offshore islands such as Sule Stack and Sula Sgeir, but may often be seen plunge diving around the

Kittiwake

Razorbill

Great Skua

Guillemot

Fulmar Petrel

Gannets breed on offshore islands and are often seen fishing around the coast

coast. Small fish such as Sandeels are the favourite food of auks, which can dive to over 140m and return with a beakful of little fish. They will also forage far and wide in search of shoals.

Larger pelagic species, like Mackerel and Herring, also hunt Sandeels and other smaller shoaling fish. They in turn attract cetaceans such as Killers or Minke Whales, Risso's or Bottle-nosed Dolphins and Porpoises.

Terns In contrast, terns are surface feeders. They are commonly seen and heard over estuaries and sandy bays diving and screeching. Terns breed on shingly beaches, on sand dunes and links, but are especially fond of maritime heath. They are prone to disturbance and have variable breeding success, depending on food availability and the weather during the critical few days after hatching.

Arctic Tern

Shag

BREEDING SEABIRDS

Fulmar Petrel
Storm Petrel)
Manx Shearwater
Black Guillemot
Guillemot
Razorbill
Puffin
Greater Black-backed Gull
Herring Gull
Lesser Black-backed Gull
Common Gull
Black-headed Gull
Kittiwake
Arctic Tern
Common Tern
Sandwich Tern
Little Tern
Cormorant
Shag
Great Skua
Arctic Skua
Eider Duck

WHERE TO SEE BREEDING SEABIRDS

CAITHNESS

Duncansby Head
Dunnet Head
Stroma

SUTHERLAND

Melvich Bay to Strathy Point
Whiten Head
Faraid Head
Cape Wrath and Clo Mor
Handa Island
Stoer cliffs
Loch Fleet
Dornoch Firth

ROSS-SHIRE

Summer Isles
Cromarty Firth
Inner Moray Firth

Golden Eagle

White-tailed Sea Eagle

Laurie Campbell

any of the rest survive. The adults drive off the young before winter. The 25% or so which reach the breeding age of about four years may survive and breed for a further ten.

Golden Eagles are most commonly seen in remote parts of the west and north but they also do come east. Over 400 pairs breed in the Highlands. GPS tracking is now being used to study their behaviour. Hunting is by surprise attack on Rabbits, Hares, Red Grouse, Ptarmigan or even seagulls. They also consume a large amount of carrion.

The White-tailed Sea Eagle and the Osprey, both of which catch fish for much of their diet, pay less attention to people. Both were shot to extinction in the early 20th century. The former was reintroduced from Norway in 1975 and later and is now firmly re-established in Skye, Rum, Mull and Wester Ross.

With its huge 8 foot wingspan, yellowish white head and white tail the White-tailed Sea Eagle is unmistakeable. It resembles and behaves like its relative the American Bald Eagle.

The Osprey is a migratory species and eventually returned on its own, first breeding again at Loch Garten in 1954. They now breed at several locations and may regularly be seen fishing at Loch Fleet, the Beauly Firth, Loch

RAPTORS The North Highlands are home to several species of birds of prey, all of which may be observed by being in the right place at the right time. They range from the majestic Golden Eagle to the tiny, fast flying Merlin.

All of the smaller species, including Buzzards, perch on objects such as fence posts, electric poles and may be observed by using the car as a hide. Golden Eagles are most commonly seen soaring over mountain ridges and remote areas, and are very wary of humans.

Golden Eagles usually build their nests on cliffs or trees in high and remote areas, but they have been known to breed near houses on the coast beside an airport. They are at their most spectacular and least timid in early spring when they perform their dramatic tumbling courtship displays and upside down prey transfers.

Eyries may be used for many years and can be quite large, at least 2m or more across. Up to four eggs are laid, but the first chick aggressively ejects its younger siblings so that in only about 20% of broods do

Shin or similar places where Salmon or Sea Trout are present.

Ospreys build their nests in trees and often use artificial platforms. Their distinctive light underwings and faces make them unmistakeable. There are now over 100 Osprey nests in the Highlands. Recently GPS has been used to study their migration routes through Spain to Africa and back.

Red Kite Having been extinct in Scotland since 1879 due to persecution, the Red Kite has been successfully re-introduced from Wales in several areas, including the Black Isle. About thirty pairs now breed in the woods there, and the birds are a common sight as they patrol field margins and ditches.

There has been a very high mortality rate here, initially attributed to persecution. Red Kites are scavengers and very adept at finding dead rodents, such as rats and mice. They are also especially susceptible to some modern rodenticides, which has resulted in the early death of about 30% of all the birds released or bred in recent years.

The birds nest high in trees and raise 1one to three young, depending on food availability. From April to July the male, then both adults, are very active searching for food for the fledglings, making this the best time to observe them.

Laurie Campbell

Red Kite

Golden Eagle

Laurie Campbell

Osprey

Osprey

Laurie Campbell

Meadow Pipits, Grouse and waders.

Hen Harriers have a spectacular sky dancing courtship display in spring when they are quite unconcerned with human spectators. The food pass manoeuvre is particularly amazing. They are most likely to be seen quartering ditches, marshes and lochsides in search of voles.

The Peregrine is the largest British falcon. This powerfully built predator is also the fastest falcon. It can reach 200mph in a stoop. The females are larger than the males, but both are grey above and grey-barred white underneath.

Common Buzzard

The Common Buzzard is perhaps the most common bird of prey in UK. It is often seen perched by the road or soaring overhead. Their preferred territory is moorland or woodland near farmland, where they feed on rodents, worms and small birds.

The Hen Harrier was persecuted to near oblivion but thanks to its stronghold in Orkney has since recovered to a population of over 100 pairs in the North Highlands. This attractive bird breeds on heather and grass moorland and in winter moves to communal roosts on lower ground or the coast.

The adult male is pale grey with black wingtips and a lighter body and rump. The larger female is dark brown on top with a white banded rump and banded brown chest and tail. Their favourite prey is voles, but they also take

They are still persecuted as their favourite prey species is the pigeon. They will take anything from Starlings to Herons, but with Fulmar Petrels they have their match as they cannot cope with their regurgitated fish oil.

Peregrines nest on long held sites on cliffs and quarries, but

Peregrine Falcon

Merlin chicks

Laurie Campbell

Short-eared Owl

Long-eared Owl

Kestrel

will also use high ledges in towns. They may be seen where suitable prey is available and as always are most active when feeding their young. They give themselves away by their high pitched screaming call as well as by their rapid dives into flocks of Pigeons. A cloud of feathers results when a victim is struck.

Merlin The smallest British falcon is also perhaps the most aggressive. It breeds on moorland, where is may be seen flying fast and low in pursuit of Meadow Pipits and other small birds. The male is smaller than the female with a striking blue-grey back with a brown and white streaked

chest. The female is greyish-brown above with a streaked brown chest.

Kestrels are seen hovering over roadside verges in search of voles and insects. They prefer open agricultural land, but also can be seen on the coast and moorland. Kestrels nest on ledges in holes in trees and on the ground.

Short-eared Owls are diurnal and are commonly seen on fence posts. This light-coloured owl has a distinctive flight and usually nests on moorland. They are usually seen patrolling field edges, ditches and moorland for voles, their preferred prey.

Long-eared Owls are usually observed in conifer woods near lowland moors. They often use abandoned crows' nests and they prefer voles but will also take small birds such as House Sparrows. Long-eared Owls are also winter visitors and migrants.

RAPTORS WHICH BREED IN THE NORTH HIGHLANDS

Golden Eagle
White-tailed Eagle
Common Buzzard
Red Kite
Osprey
Peregrine
Hen Harrier
Kestrel
Sparrowhawk
Merlin
Short-eared Owl
Long-eared Owl

Male Hen Harrier

Female Hen Harrier with chicks

Ptarmigan in summer plumage, which turns white in winter

Dotterel nest high up

LANDBIRDS A large selection of passerines breed in, or are migrants, to the North Highlands. The diverse range of habitats means that species absent or hard to see elsewhere may be observed here. Tips are made throughout the gazetteer section.

Montane Ptarmigan and Dotterel breed on the tops but may often be seen lower down. Ring Ouzel breeds in the area as a summer visitor, but is rare in Caithness.

Moorland and Cliffs Red Grouse frequent lower heather moorland, and are more likely to be heard before they are seen. Ravens may be seen anywhere, both inland and on the coast, where carrion is available. Hooded Crows and Jackdaws are common, but Magpies rare.

Streams and Rivers are home to the Dipper, which has an unusual manner of catching invertebrates by walking under water. With its white bib and confident behaviour it is easily observed, especially while the young are being fed. Kingfishers are also present in some places and Grey Wagtails are common.

Woodland Crested Tits, Siskins, Goldcrests and Crossbills may be present in Pinewoods. Capercaillie was formerly quite common, but is now in decline, although they are still occasionally seen in the Black Isle. They are more likely to be heard, or seen

Red Grouse

Stonechat

Wheatear

Rock Pipit

Raven

Ring Ouzel nest in the hills

Laurie Campbell

Dippers feed on insects in streams and rivers

fleetingly crossing the road in woodland. The Black Grouse has become even rarer.

Small Passerines such as Stonechats, Rock Pipits, Skylarks, Meadow Pipits, various warblers, Reed Buntings and Wheatears remain quite common. House Sparrows also continue to thrive.

Rarities Species such as the Corncrake and Corn Bunting, once common, are now rare almost everywhere. The

Corncrake holds on in small numbers around Durness, where the unmistakable *crex*

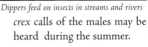

Male Capercaillie displaying - they are rare now in the North Highlands

crex calls of the males may be heard during the summer.

Crested Tits prefer Pinewoods

Laurie Campbell

Reed Bunting

Skylark

Hooded Crow replaces the Carrion Crow in the north

Corncrake strutting across the road

Greenshank

summer they are most likely to be seen whilst on passage to their wintering grounds in Africa. Their distinctive call, green legs and grey back make them unmistakable.

Whimbrel breed in small numbers in Caithness and Sutherland, and are very apparent from their Curlew-like call. It is smaller than its cousin and has a distinctive darker eyestripe and a lighter crownstripe.

WADERS form a large family of birds which inhabit shorelines, wetlands and moorland. A number of species breed in the area, including the iconic Greenshank. Many more are passage or winter migrants. Waders generally eat invertebrates found on the tideline, mudflats, in bogs, lochsides and on farmland.

The group comprises a number of families, including plovers, sandpipers, curlews, godwits, snipes, phalaropes and shanks. Summer, winter and juvenile plumages can be confusing so a good bird book is recommended.

Greenshank are on their breeding areas between May and August. In April and late

Peatlands The Flow Country of Caithness and Sutherland covers over $1,500m^2$, or about 52% of the two counties. Greenshank, Dunlin and Golden Plover all breed here, their calls being the pervading sound of early summer. The RSPB Reserve at Forsinard is a good example.

Moorland and Marsh Species including Whimbrel, Curlew, Snipe, Oystercatcher and Lapwing prefer drier areas and often feed on adjacent farmland or nearby shallow bays where large areas of sand and mudflat are exposed at low tide.

Redshank

Dunlin

Common Sandpiper

Curlew

Ringed Plover

Coastline There are many coastal areas suitable for waders to feed and roost in the North Highlands. Outwith the breeding season both residents and migrants can be observed, often in massive flocks, some of which overwinter while others carry on further south.

Around high tide is usually the best time to see wheeling

or roosting flocks of Sanderling, Knot, Purple Sandpiper or Dunlin. Vagrants from North America frequently also turn up for the sharp eyed to recognize.

Further suggested places to visit are listed in the gazetteer. There are a number of bird hides, but the car (carefully parked) also makes a good observation post.

Lapwing

Laurie Campbell

Golden Plover

Whimbrel

Oystercatcher

**BREEDING WADERS
TO SEE**

Oystercatcher
Ringed Plover
Golden Plover
Lapwing
Dunlin
Snipe
Whimbrel
Curlew
Greenshank
Redshank
Common Sandpiper
Woodcock

Red-throated Diver

Black-throated Diver

and lochans. Many of these are remote, but some may be seen from the road or paths in the hills. The parents can be heard noisily calling as they fly in and out from their feeding grounds at sea. Both species are present in west coast bays in winter.

Sea Ducks, including Eider, Shelduck and Red-breasted Merganser breed around the coast. Eider females are very hard to spot while they brood in grass, heather or clumps of vegetation near the shore. The males take no part in bringing up the ducklings, but whole families of females and young congregate for safety from skuas and gulls.

Shelduck nest mostly round the coast in sand dunes often in old rabbit holes. They are conspicuous with their black, white and reddish colouring. They can often be seen on the east coast feeding on mudflats or farmland.

Red-breasted Mergansers have long, serrated bills which help them catch fish such as Salmon and Trout. They

WATERFOWL Divers, Ducks, Geese, Swans and Herons are to be seen in the North Highlands in all seasons. Obviously, during the breeding season, great care must be taken to avoid disturbance. In practice excellent views can be had of most species from a distance without compromising nature.

Divers Both Red and Black-throated Divers nest on lochs

Laurie Campbell

Eider Ducks

Red-breasted Merganser

Tufted Duck

Grey Heron in typical pose

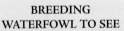

Greylag Geese with young

breed around the coast and inland near lochs. In winter they congregate in large numbers at places such as Udale Bay. Their relative, the Goosander, was persecuted to near oblivion by gamekeepers.

Geese Greylag Geese are resident and breed in various localities all over the area. They can be seen in summer in the Flow Country, especially around Forsinard. Family groups congregate for safety.

Mute Swans are resident on some of the lochs near the east coast in small numbers, especially in Caithness.

Heron The Grey Heron can be seen fishing around estuaries, sheltered low coasts or on lochsides. They normally stand quite close to the shore and may remain motionless for some time until the next unfortunate fish gets snapped up. Although usually solitary they nest in often substantial colonies, such as that at Culag Woods in Lochinver. Although wary of people, they may be closely observed using the car as a hide.

Mute Swan with cygnets

**BREEDING
WATERFOWL TO SEE**

Red-throated Diver
Black-throated Diver
Red-breasted Merganser
Shelduck
Eider
Mallard
Tufted Duck
Wigeon
Shoveller
Mute Swan
Grey Heron
Greylag Goose

Whooper Swans in formation

Barnacle Geese

Laurie Campbell

south in autumn and large numbers of Arctic breeders overwinter in Scotland. Thus a varied range of species can be observed during the year.

The Estuaries are internationally important for wintering waterfowl and waders. Great numbers of Pochard, Widgeon, Tufted Duck and others arrive each autumn. Huge flocks may be seen on Loch Fleet as well as on the Cromarty and Beauly Firths.

The many geese which pass through or stay all winter also roost on the lochs and graze on the surrounding farmland. Greylag, Pink-footed and Greenland White-front are the commonest types of geese, but Barnacle Geese may be seen on passage. Whooper Swans are winter visitors to the east coast. Many overwinter in the Firthlands.

The Sea The large areas of sheltered, shallow sea water often with gently shelving beaches provide good feeding and overwintering areas for many species. While Shag, Cormorant and Eider are resident around the coast, they are joined over the winter by

Migration After the breeding season many birds migrate southwards or out to sea for the winter. Spring and autumn bring interesting and unusual vagrants every year, while species which breed further north migrate annually. Many pass through on their way north in spring and back

Greenland White-fronted Geese

Greylag Geese

Goldeneye

Long-tailed Duck

Great Northern Diver, Velvet Scoter, Long-tailed Duck, Goldeneye, Slavonian Grebe and others.

Iceland and Glaucous Gulls are regular visitors and may sometimes be seen at Scrabster, Kinlochbervie or Lochinver Harbours in winter, or at sewage outfalls and rubbish tips. The occasional Ring-billed Gull also may appear.

Little Auks sometimes come inshore in winter, particularly after an extended period of strong easterlies, when there may be a "wreck" of auks, mostly young Guillemots, presumably caused by exposure and inexperience.

The Shore The intertidal zones provide rich feeding ground for the many waders, both resident and migrant. These include Purple Sandpiper and Curlew, Ringed Plover, Turnstone, Sanderling, Redshank, Bartailed Godwit, Golden Plover, Lapwing and Dunlin. The mudflats of Loch Fleet and the Cromarty Firth are particularly attractive to waders.

Raptors Merlin are more common in winter, as adults from Orkney, Shetland and Iceland move south and the previous summer's young are still lingering about. The occasional Gyrfalcon may appear on passage and White-tailed Sea Eagles are also sometimes seen on the east coast. Long-eared Owls arrive every winter from Norway and roost in woodland.

Migration Time Unusual Continental migrants are often blown in on easterly winds. During the spring especially, east winds can blow strongly for some days, due to the development of a Baltic high pressure and often bring falls of interesting birds. While very exciting for the birder, one cannot but speculate on the fate of many of these birds, which are often many thousands of miles away

Great-northern Diver, a winter visitor to sea lochs and estuaries

Velvet Scoter

Sanderling flocks wheel and turn, flashing light underwings and darker topsides in turn

from their normal destination. North American species also get caught up in weather systems, and are seen on occa-

A rare Scops Owl

Bullfinch

sion. They are usually waders or waterfowl and may be solitary or among flocks of local birds.

Sea and Land Watching
There are a number of notable places to observe seabirds on passage, including headlands such as Point of Stoer, Cape Wrath, Strathy Point, Dunnet Head, Duncansby Head, Tarbatness and Chanonry Point. During the migration periods large numbers of birds

can be seen passing. These can include auks, terns, divers, shearwaters, Gannets, Shags and Cormorants.

Dunlin

Twite

Hugh Harrop

Bar-tailed Godwit in winter plumage

Turnstone in winter plumage

Golden Plover in winter plumage

MIGRATION TIMES
From mid March to early June
May best
From end July to early October
September best

**SOME MIGRANTS
WHICH MAY BE SEEN**
Turnstone (common)
Red-necked Phalarope (scarce)
Purple Sandpiper (common)
Sanderling (common)
Knot (common)
Ruff (scarce)
Snow Bunting (common)
Wheatear (common)
Robin (common)
Great Northern Diver (common)
Long-tailed Duck (common)
Bluethroat (scarce)
Redwing (common)
Fieldfare (common)
Greylag Goose (common)
Pink-footed Goose (common)
Greenland White-front Goose (common)
Barnacle Goose (scarce)
Pochard (common)
Tufted Duck (common)
Wigeon (common)
Goldeneye (common)
Velvet Scoter (scarce)
Slavonian Grebe (scarce)
Iceland Gull (scarce)
Glaucous Gull (scarce)
Ring-billed Gull (rare)
Little Auk (scarce)
Whooper Swan (common)
Swallow (common)
Long-eared Owl (scarce)
Waxwing (eruptive)
Crossbill (eruptive)

Flocks of waders, including Ring Plovers, Sanderlings, Knots, Turnstones and Purple Sandpipers are often present on nearby beaches. Large numbers of thrushes, finches and other small passerines also often make landfall near such headlands, especially on the north and east coasts. These can include Redwings, Fieldfares, Bullfinches, Bramblings, Snow Buntings, Waxwings and Crossbills. Rarer species can also put in an appearance.

Waxwings are attracted to Cotoneaster berries especially, but also like apples

Hugh Harrop

Thrift at Duncansby Head, Caithness

This allows a variety of very hardy plants to dominate. Many are low growing or dwarf versions which elsewhere grow much larger.

Primula scotica Unique to the coasts of Caithness and North Sutherland and to Orkney is *Primula scotica* (the Scottish Primrose). This species only exists on exposed maritime heath. It is very small, yet sturdy. There are between two and eight small magenta flowers with yellow throats per head.

Maritime Heath is one of the most interesting of habitats. It occurs particularly on soils overlying Old Red Sandstone, on areas with considerable salt gusting exposure. In summer it is very colourful, with a tight carpet of flowers up to 10cm high. The hardy sedges and heather, with Grass of Parnassus, Thrift, Moss Campion, Eyebright, Mountain Everlasting, Sea Plantain and Spring Squill all add to the display. The heath flora becomes more diverse further away from the salt blasted coast, eventually merging into moorland or pasture.

Throughout late spring and early summer there is a constantly changing display of wild flowers on these clifftops. Where the underlying rocks are harder Middle or Upper Red Sandstone, Torridonian Sandstone or Lewisian Gneiss, the soils are more acidic and less free draining leading to a flora more like that found on moorland.

The range of plants which thrive on clifftops and rocky shores depends also on the degree of exposure. Most species cannot cope with the salt, wind and lack of water.

Conveniently for visitors, there are two flowering periods, in May, and in July. *P. scotica* is self-fertilizing like other primrose species in the north, which may confer advantage by making sure that at least some seed is set, but in very small colonies this may increase the risks to survival due to lack of genetic diversity in the longer term.

Lichen Apart from flowering plants, many lichens grow on exposed rocks where nothing else will succeed. These

Primula scotica - unique to the north

Spring Squill

Eyebright

White Sea Campion

colourful plants are symbionts of algae and fungi which can thrive in places where no other plants can, gaining their nutrients from the air, rain, sea spray and their rocky substrates. They make a good subject for photographs with their huge variety of colours and morphology.

Grass of Parnassus

Mountain Everlasting

Threats Like most habitats maritime heath is exposed to threats, not least being the constant erosion of the coast by wind, sea and rain. Light grazing by cattle is actually beneficial, but application of fertilizers kills many of the plants which grow in such localities.

Moss Campion

Sea Plantain

Thrift

Red Campion

Sea Aster

Coastal areas Thrift grows in many coastal areas, forming vivid carpets of colour. It is often accompanied by Sea Campion, red or white. Oyster Plant used to be common in Scotland, but Orkney is now its main stronghold. It grows on the top of shingle and sandy beaches where virtually no other land plant will grow. It has strong, thick blue-green leaves. Scurvy Grass, so called because sea-men ate it for its vitamin C content, also grows on the top of the shore and low clifftops.

Sea Rocket, Orache, Sea Milkwort, Oyster Plant, Scentless Mayweed, Yarrow, Sow Thistle and Silverweed all grow near or on beaches. Sea Aster, Thrift and Sea Spurrey give colour to salt-marshes. Brilliant yellow Goldenrod, together with Devil's-bit Scabious and Scots Lovage enliven sheltered cliffs.

Saltmarsh, Dunes and Machair Saltmarshes occur frequently at the heads of long, shallow inlets and in low-lying but sheltered areas of the coast which get periodically flooded at high tides. Many salt tolerant plants thrive in these zones, which may be a sea of pink, blue and yellow in early summer. Thrift, Spring Squill and

Silverweed

Oysterplant

Scurvy Grass

Orache

Yarrow

Scots Lovage

Silverweed are a few of the many colourful wild flowers to see here. Later, Sea Aster turns many saltmarshes mauve.

Large areas of sand dunes have remained unspoilt in many of the remoter areas. These include Gairloch, Oldshoremore, Sandwood Bay, Kervaig Bay, Balnakeil Bay, Torrisdale Bay, Melvich, Sandside, Dunnet Bay, Freswick, Brora, Golspie and Dornoch, to mention but a few.

Machair often forms behind the dunes. It is a free soil of sand and peat which has been fertilised with seaweed and manure in the past. It supports a wide variety of colourful wild flowers.

Ladys' Bedstraw

Goldenrod

Sea Milkwort

Sea Rocket

Scentless Mayweed

Whin flowers even in snow, early in the year

Whin or Gorse

Roadside Verges The lack of crop spraying (except in Easter Ross and to some extent Caithness) has helped retain a diversity of plants on roadside verges, uncultivated meadows, ditches, and burnsides which provide a wonder-

Coltsfoot flowers early

ful variety of wild flowers. The plants growing alongside the roads which are salted in winter tend to include many coastal species, even well inland.

Yellows predominate in springtime with wonderful displays of Whin (Gorse), especially from Helmsdale northwards. The Whins often flower in winter, even under snow, but are at their most glorious in May. Daffodils, Dandelions, Coltsfoot and Celandine are also early to flower. Hawkweeds provide colour until late autumn, while Ragged Robin and Red Campion add reds and pinks.

Primroses or May Flowers, appear in profusion in April and May on many verges and roadside banks, in company with Violets and Speedwell. Buttercups add colour to many fields, while Red and White Clover are everywhere near cultivated land.

Later several species of Orchids, Vetches as well as brilliant yellow Broom and, in damp places, Meadowsweet, all continue the colourful displays. Rosebay Willowherb and Foxgloves often grow in abundance where they have

Lesser Celandine

Orchids and Birds-foot Trefoil

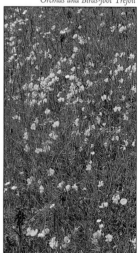

Primroses flower in April and May

Lesser Twayblade

Broom enlivens many roadsides in early summer

Buttercups in an old meadow

escaped enthusiastic verge trimmers.

In the less intensively farmed but fertile areas the whole place takes on a colourful appearance in summer, especially where fields have not been cultivated for a long time.

These old meadows persist in many places as havens of enchanting rustic beauty.

Meadowsweet with entwined Vetch

Orchid

Kidney Vetch

Foxglove

Dandelion clocks

The Flow Country at Forsinard, Sutherland

Blanket Bogs form over relatively flat terrain with impermeable rocks which prevent rain from draining away quickly. The Flow Country consists of Moine Schists and some Granite, both of which are very hard and impermeable.

Peat forms from plant remains, mostly Sphagnum Moss, which build up in acidic and anaerobic conditions. The rate of deposition depends on how waterlogged a particular place is. The peat can be 3m deep in places.

Wetlands and Bogs The blanket bogs of the Flow Country of Caithness and Sutherland cover about 400,000ha, or about 50% of the two counties. Sphagnum mosses are the main constituent of the bogs, but Cross-leaved Heath, Bog Asphodel, Bog Cotton, Sundews and Butterworts are also present along with a variety of sedges and rushes.

These bogs are of international importance for their plant communities and breeding waders. In the past they were under threat by grant assisted afforestation, but when the financial support ceased it was soon realised that this was not a suitable place to plant trees, and now they are being cleared and ditches blocked to return the area to nature.

Lochs and Rivers The North Highlands has hundreds of lochs ranging from Loch Maree and Loch Shin to the smallest of lochans. Depending on the surrounding geology, depth and con-

Sundews trap and digest insects

Butterwort also attract and eat insects

Sphagnum Moss hummock

Bog Myrtle in flower

Laurie Campbell

Water Lilies grow on many lochans

Bogbean grow in shallow pools

Small Cranberry in flower

Laurie Campbell

Cranberry

Laurie Campbell

quite short. Partly because of this, the marshy areas in the west are smaller than the very extensive bogs in the north and northeast.

Other Plants Sundews and Butterworts survive in these nutrient poor locations by attracting insects to their sticky leaves and then digesting their unfortunate victims. Other specialist plants include Water Lilies and Bogbean which grow on many lochans, adding colour to otherwise dark and peaty water.

Cranberry is a dwarf shrub which grows in this area while Small Cranberry is restricted to Caithness. Both species are well adapted to thrive in this habitat, having waxy leaves and thin, string stems. They

tours they may be very productive or quite hostile to plants. One thing they all have in common is to add depth and interest to a sometimes bleak landscape.

The watershed for most of the area is far to the west, so the larger rivers drain into the firths on the east coast. Only the River Thurso along with several smaller rivers reaches the north coast, while all of the rivers flowing west are

are pollinated by bumblebees, while Red Grouse are partial to the bright red berries.

Cross-leaved heath

Bog Myrtle fruits

Marsh Marigold

Laurie Campbell

Strathfleet above Pittentrail, Sutherland

Moorland covers vast areas of the North Highlands. Its character varies depending on the underlying rocks, the terrain, altitude and exposure. In the west Lewisian Gneiss, Torridonian Sandstones and Quartzites do not produce very good soils, therefore creating a wild and rocky landscape, especially higher up.

In contrast, the Limestone band just west of the Moine Thrust is verdant, with a striking array of bright green grasses and wild flowers. Further east the large expanse of Moine Schist is mostly grassland heath with areas of heather.

In former times large areas were covered in Scots Pine forest, with Oakwoods, Ash, Hazel, Birch and Rowan. These were largely removed by man over the centuries. Overgrazing by huge numbers of sheep in the 19th and 20th centuries has drastically changed the vegetation and prevented regeneration of forests and moorland.

Stocking of sheep has fallen considerably and as a result there is now more food for the deer. In some places, such as the locally owned Assynt Estate, deer fences have been erected and native trees planted to start regeneration of woodland and the surrounding moorland.

Heather Moorland is dominated by Heather (Ling), Cross-leaved Heath and Bell Heather, but Wood-Rush, grasses, rushes and sedges, as well as many other plants may be found.

In wetter areas, where moorland merges with marshland, these may include Pale Butterwort, Yellow Saxifrage, Cotton Grass, Bog Asphodel, Sphagnum and other mosses.

Ragged Robin

Pale Butterwort

Northern Marsh Orchid

Laurie Campbell

Bog Asphodel

Higher up, Blaeberry starts to replace the Heather and the delightful Dwarf Cornel may be found sheltering under the canopy, often along with Cloudberry. Goldenrod and Crowberry also frequently add variety.

Grassy Heath On more fertile soil grasses dominate the landscape, so that many of the inland hills and mountains are all green. Plants such as Tormentil, Ragged Robin, Buttercups, and Sheeps-bit Scabious all add colour.

Lichens grow everywhere, especially on rocky outcrops, fence posts and any other suitable substrate. The large variety of colours and forms add yet more interest to the landscape.

Bog Cotton and Buttercups

Laurie Campbell

Dwarf Cornel

Tormentil

Bell Heather

Heather (Ling)

Lousewort

Cross-leaved Heath and Wood-Rush

Kyle of Durness with rich Limestone-based grassland

Limestone is largely composed of calcite (calcium carbonate) and formed from the deposition of marine organisms. From Kishorn in the southwest to Loch Eriboll in the northwest of the North Highlands there are exposures of Durness Limestone on the west side of the Moine Thrust.

Calcicole (lime-loving plants) such as Mountain Avens and Yellow Saxifrage grow in rich grassland on this limestone corridor in striking contrast to the moorland all around. The crags support rare plants like Norwegian Sandwort and Dark Red Helleborine.

Kishorn Rassal Ashwood (ON *Yggrasil*, Tree of life) is a National Nature Reserve north of Kishorn. Ash is tolerant of basic soils, unlike many trees. The orchid, Dark Red Helleborine grows here along with a wide variety of other lime loving plants, many of which shelter from wind and grazing animals in *grikes* or cracks in the hard crystalline Limestone. Rowan, Willows, Birch and Hazel also grow here.

Inchnadamph has the largest outcrop of Durness limestone, where the Moine Thrust was held back by the great Torridonian Sandstone mass of Ben More Assynt. This wide valley, surrounding glens,

Frog Orchid

Eyebright

Seaside Centaury

caves and cliffs hold many interesting plants.

Durness On the north coast most of the Durness area, including Faraid Head, Loch Eriboll and Whiten Head are composed of Limestone. In consequence there is a large variety of plants, which are normally rare in most of the North Highlands.

Besides those already mentioned Seaside Centaury, Spring Sandwort, various Eyebrights, Frog Orchid and Purple Oxytropis all grow in some abundance. Sheltered places above the shore and in the rich grassland around Durness are good places to look. *Primula scotica* also thrives in the short turf near the shore.

Purple Oxytropis

The Durness area has the largest area of Mountain Avens Heath in Britain. This striking plant with brilliant white petals, yellow stamens and dark green evergreen leaves is one of the floral gems of the Durness Limestone, along with the equally resplendent Yellow Saxifrage.

Mountain Avens

Spring Sandwort

Yellow Saxifrage

Scots Pines with Beinn Eighe behind

Twisted old Scots Pine

Balblair Pinewoods near Golspie

Natural Woodland Very little natural woodland remains today, but in many areas planting of native trees has been or is being done. There are many forestry plantations all over the area, as well as a number of very attractive gardens, such as those at Inverewe in Wester Ross.

Pollen studies show that by around 6000BC there was mixed woodland vegetation with Oak, Pine, Willow, Birch, Hazel and Alder. By 3000BC the more fertile parts of these had become open grassland, while many were heather moorland. The change was obviously influenced by the arrival of man and his grazing stock but was also probably part of natural vegetation progression due partly to variations in climate.

Intense grazing prevents regeneration of native trees, except where protected by fences or on islands in lochs. Reduced stocking of sheep may help this, so that now the vast numbers of Red Deer are the main factor in keeping the area relatively treeless.

Pinewoods once covered vast areas of the Highlands. The largest semi natural woodland is at Beinn Eighe in Wester Ross, but many more have been planted. The large plantation at Balblair just south of Golspie is now part of the Loch Fleet NNR. Several rare plants, typical of Pinewoods, grow here.

These include One-flowered Wintergreen, Creeping Lady's Tresses and Common Wintergreen. The mature Scots Pines are over 100 years old and the relatively clear and shady understorey provides an ideal habitat for these plants as well as birds and mammals typical of such woods.

Sessile Oakwoods occur at Ardvar and Loch a'Mhuillin in Northwest Sutherland. They are mostly Oak and Birch in varying proportions and are famous for the mosses, liverworts and lichens which like the damp, cool conditions. These woods make up the most northerly remnants of the Oakwoods which once covered much of Britain.

Woodland Plantations The many Forestry Commission and private plantations of mostly conifers are very accessible to walkers and cyclists. Most have parking places and trails marked. Leaflets and display panels are often available at these woods.

When to visit Woodlands can be enjoyed in every season as a haven of calm on windy winter days or in spring when everything is coming back to life. Early summer is best for birds which are very active feeding their young. Wild flowers are dependent on location and weather, but of course are best in summer. Later, in October, rich autumn colours can be seen for a time, before the trees are battered by storms.

One-flowered Wintergreen

Harebell (Scottish Bluebell)

One-flowered Wintergreen

Creeping Lady's Tresses

Twinflower

Adam Ward

Laurie Campbell

Mountain Saxifrage

by Mountain Avens and Moss Campion. It reaches to 1,200m on Ben Lawers, but in the far north it grows near sea level. This splendid plant flowers very early in March or April.

Na Tuadhan and Coire a Mhadaidh from Conival, Assynt

MONTANE habitats normally exist above the tree line, which in the North Highlands may be as high as 700m but as low as 200m or even sea level in the far north. As a result of soil types and exposure several plants which are normally alpine flourish at much lower levels than elsewhere at these latitudes.

Plant communities include moss, lichen and grassy heaths, blanket bogs and dwarf shrubs. In this landscape, man has had only a limited effect on montane vegetation.

Purple Saxifrage grows on outcrops of calcareous mountain ledges often accompanied

Cyphel is found in several places in the area, normally growing above 450m. Ben Klibreck and Ben Griam are the classic sites but it is also found in other parts, including Caithness.

Trailing Azelea normally grows at over 650m, though down to 400m in the far north. It grows on many mountains in the area including Ben Wyvis and Scaraben. Its red buds first open between May and July, followed by pink flowers, which change to white later.

Mountain Bearberry is another true alpine which lives on bare rocky ground above 600m, though in the far north it can be found at 300m. Buds

Calcite scree on Ben More Assynt

Adam Ward

Mountain Bearberry in autumn

Laurie Campbell

Mountain Bearberry in July

open in May and bright red berries are later produced which attract Red Grouse. In autumn the leaves turn a spectacular dark red.

Other flowers which grow in these areas include Roseroot, Alpine Lady's Mantle, Cloudberry, Yellow Saxifrage and Mountain Avens. Clubmosses, stunted Juniper and Willow also grow in the shelter of rocks. Hawkweeds and hardy grasses inhabit the high ground where conditions are right.

In sheltered, wet places lower down near the treeline, Globe Flower, Water Avens, Butterwort and Mountain Saxifrage may be found, often in quite unlikely spots. Stunted and knarled Scots Pines mark the treeline.

Laurie Campbell

Cyphel

Clubmoss

Globe Flower

Water Avens

Dwarf Juniper

Mountain Azelea

Laurie Campbell

Fauna - Land Mammals

Red Deer Stag

During the rut, from September to November, stags attempt to dominate groups of hinds with roaring contests, and often serious fights where antlers are locked. Calves are born in May or June. Golden Eagles and Buzzards prey on the young. Other predators like Badgers, Foxes, Pine Martens and Ravens consume carrion.

Roe Deer

Roe Deer are smaller than their cousins. They are found in most of Scotland and frequent mixed woodland. The Roe Deer prefers lower altitudes and is also more solitary. They have a white chin, black moustache and a cream-coloured rump. The males have small antlers with three or less points.

Laurie Campbell

LAND FAUNA During the last Ice Age sea level was 100 to 150m lower than today. Scotland was connected to Europe by a land bridge for a time until the glaciers retreated. The rapid rise in sea level after the melting of the ice, ensured that the Highlands became isolated and most of the Arctic species died out.

Red Deer are prevalent on moorlands in the Highlands. Stags and hinds are separate for most of the year, the former tending to range higher into the mountains, while the latter remain on richer pasture. In winter they move to lower, more sheltered ground, where they may be fed by farmers and are easier to see.

During the rut, in July and August the males compete aggressively with each other to mate with the females. Implantation is delayed until January so that kids are born in late May. Roe Deer are most active around dawn and dusk.

Otters are relatively common around the coasts, particularly where burns and rivers enter the sea. They are rarely seen, however, their spraints are frequent sights around the coast, or along the loch shores, often being left on small green mounds.

Most glimpses of Otters are fleeting as they dive into ditches, run across the road or, swim among the seaweed

Otter

along the shore. They are carnivores, and although they normally live on littoral species such as Blennies, Butterfish, Eels, and Crabs, they will also take Black Guillemots, breeding ducks, rats and mice.

The best time to see Otters is in early morning, when they are most active and no one is about. By keeping quiet it is possible to observe these elusive creatures at quite close quarters, but a great deal of patience is needed.

Scottish Wildcats are very timid and rarely seen near human habitations. They are larger than domestic cats and brown with black stripes. They are carnivores which hunt at night and, apart from mating, are solitary and silent. Like the domestic cat, females caterwaul to attract males during the breeding season.

Now confined to the Highlands, under 500 Wildcats exist in the wild. They have highly developed senses of sight, hearing, memory and touch making them very efficient predators. Although primarily forest creatures, they have been forced to roam far and wide in search of prey. The biggest threat to their survival turns out to be interbreeding with feral Domestic cats.

Short-tailed Vole The Vole is much more stumpy than a mouse, with short rounded ears, and a short tail. It is nor-

Laurie Campbell

Scottish Wild Cat

mally darkish brown, but a range of colours have been observed. A variety of habitats are occupied, including heather moorland, marshland, grassland, cereal crops, field margins and ditches. Long runs are made from the nest and the animals are not often seen. They are the favoured prey of Hen Harrier, Short-eared Owl and Kestrel, all of which are common in the North Highlands.

Pipistrelles are the smallest and commonest bats in UK. Their bodies are mouse sized and they are nocturnal insect feeders which use echo location to find their prey. They commonly eat several thousand midgies in a night. Bats roost in hollow trees, build-

ings or caves and hibernate in winter. They are most likely to be seen in late evening just before dark in places with plenty of insects.

Red Squirrels are under threat from the larger Grey Squirrel but, for now, the latter has not gained a hold in the North Highlands. Their favourite food is pine cones and piles of chewed debris are a sure sign of their presence.

Although elusive, they leave scratches in trees and build large dreys in tree forks which are often conspicuous. During courtship in early spring or summer they become much more obvious as males chase females through the trees. They are preyed on

Pipistrelle Bat

Laurie Campbell

Laurie Campbell

Red Squirrel

Pine Martens are members of the weasel family which inhabit Pine forests. They are about the size of a domestic cat. They were persecuted almost to extinction in the UK by the early 19th century for their fur and because they prey on gamebirds' eggs and chicks. They are curious as well as aggressive hunters.

by Pine Martins, Wild Cats, various raptors and owls.

Mountain Hares have a bluish grey coat well suited as camouflage in their rocky terrain. In winter it turns white, making them almost invisible in the snow. There can be three litters in a season, but many leverets fall victim to Golden Eagles and Buzzards.

In spring, Mountain Hares become quite conspicuous until their summer coat grows in. This coincides with their breeding season, when mad March hares box each other and jump around and are much more easily seen.

Foxes are very adaptable both in diet and habitat. In the North Highlands they can be found everywhere from salt-marshes to mountains and even towns and villages. Although hunting foxes with hounds is now illegal, they are still heavily persecuted.

They are opportunistic hunters, living on rodents, insects and fruits. They also may take eggs, nestlings and sickly lambs. Foxes are understandably very shy of humans, although in urban environments they can become quite tame. Vixens usually have one litter of cubs in late spring, which are born blind. Foxes normally live in loose family units.

Their fur is darkish brown with a yellow bib. They are active around dusk and at night, sleeping in dens during the day. A piece of bread and jam appeals to their sweet tooth and attracts them. During courtship males will chase females noisily through the trees. Pine Martens have been shown to limit the northwards expansion of the Grey Squirrel and so may help the Red Squirrel hold on in the north.

Badger Though commoner in the Lowlands than in the north, the Badger is present in the North Highlands. A member of the weasel family, it is instantly recognisable. They are normally active after dark. Their distinctive black and white-striped face is familiar from photographs but rarely seen.

Badgers breed in winter and cubs are born in February in the sett. These underground dens are often traceable by following trails left in the undergrowth. Sett watches are often organised where people can observe these animals as they forage for food.

Pine Marten

Laurie Campbell

Laurie Campbell

Mountain Hare

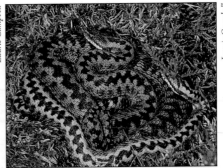

Laurie Campbell

Adder

Laurie Campbell

Badgers foraging

Adder Scotland's only poisonous snake is not dangerous if not aggravated. They are recognizable from the dark zig zag pattern on their backs. Females are longer and duller in colour with orange eyes. Adders are often spotted basking in the sun around large stones, on paths or boulders, and on open stretches of moorland in summer. They can be difficult to see, given their sensible tendency to avoid humans.

Nobody has died in Scotland from an Adder bite for at least 20 years. Nevertheless, their bite is potentially lethal if untreated. They inhabit woodland margins and open heathland and prey on small rodents, especially voles, frogs, newts and young birds which are killed by lethal injection.

Adders hibernate in the winter. In spring the *dance of the Adders* may be seen where males fight with each other for supremacy. The snakes writhe round each other and may also move very fast. They mate in April or May and the young are born about four months later. The snakes frequently hide under old sheets of corrugated iron or pieces of wood, which are also favourite hiding places for voles and other prey.

Red Fox

Laurie Campbell

LAND ANIMALS

Red Deer
Roe Deer
Wild Cat
Pine Marten
Red Squirrel
Fox
Badger
Bats
Otter (shy, but common)
Pigmy Shrew (common)
Vole (abundant)
Rabbit
Mountain Hare
Hedgehog
Brown Rat
Field Mouse
House Mouse
Adder
Pipistrelle Bat

Grey Seal mother and pup in October

Grey Seals can be seen at all times of year, but most often during the breeding season. Females come ashore on small islands and sheltered coves from late September onwards to have their pups and mate, before leaving again for sea after the pup is weaned at about four weeks.

Adult males are up to 2.3m long and weigh up to 300kg, while females reach only 2m and 120kg. The males become sexually mature at 6 or 7 years, but do not gain the social status to breed until at least 10 years old. They do not survive much beyond 20 years. Cows, on the other hand, commence

breeding at 6 to 7 years and may survive and bear pups until at least 35 years old.

Baby Grey Seals are born with a very attractive silky white coat, and gain weight rapidly on their mother's very rich milk. The mothers identify their pups by smell, and they are very defensive, because if separated they may not be able to find their pups again.

Grey Seals will feed pups that are not their own, but these pups do not do so well. The pups moult at about 3-4 weeks to a beautiful silver-blue-grey coat, and are ready for sea five or six weeks after birth. Although they can swim and dive before moulting they do not normally leave the land until fully moulted.

The cows are ready to mate at about 3 weeks after giving birth and may copulate with several bulls. The aggressive reaction of the cows to the bulls prior to intimacy may well encourage mating with the most dominant nearby bull. Neither sex does much feeding during the breeding season, especially the dominant bulls.

Grey seals were killed for their skins on a large scale in the past, and have also had periodic attacks of a fatal disease. Controversy over competition with commercial fishing has led to much research on Grey Seal diets, with very interesting conclusions.

Grey Seal pups only take to the water after a few weeks

Grey Seal pups have a white fur which moults

Study of faeces has shown that Sand Eels make up about 60% of the diet and total fish consumption is estimated at 5kg per seal per day. Thus, although there is little evidence that seals consume much white fish, they could be in competition with birds and other mammals for Sand Eels. There are about 100,000 Grey Seals in Scottish waters, about 36% of the world population.

Common Seals are very inquisitive and can be quite confiding

Common Seals are smaller than their cousins, at about 1.9m, and are also more coastal in habitat. They may be seen all round the shores on skerries, small islands, and sand banks at low tide.

Pups are normally born in late June and July, in their adult coat, having moulted in the uterus. Those born with a white coat moult in a few days. Though they can swim within hours of birth, it takes about three weeks before they become strong enough to haul themselves up the beach.

They suckle for several weeks on the tide line and keep a close relationship with their mother

for an extended period. Common Seals seem to be very good mothers and this close relationship may well greatly assist the survival of the pups.

There are at least 26,000 Common Seals in Scottish waters, about 5% of the world population, but numbers have declined in recent years. The reasons are unclear but predation by Killer Whales, or disease, could be causes. In general the species is much less social than Grey Seals, although they do haul out in large groups in several places, especially round the shores of the Cromarty Firth.

Epidemics, possibly exacerbated by pollution, have killed

large numbers in the Baltic and the Southern North Sea in the past. The population here seems to have generally escaped this fate There has not been excessive shooting for several decades, though some rogue seals do learn how to attack salmon cages and creels, and are dealt with, but these are a small minority.

Common Seals have dog like heads

Common Seal mother with pup clinging to her back

SEA MAMMALS

Common Seal (abundant)
Grey Seal (abundant)
Killer Whale (quite common)
Minke Whale (quite common)
White-sided Dolphin (regular)
Risso's Dolphin (regular)
White-beaked Dolphin (regular)
Harbour Porpoise (common)
Sperm Whale (almost annual)
Pilot Whale (now rare)
Humpback Whale (very rare)
Fin Whale (very rare)

Bottle-nosed Dolphins at Chanonry Point

Risso's Dolphin

Laurie Campbell

whale used to be driven or *caa'd* ashore in large numbers as it still is in the Faeroes, but this stopped in the 1860s. They are jet black in colour, with a low but prominent dorsal fin and reach up to 6m in length.

Baleen Whales (Rorquals) are sometimes sighted. By far the most common in coastal waters is the **Minke Whale**. They can be seen close inshore near headlands, but are more frequently seen at sea, especially around the Pentland Firth. They are quite distinctive, with their relatively large dorsal fin, small size and white striped flippers.

The Minke is known by fishermen as the *Herring Hog* on account of its liking for that species. Most sightings are between April and October, especially between July and September, when shoals of Herring and Mackerel may be inshore.

Other Rorquals, such as **Fin**, **Sei** and **Blue Whales** are sometimes seen offshore as they migrate south along the continental shelf in late summer and autumn, but more usually when

CETACEANS About twenty species of whales have been recorded around the coasts of the North Highlands. In recent times increasing numbers have been observed in these waters. There is a good chance of seeing one or more species, either from various headlands, or from a ferry. Chanonry Point on the Black Isle is probably the best place to regularly see Bottle-

nosed Dolphins close up.

Blackfish (smaller, toothed whales) usually live in groups, although they may be seen singly. The Long-finned **Pilot or Caain' Whale** is mostly a pelagic species. It is now rarely seen inshore, but was formerly quite common, especially in the winter, either singly or sometimes in large groups. This

Long-finned Pilot Whales

Hugh Harrop

White-beaked Dolphin

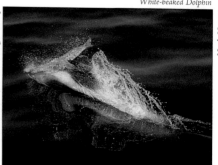

Hugh Harrop

Laurie Campbell

RSPB

Minke Whale

Killer Whales attacking Common Seals

they come ashore dead. **Humpbacks** have been observed in the vicinity of Orkney and Shetland as well as offshore in recent years, suggesting that numbers may be recovering.

Sperm Whales are seen most years, usually between September and January. The head shape, small dorsal hump and back knuckles are diagnostic. Dead specimens are washed up sometimes, and there are occasional major strandings. Small pods of young males regularly visit the Pentland Firth area.

Dolphins Several species of Dolphin frequent these waters, including **Harbour Porpoise**, which is often seen in bays feeding on small fish, or, from boats, usually in the summer. **White-beaked Dolphin** also occur in summer and autumn in small herds, usually off to the west, but sometimes in the Pentland Firth. The **White-sided Dolphin** and **Risso's Dolphin** tend to be more oceanic, but can also be seen to the west, usually from boats, or from headlands.

The **Bottle-nosed Dolphin** is present all year in the Moray Firth, but is regularly seen all round the coast, especially in the east and on the Pentland Firth, where they often chase shoals of Herring or Mackerel.

The **Killer Whale** or **Orca,** prefers deeper water. They are seen occasionally off headlands, sometimes very close in to the shore, usually in the deeper water of the Pentland Firth or off the west coast. The tall dorsal fin, white chin and eye patch are unmistakable.

Males average 7.3m and females 6.2m in length and they rarely strand. Groups have different behaviours and preferences, some seem to prefer seals as prey while others are more partial to Herring and Mackerel.

Whale watching trips are run from a number of locations around the coast, including from Kyle of Lochalsh, Gairloch, Ullapool and various places in the Moray Firth area. The ferries across the Pentland Firth, especially the eastern routes, can also be good for seeing whales.

Porpoise breaching

Sperm Whale blowing

Richard Jones

The Small Tortoiseshell Butterfly is very common in some years and rare in others

Insects The North Highlands may not be the obvious environment for insects, but in fact it supports a wide range of species. The ubiquitous Midge is not much of a problem, except on heather moorland in certain conditions. The diversity of wild flowers and lack of use of chemicals mean that many species of insects survive here which have elsewhere disappeared.

Perhaps the most prominent are the **bumblebees**, many of which have become rare elsewhere in UK due to industrial farming. There are several species, which may be distinguished by their size, head shape, tongue length and prominent black, yellow and white stripes. They are easily seen feeding anywhere there are wild flowers, roadside verges are especially good.

Several species of **butterfly** are resident in the North, and more arrive most years as immigrants from South Britain or Europe. Cabbage White are the bane of all vegetable gardeners. Green-veined Whites and Small Tortoiseshells appear in May, while the Common Blue and Meadow Brown appear later. Dark Green Fritillaries and the Large Heath appear later still.

Larvae and adults of each species have their own plant preferences and most prefer to fly on bright days. The Meadow Brown, by contrast, flies on the dullest and windiest of days. Butterfly numbers, especially of immigrants, vary annually due to food availability and weather conditions.

Peacock Butterfly

Dark Green Fritillary Butterfly

Common Blue Butterfly

Meadow Brown Butterfly

Dragonflies are best seen during July and August beside pools and burns, especially on sunny days, when they bask on warm rocks. Peatbogs are especially good places to find them. There are several resident species as well as a number of **damselflies**.

Over 250 species of **moths** have been recorded here. Most are nocturnal and thus only generally observed by specialists. However, a number of the most spectacular species are commonly seen in daylight hours. These include the large Emperor, and colourful Garden Tiger, while the Magpie may be seen feeding on Heather flowers on summer evenings.

Emperor Moth - found on moors and marsh, male flies in afternoon daylight

Bumblebee on Mint

Magpie Moth - feeds on Heather

Green-veined White Butterfly in early May

Garden Tiger Moth

Bumblebee on Hawkweed

Dragonfly on rock

BC
c.10000 Ice retreats
c.6000 Grassland, Oak and Pine forest,
Birch and Hazel-scrub and ferns
cover the landscape
c.6000 First (Mesolithic) people arrive??
Evidence at Sand, Applecross
c.4000 First known farmers
Vegetation becoming more open
3800 Climate deteriorates
3000 Chambered Tombs being used
2700 *Start of Great Pyramid Age*
2600 Trees in decline in many areas
c.2500 Bronze Age,
Achavanich Stone Setting
1300 Peat bogs developing
1159 Hekla erupts
700 Iron Age round houses
600 Oldest Broch deposits
c.325 Pytheas circumnavigates Britain
214 *Great Wall of China constructed*
100 Brochs in peak period
AD
33 *Death of Christ*
43 Orkney said to submit to Claudius
83 Agricola's fleet said to visit the north
c.100 Brochs falling into disuse
297 Eumenius first refers to "Picts"
c.500 Celtic monks arrive
Scotti moving over from Ireland
c.550 Portmahomack monastery estab.
600 Norsemen start to appear in West
632 *Death of Muhammad*
c.673 Applecross Monastery founded
793 Major Viking raids begin
800s Norse migration
839 Major battle Vikings versus Picts
843 Kenneth MacAlpin rules combined
Pictish/Scottish Kingdom
c.872 Harald Fairhair King of Norway
Sigurd of More first Earl of Orkney
955 Earl Sigurd the Stout baptised
1000 Leif Ericson discovers America
1014 Thorfinn becomes Earl of Orkney
1035 Battle off Tarbat Ness
1065 Earl Thorfinn the Mighty dies
1066 *William - a French Viking takes England*
1098 Magnus Barelegs expedition
1116 Murder of Magnus
1124 Diocese of Ross
1145 Diocese of Caithness founded
1151 Earl Rognvald goes to Holy Land
1153 St Duthac buried in Tain
1171 Sweyn Asleifson killed at Dublin
1197 Thurso Castle slighted by King
William the Lion
1216 Rosemarkie a Royal Burgh
1221 Fearn Abbey established
1222 Bishop Adam burnt at Halkirk,
Bishop Gilbert appointed
1224 Dornoch Cathedral building started

1231 Last Norse Earl murdered
in Thurso (John Harraldson)
c.1235 First Earl of Sutherland
1263 Battle of Largs, King Haakon dies
c.1264 Dingwall and Cromarty became
Royal Burgh
1290 Margaret, Maid of Norway, dies
1300 Dutch already fishing herring
1314 Battle of Bannockburn
1379 Earl Henry Sinclair I
1398 Henry Sinclair visits America??
1455 Royal Burgh of Fortrose and
Rosemarkie
1468 Orkney impignorated to Scotland
1470 Sinclairs resign Orkney Earldom to
the King but retain Caithness
1492 *Columbus reaches America*
c.1500 Jan de Groot starts ferry
1513 Henry Sinclair II killed at Flodden
1517 Battle of Torran Dubh, Rogart
1528 Battle of Summerdale
1529 Coal mining at Brora
1540 King James V visits North
1567 James VI becomes King
1586 Battle of Leckmelm
1588 Spanish Armada - many wrecks
1589 Wick became a Royal Burgh
1600s Herring fishery becoming
important
1602 Strome Castle blown up
1603 Union of Crowns
1607 Iron smelting at Loch Maree
1633 Thurso a Burgh of Barony
c.1660 Brahan Seer put to death
1666 *Great Fire of London;*
Newton realises gravity of situation
1698 Herring Fishing in Loch Broom
1715 First Jacobite Rebellion
1719 Eilean Donan castle blown up
1721 Kelp-making introduced
1723 Bernera Barracks, Glenelg
1725 Pirate Gow captured at Calf Sound
1739 Reay Parish Kirk
1745 Second Jacobite Rebellion
1747 Hanoverians burn Coigach Forest
1769 Whaligoe first mentioned
c.1770 Grass, clover and turnip seeds
introduced, farming reforms
1772 Cromarty harbour developments
1773 First immigrant ship sails from
Loch Broom to Nova Scotia
1776 *American Declaration of Independence*
1788 Ullapool village established
1790 Balblair Distillery established
1794 First lighthouses Pentland Skerries
Plockton founded
1798 Thurso new town laid out
1800 Over 200 boats at Wick
First clearances at Strath Oykel
1802 Lybster development begins
1803 Wick Harbour developments

1810 Shieldaig Village started
1814 Helmsdale planned village
1816 The Mound constructed
1819 First pump room at Strathpeffer
1822 Bealach na Ba road opens
1825 First cargo of flags from Castlehill
1826 Old Pulteney Distillery
1828 Cape Wrath lighthouse first lit
1830 Collapse of Kelp Boom
Sandside Harbour built
1831 Dunnet Head lighthouse lit
Keiss Harbour built
1836 First Black Isle Show
1845 Croick Kirk clearance graffiti
1855 Steamer between Stromness
and Scrabster
1862 Peak of Wick Herring Fishing
Inverewe Gardens started
1868 Kildonan Gold rush
1874 Railway reaches Thurso and Wick
1882 Thurso Esplanade
1894 Kyle Line opens
1884 Napier Report on crofting
1892 SS *St Ola I* starts her long service
1913 Brora gets electricity
1914 World War I
1915 HMS Natal blows up at
Invergordon
1920 New Zealand Wild White Clover
introduced
1937 End of herring boom
1939 World War II,
1941 Anthrax on Gruinard Island
1951 MV *St Ola II* commissioned
Beinn Eighe NNR
1952 Queen Mother buys Castle of Mey
1955 Dounreay NPDE work started
1956 Stroma evacuated
1959 *Russia launches first satellite*
1969 First landing on the Moon
1973 Ro-ro ferries start with MV *St Ola III* Scrabster to Stromness and MV *Suilven* Ullapool to Stornoway
1974 Local Authorities formed
1975 Kishorn construction yard opens
1976 Discovery of the Beatrice Oil Field
1979 Cromarty Bridge
1982 Kessock Bridge
1984 Kylesku Bridge
1991 Dornoch Bridge
1992 *St Ola IV* enters service
1994 Dounreay shut down, start of
de-commissioning work
1995 Skye Bridge opens
2002 NorthLink takes over
new pier at Scrabster
2005 Mey Selections established
2008 Caithness Horizons opened
2009 *North Highlands Guide Book*

Sunrise over the Atlantic Ocean

After the end of the last Ice Age, about 10,000 years ago, Mesolithic nomadic hunters arrived in Scotland. By 4000BC, Neolithic farmers were well settled in the North Highlands and for over 1,500 years their culture flourished. The houses, tombs and standing stones that we can see today are among the most spectacular Neolithic monuments in Europe.

The Bronze Age succeeded the Neolithic Age and these peoples left behind burnt mounds, middens, cist, and barrow graves as well as ruins of small houses. This period was marked by a deterioration in climate and changes in society as well as the appearance of bronze tools and weapons.

About 700BC larger round houses started to appear and later the spectacular brochs, some with large settlements around them, were developed. The introduction of iron for tools and weapons would have been a revolution in itself. From about AD43, as part of the Pictish Kingdom, the North Highlands, had more outside cultural influence from Romans, Christians, the British and the Scotti from Dalriada.

Beginning in the 8th century the Scandinavians began to appear, probably not in huge numbers at first. Large scale migration took place during the 9th century, followed by the Golden Age of the Vikings. The Norse domination of much of the North Highlands

lasted for nearly 500 years and this influence can still be seen in many placenames today. The North of Scotland was of great strategic importance during Viking times, and the exploits of the Earls and their supporters are related colourfully in the *Orkneyinga Saga*.

Medieval times saw a large influx of Lowland Scots attracted by the rich lands of Easter Ross. However the remoter areas of the west and northwest remained so for centuries to come. During the 19th century the notorious clearances removed many thousands of native inhabitants from the land. Partly as a result of this, many areas remain virtually uninhabited today.

The region was opened up with the advent of steam power in the 19th century when sea transport became more reliable and railways were built. During the later 19th and then the 20th century there have been the effects of the boom in Herring fishing and two World Wars.

There were further great strides in agriculture, North Sea Oil brought work for a time, and an influx of large numbers of immigrants from England and the Lowlands helped to reverse the population decline. The North Highlands now has a diverse economy, mainly based on its natural resources.

Camster Long Cairn, Caithness

NEOLITHIC AGE Farming was well established in the North Highlands at least 6,000 years ago. Domestic sites like Skara Brae in Orkney have not been found, but there are many burial sites, known as chambered cairns. Artefacts including human and animal bones, pottery, carved stone axe heads and other objects were often found.

Nothing is known of the language or culture of these people, except that which can be gleaned from archaeology. Barley and some wheat was grown, while cattle and sheep plus some pigs, goats and deer

were kept. Seabirds, sea mammals and fish were also an important part of their diet.

Burial of the dead Burial rituals were clearly very important, and, at least in some cases, excarnation was practised. Bodies were left outside to allow the flesh to decay, and only the bones were placed in the tombs. Some studies suggest that the people had short and unhealthy lives, but there is no evidence to suggest that this was universal.

The fact that they were able to construct such elaborate monuments for their dead as well as impressive stone circles suggests that their society was prosper-

ous and well organised rather than primitive and subsistence only. There are similarities between pottery and other artefacts found in Portugal, Southern England, Ireland and the North of Scotland, suggesting that there was cultural contact with people in these areas.

Little is known about the boats of the time, but vessels able to transport people and their animals across the Pentland Firth and the Minch or to fish offshore would have been more than adequate to undertake longer trading journeys as well.

Climate and climatic change may well have had a lot to do

Cairn of Get, Caithness

Chambered Cairn, Yarrows, Caithness

with early settlement. Analysis of pollen shows that by about 5900BC the land was covered with Pine and Oak forest, grassland, Birch-Hazel scrub and ferns. After the arrival of farming in about 4000BC, this was replaced in the settled areas by more open vegetation, probably due to grazing animals and clearing for cultivation.

These vegetation changes continued for some time and by 2600BC there were far fewer trees in the more fertile valleys and coastal areas, where most settlement took place. Recent tree-ring studies of old Irish Oaks suggest that there was a sudden deteriora-

Camster Round Cairn, Caithness

tion of climate during 2354-2345BC, which is around the time of the latest Neolithic dates. One theory is that a large comet or asteroid struck the Earth at this time, causing a nine year winter.

By 1300BC extensive peat bogs were developing, making much marginal land unworkable, and overwhelming remaining woodland in places such as the Flow Country. The landscape would then have been very similar to that of the early 20th century.

Chambered Cairns are tombs which are characteristic of Neolithic times. They are stone built and typically have a central chamber with an entry passage and sometimes one or more cells off the main chamber. Variations include round, long and heel shaped cairns, sometimes with horns enclosing a forecourt.

Interior of Camster Round Cairn, Caithness

Interior of south chamber, Camster Long Cairn, Caithness

Sutherland and Caithness have around 80 surviving examples of these houses for the dead, while there are about 60 known in Ross-shire. Doubtless many more have been robbed for stone or cleared by farmers. These tombs were built from before 3200BC, and many continued in use for 800 years or more before finally being sealed.

ARCHAEOLOGY AND HISTORY

Achavanich Stone Setting, near Lybster, Caithness

The commonest type has been defined the *Orkney-Cromarty* (OC) type, due to its widespread distribution. They are characterised by having upright stalls set into the side walls, shelves at one or both ends as well as sometimes along the sides and rounded corbelling for the roofs. Low roofed cells occasionally lead

Chambered Cairn at Achavanich

off the main chamber. The pottery type found in these cairns was Unstan Ware. These are wide, round bottomed pots, which may or may not be decorated, and are also associated with some domestic sites in Orkney.

Unfortunately most sites were cleared out in the 19th or early 20th centuries without proper recording, or the benefit of modern techniques. Many of the artefacts also became dispersed and lost. Luckily a few intact chambered cairns have been investigated more scientifically, with very interesting results.

That the Neolithic people placed such emphasis on the ritual of housing their dead, is symbolic of their reverence for their ancestors. Much has been discovered about the material aspects of these people's lives. However little has been revealed about the ritual and social aspects of their lives except that the very large effort implied in the construction of these monuments suggests a society which was well organised and had plenty of resources and expertise.

Standing Stones are prominent in the landscape, especially in the east. There are good examples in Caithness at Yarrows, above Loch Rangag and near Houstry, north of Dunbeath. In Sutherland Clach Mhic Mhios stands at the top of Glen Loth, while at Ospisdale, west of Dornoch a large stone stands at the side of the A949. In some cases older stones have been re-used as at Edderton by a Pictish carver.

Clach Mhic Mhios, Glen Loth, Sutherland

Stone Circles In the North Highlands these exist only in Caithness. At Guidebest, near Latheronwheel a circle over 50m in diameter has at least eight stones remaining standing, as well as several stumps. Although now partially hidden by trees, it must have been very impressive in its time.

The Achavanich U-shaped stone setting, inland from Lybster is unique. Forty stones remain out of a possible fifty-four, the highest exceeding 2m. This site is spectacularly located in moorland overlooking the Loch of Stemster. Unusually, the narrow faces of the uprights face inwards. A chambered cairn lies just to the southeast. The remains of several cist burials, with stones set on edge, are just to the east of the setting.

Ledbeg Chambered Cairn, Wester Ross

Ledmore Chambered Cairn, Wester Ross

NEOLITHIC TIMELINE

BC	
c.8000	First hunter-gatherers
4000	First farmers
3600	Oldest houses in Orkney
c.3200	Chambered Tombs
c.2000	Chambered tombs sealed up

CHAMBERED CAIRNS TO VISIT

CAITHNESS
Grey Cairns of Camster
Cairn of Get
Cnoc Freiceadain
South Yarrows
Houstry
SUTHERLAND
Ord Hill
Coille na Borgie
Kyle of Sutherland
Skelpick
Inchnadamph
Ledbeg & Ledmore
Embo
ROSS-SHIRE
Kilcoy, Black Isle
King's Head, Kilmuir
Mid Brae, Resolis
Scotsburn Wood, Easter Logie

Hill o'Many Stanes, Mid Clyth, Caithness

BRONZE AGE In contrast to the spectacular monuments of the Neolithic, the Bronze Age has not left many such remains to visit. Metal working reached Britain around 2700BC, but none of the few bronze artefacts found in the North Highlands dates to earlier than 2000BC. Copper ore does occur locally but there is

Beaker from Caithness

no evidence that it was exploited at this time.

Artefacts which have been found all appear to be imported. Beaker pottery, a finer and more decorated type characteristic of the period elsewhere, is also rare here. This lack of artefacts may suggest that the Highlands were relatively isolated from the rest of Scotland, perhaps due to climate changes making life much harder. However, intriguing finds in several graves suggest that this is not the whole picture.

Stone Rows are parallel or fan shaped rows of small stones set into hillsides in eastern Caithness and Sutherland.

The most impressive, the Hill o'Many Stanes, is at Mid Clyth, north of Lybster (ND295384). It has over 200 stones in 22 rows, which fan out towards the south. Other examples can be seen at Yarrows, Learable Hill and Garrywhin. One theory suggests that they were observatories used to follow and pre-

Beaker in Dornoch Museum

dict the movements of the moon.

Burial Mounds Around 2000BC there was a change in funereal practice, from communal burials in chambered cairns to individual interments in stone lined cists, often then topped with a barrow of earth or a cairn of stones. There was also a change from inhumation burials to cremation.

Pottery beakers are often found associated with burials from this period. They may have contained food or drink for the deceased's journey. The inclusion of these beakers may well reflect a fashion adopted from elsewhere, rather than due to any large influx of new people.

Hut Circles There are numerous circular house foundations, with associated field systems, walls and clearance cairns marked on the map. Although all that can be seen today are the foundations, some of these huts would have been quite substantial houses. Many of these

are located in what is now moorland or marginal agricultural land, suggesting that conditions then were better for farming.

Burnt Mounds are large piles of burnt stones. They are usually crescent shaped and near a water supply, such as a burn or spring. They always had a hearth and sometimes a large trough and remains of buildings also often survive. Good examples can be seen in Achany Glen, south of Lairg.

It has been thought that these sites were used to boil water for cooking of large joints of meat for communal feasting, but it is also argued that they may have been Bronze Age bathhouses or saunas. They date from about 2000BC to 800BC and may also have been used for dyeing and preparing textiles and leather.

Climate Change During this period there is evidence from pollen and isotopic studies that the climate became cooler and wetter, making farming much harder, especially in upland areas. The eruption of

Achentoul standing stone

Hekla in Iceland in 1159BC may have caused a sudden change for the worse in the weather, and further encouraged the development of peat in areas previously available for farming.

This could have resulted in increasing crop failures, leading to a sudden decline in the upland population which may have ensued as settlements were abandoned in favour of lower, more fertile ground.

Trough and lid beside a burnt mound

BRONZE AGE SITES TO VISIT

CAITHNESS
Tulloch of Assery animal bones
Achavanich cist burial
Hill o'Many Stanes
Garrywhin stone rows
SUTHERLAND
Achany Glen, Lairg
Ord Hill, Lairg
Learable Hill stone rows
Kildonan hut circles
Embo, Dornoch cist burials
Migdale, bronze hoard
ROSS-SHIRE
Fodderty, cist burial
Heights of Brae, Dingwall, gold

Carn Liath, north of Golspie, has a prominent tower and surrounding houses

BROCHS (ON *Borg*, stronghold) are a type of building unique to Scotland, especially the North, and of which there are over 200 examples in the North Highlands. Most of the brochs which have been excavated were cleared out in the 19th century. More recent excavations, combined with a re-appraisal of many other sites have thrown much light on the subject.

About 700BC a new type of house appeared, typified by those at Jarlshof and Old Scatness in Shetland and in the Western Isles. They have now been shown to have been built in Orkney and elsewhere. These were large and well built, with occupation continuing for at least 500 years. They represent a sharp contrast to the preceding millennium, from which domestic building remains are sparse. Unfortunately none of these interesting ruins are able to be viewed in this area. It may be that the appearance of the roundhouses reflects changes elsewhere in Scotland.

Brochs were developed in the late Iron Age as the ultimate version of the roundhouse. Many excavations clearly show how there was a progressive evolution in design until the final massive round tower, with surrounding settlement, was developed. These towers were up to 20m in diameter, with walls up to 5m thick at the base. If Mousa in Shetland, or Dun Telve and Dun Troddan in Glenelg are typical, brochs may have been up to 14m high, the walls being hollow with an interior stairway.

The single entrance is usually guarded by cells, and would no doubt have had a substan-

Broch beside Loch Naver, Sutherland

South Yarrows Broch has a well-preserved interior, now flooded

tial door. There is evidence of one or more floors in several, but whether these were galleries is not clear. Most brochs are situated in defensive positions on the coast, and usually amid prime agricultural land. This may be coincidence, as not only are there many inland brochs, but others probably occupied sites which are now modern farms.

That they were primarily defensive structures seems clear. The massive construction, ditches and ramparts were not just for show. However, the presence of contemporary houses suggests that they were often the centre of a whole community. In cases where no domestic buildings surrounded them, they must have been very imposing farmsteads.

The radiocarbon dating from several sites imply an early date of about 600BC, suggesting that roundhouses were already being developed into proto brochs by this time. One theory is that brochs are

Ousdale Broch, just north of the Ord of Caithness

a local product, which developed quickly from roundhouses, in themselves perhaps the true architectural innovation of the early Iron Age. Excavations have revealed

Carn Liath intra-mural stairway

whole unexpected sequences of occupation from an early Iron Age roundhouse, itself built on the remains of a Neolithic tomb, through to the final broch at about 200BC or earlier.

Recent work at Old Scatness in Shetland and elsewhere suggests that brochs may date from about 400BC, a much earlier date than previously envisaged for such structures. Thus it appears that the brochs were in existence well before the Romans reached Scotland.

By AD100 roundhouses had fallen out of use, and the later houses were of much poorer quality. The Greek explorer, Pytheas, circumnavigated Britain about 325BC, yet no Mediterranean artefacts have been found from this time. Roman artefacts were only present from about the 1st century AD. At the very least there was some form of contact with Roman Britain, perhaps due to Agricola's fleet in AD83.

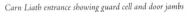

Carn Liath entrance showing guard cell and door jambs

Stairway at Dun Troddan, Glen Elg

which first appeared around 600BC. A typical example is at Ham in Caithness. Sadly, although many have been found, none are formally presented for visiting by the public. These underground structures are thought to have been used for storage, and probably formed cellars to long disappeared roundhouses.

There were similar structures under some brochs, the superficial resemblance to chambered cairns is probably more to do with common materials than anything else. There is another example, now flooded, at Laid, next to Loch Eriboll, in West Sutherland.

Wags (G little cave) are only known from the south of Caithness. These houses have upright stone pillars which supported the roof. They date from the first centuries AD and are in some ways similar to the wheelhouses found in the Western Isles and Shetland. They may be round or long in plan.

Wag of Forse (ND204352) is

Little is known of the people who inhabited the brochs. They may have been descendants of the first settlers, who developed the society themselves, or they may have been influenced by Celtic ideas or incomers. Their boats would certainly have been very seaworthy and, apart from their impressively built brochs and roundhouses, they were also accomplished farmers and fishermen.

Earthhouses Another interesting development is the earthhouse, or souterrain

Triangular lintel at Dun Dornaigil, Sutherland

Corbelled roof of cell at Dunbeath Broch

just north of Latheron. This complex site started as a small settlement. A broch was then built and the stones from it were used to construct two longhouses, one of which has two rows of pillars which supported lintels.

Access is through a long passage and doorways lead to further rooms. This complex and partially excavated site includes further Iron Age buildings as well as earlier hut circles, burnt mounds and field walls.

At South Yarrows, there is another wag like structure in the complex of outbuildings next to the broch. This also had rows of upright stones as roof supports, joined by lintels to the walls and each other.

Magnus at the Wag of Forse

Sallachy Broch, Loch Shin, Lairg

Dun Telve, Glen Elg

IRON AGE TIMELINE

BC	
c.2000	Bronze Age
	Beakers first appear
1500	Peat bogs developing
c.800	
700	Iron Age round houses
600	Oldest Broch deposits
100	Brochs at peak
100AD	Brochs abandoned

IRON AGE SITES TO VISIT
CAITHNESS
Ham
St John's Point
Skirza
Nybster
Wag of Forse
Houstry
Yarrows
Wag of Forse
Dunbeath
Ousdale
SUTHERLAND
Surgical
Carn Liath
Dun Dornaigil
Strathnaver
Kildonan
Sallachy
Laid, Loch Eriboll
ROSS-SHIRE
Dun Telve, Glenelg
Dun Troddan
Totaig Broch
Dun Lagaidh
Dun Ruigh Ruaidh

Ulbster Stone, Thurso, Caithness

symbol stones have been found in the North Highlands. By far the majority are from Easter Ross, East Sutherland and Caithness, although a few have turned up in the north and west.

The Picts were first mentioned by Eumenius in AD 297, as **Picti.** Their ancestors were also earlier referred to by Pytheas as **Pretani.** He also called the headland facing Orkney **Cape Orcas.** The *Pretani* are said to be one of the first Celtic tribes to arrive in Britain and seem to be connected with the Picts. Celtic people thus seem to have been living in the north of Scotland at least as early as the fourth century BC.

Irish legend refers to the Picts as **Cruithni,** descendants of a king called Cruithne and his seven sons. They were a Celtic people who inhabited Northern and Eastern Scotland and who spoke a form of Brittonic Celtic. They left numerous sculptured symbol stones, some houses and forts, but virtually no language apart from some place names. A form of Irish Ogam script was used, but most of the inscriptions have so far proved indecipherable, although this may soon change.

In AD43 Orkney leaders submitted to Claudius and reference is made to *Islands of the Picts.* The Romans returned again in AD83 when Agricola specifically sent his fleet to

PICTS Although often referred to as the Dark Ages, the first millennium AD was in fact a time of great change and development. The Roman invasion and the forceful spread of Christianity, came before the emergence of local, regional, and finally national power. The Pictish influence was felt in the North Highlands, to be followed by Norse domination by the end of the millennium. The people probably continued with their pastoral agriculture and fishing as previously, but much improved ships allowed more contact with the outside world. Certainly by the 8th century many families were living in remarkably good houses with a reasonable standard of life.

Symbol Stones Many Pictish

subdue Orkney. It is interesting that the decline of the brochs occurs at about the same time. This of course may all be Roman propaganda as part of their policy their potent reputation. Without hard evidence these Classical references must be held in some doubt.

It is likely that the origins of the Picts in the North Highlands go at least as far back as the early Iron Age and perhaps further still, with continuity of settlement the main theme. The sea would have been very important both for food and raw materials, as well as for communications. No doubt there were accomplished seamen and good boats. The incursions of the Romans at the height of the

development of the Brochs culture may well have stimulated a common purpose between the various tribes, who then became what the Romans called the *Picti*. The tribal groupings of the 1st century then became the Picts of the 4th century.

Although Orkney was said to be *the Cradle of the Picts*, in fact the main northern Pictish centres of power were in the Inverness area, where they had a large fort at Burghead. The Picts in the area were probably descendants of the earlier population, enriched by Celtic immigrant blood.

The Pictish Kingdom gradually developed and became more centralised, with a probable loss of power and prestige

Pictish symbol stone, Dingwall

on the part of the regional chiefs. By St Columba's time the northern Picts were embracing Christianity and in the mid 9th century the Picts

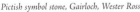

Pictish symbol stone, Gairloch, Wester Ross

The Eagle Stone, Strathpeffer, Easter Ross

Shandwick Stone, Fearn Peninsula, Easter Ross

and Scots had been unified under Kenneth MacAlpin. The Northern Isles were already under Norse threat, which soon spread southwards.

There has been speculation that Christianity may have partly caused the downfall of Pictish power. Inheritance may have followed the female line, at least for the kings. Many of the beliefs of Pictish society, as deduced by some experts from their symbol stones, may have been quite different to Christian thinking. Finally, the increasing numbers of pagan Norse raiders and settlers could have exploited the disintegrating society, and taken over easily.

Although the *Orkneyinga Saga* makes no mention of the Picts, it nevertheless refers to the Pentland Firth as *Peetalands Fjordur*, Fjord of Pictland. There are also numerous *Pett* names which suggest Picts. The vast majority of place names in the North Highlands are derived from Old Norse, English and Gaelic, but there remain several which may derive from the old Celtic language.

The Moon was masculine in the Norn, the Old Norse language spoken in Caithness until a few hundred years ago. This is most unusual, and perhaps reflects the Pictish form. However, these forms may derive from later Scots Gaelic. What is sure is that the Picts left an immense legacy of pla-

Pictish symbol stone, Poolewe, Wester Ross

Pictish fragment, Portmahomack

Pictish stone fragment, Strathnaver Museum

Edderton Stone detail

Shandwick Stone, Fearn Peninsula, Easter Ross

Dunbeath Pictish symbol stone

Site of Pictish monastery at Dunbeath Strath

cenames and symbol stones.

Chapels Many chapel sites predate the Viking settlement, including those dedicated to saints such as St Boniface, St Drostan, St Columba, St Maelrubha and St Peter, some of which may have been in use by the general population as well as monks. Many later churches are built over earlier Christian sites.

Recent excavations have revealed much about Pictish buildings. They indicate that some of the Picts lived in substantial dwellings, grew oats and bere, raised cattle, sheep and pigs. They also fished extensively offshore, showing that they had seaworthy boats. There was some communication with the outside world as shown by their artefacts.

Pictish Monasteries There are several monastic sites which date from Pictish times. In the east, Rosemarkie, Dunbeath and Portmahomack are the most prominent.

Portmahomack monastery originally dates from the 6th century. The cemetery had only older males buried in stone cists with cross-marked grave markers. There was clearly an important Christian site here around the time of St Columba.

St Boniface, also known as Curadan, and St Moluag are associated with Rosemarkie. The Pictish king, Nechtan, is said to have requested Northumbrian monks and stone masons to establish a stone church dedicated to St Peter here. A monastery was created and numerous Pictish carved cross-slabs underline the importance of the site.

At Ballachly, near Dunbeath, remains of a 6th century chapel have revealed the probable presence of an early monastery here. Part of a Pictish carved cross-slab is on display in the Heritage Centre and the suggestion is of another 6th century monastery. Later there was a major Norse ironworks here.

At all three of these sites pro-duction of carved Pictish cross-slabs was clearly important. Perhaps the most impressive of all is the Rosemarkie Stone now on display with others in the Groam House Museum in Rosemarkie.

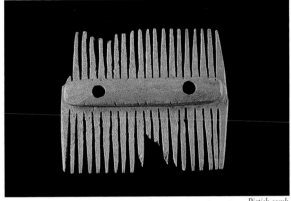

Pictish comb

Ballachly Stone, Dunbeath Heritage Centre

Pictish fragment at Portmahomack

PICTISH TIMELINE

AD
83   Battle of Mons Graupius
c.100   Decline of brochs
297   Eumenius mentions Picts
c.561   Breidei receives Columba
c.580   Pictish monasteries
c.680   First symbol stones
700s   Pictish hoards hidden
843   Unification of Scots & Picts

PICTISH SITES TO VISIT

CAITHNESS

Caithness Horizons
Dunbeath Heritage Trail
Freswick
Forse, Latheron
South Yarrows

SUTHERLAND

Strathnaver Museum
Dunrobin Castle Museum

ROSS-SHIRE

Portmahomack
Rosemarkie
Gairloch
Poolewe
Applecross
Nigg Church
Dingwall
Strathpeffer
Edderton
Shandwick
Hilton of Cadboll

Archaeology and History

Replica Viking longship Gaia

VIKINGS For nearly five hundred years much of the North Highlands was dominated by the Norse, initially invaders and then settlers from Western Norway. They rapidly colonised the Northern Isles and went on to build the Earldom of Orkney which, at its peak in the 11th century, controlled much of the west coast of Scotland, the Hebrides, the Isle of Man, Caithness, Sutherland and coastal parts of Ross-Shire.

Their westward expansion started late in the 8th century and, apart from population and other pressures, was made possible by technology. The development of large ocean going sailing ships, combined with a knowledge of seamanship and navigation, which could reliably transport people, livestock and goods for long distances, allowed them an ascendancy over other coastal Europeans for several centuries.

Orkney made an obvious base for these seafaring people, in a time when there was no quick land transport. While there is some evidence that contact may already have been going on for some time before the main influx, it now seems that the Norse takeover was abrupt and complete.

The Picts simply seem to have disappeared. Existing settlements were taken over by the Vikings, who may even have recycled some Pictish pots and other household items, but soon the invaders imposed their own farming style and land holding patterns, which are preserved as farm names and parishes to this day.

Recent excavations have suggested that there may have been a considerable Pictish population in Orkney, Caithness and Sutherland at the time of the Viking migrations in the 8th century and there have been suggestions that the Norse colonisation may have been peaceful. However, there is scant evidence supporting this idea.

Very few Celtic placenames and other words have survived in these areas, again suggesting that the Norse political takeover must have been fast and virtually total, and that no integration took place. The attractiveness of Orkney as a Viking base, due to position and natural resources, must have been overwhelming, and the Pictish people, leaders, churchmen and ordinary people either fled or were slaughtered.

This short but violent period of Viking migration at the end of the 8th century, was followed by an influx of settlers such that Norse culture and language totally replaced Pictish. This is

Norse Steatite vessel from Freswick

Norse hack silver

well stated in **Historia Norwegiae**, written in the 11th or 12th century referring to the Picts who *"did marvels in the morning and in the evening, in building towns, but at mid-day they entirely lost all their strength, and lurked, through fear, in underground houses"* It goes on to say *"But in due course... certain pirates... set out with a great fleet... and stripped these races of their ancient settlements, destroyed them wholly, and subdued the islands to themselves."*

The early 20th century Orcadian historian, Storer Clouston, had no illusions about what happened, *"Surely the common-sense of the matter ... is evident. The first Norsemen.... proposed to settle in these islands, whether the existing inhabitants liked it or not. They brought their swords, and if the inhabitants were numerous and offered resistance, they fought them. If they were few and fled, they took their land without fighting. They did, in fact, exactly what we ourselves have done in later centuries, in India, America, Africa, Australia. That is the only way in which we can settle a new land - chance your luck, but always bring your gun."*

Most of our knowledge of the

Freswick has a lovely long sandy beach

Vikings comes from the sagas, which describe the feuds of great families and the deeds of great men, but do not give much detail of more mundane events or conditions. There was a climatic improvement during the Viking era which greatly aided westward expansion, the development of more advanced agriculture and population growth.

It also seems that the Vikings had made improvements to living standards such as improved domestic hygiene and midwifery, as well as being good blacksmiths, joiners, farmers, shipbuilders and seamen. Additionally, they were craftsmen and took great pride in their work as is evident from their high quality weapons and

items of jewellery. Perhaps most important, was the advanced technology of their ships and their navigation skills.

Today, many placenames derive from Old Norse, with only a few possible Pictish remnants. The *Orkneyinga Saga* and other Norse Sagas, mainly written in the 12th century in Iceland, give a vivid account of Viking times, with many colourful characters.

According to the *Saga* the Earldom was founded by King Harald *Harfargi* (Fairhair), who set out *west over sea* to deal with the Orkney Vikings who kept making raids on Norway. During his time Norway was united as one Kingdom (in 892AD), and the lands *west over*

Runic-inscribed stone found at St Peter's Church, Wick on top of a burial

ARCHAEOLOGY AND HISTORY

Dornoch Firth

sea of Orkney, Shetland, the Hebrides and Man came under his rule.

Earl Rognvald of More became Earl of Orkney, but passed the title to his brother, **Sigurd, the Mighty**, the first Earl of Orkney to be recorded by history. He is best known for his death rather than his life. During one of his forays into Scotland, c.AD893, he incurred the wrath of a man called Maelbrigte *Tusk*.

A meeting was arranged where each was to bring 40 men and 40 horses. Sigurd put two men on each horse, with the result that all the Scots were killed and beheaded. The Vikings tied the heads to their saddles in triumph, but Maelbrigte had the last laugh as one of his protruding buck teeth scratched Sigurd's leg, causing a fatal infection. He is buried at Sigurd's Howe, now called Ciderhall, near Dornoch.

Sigurd was succeeded by another colourful character, his half-brother **Torf Einar**, who *"took the earldom, and was long earl, and was a man of great power"*. Despite only having one eye, the *Orkneyinga Saga* recounts his sharp vision.

The *Saga* tells how he found and slew Halfdan Fairhair on North Ronaldsay for killing his father, Rognvald, by burning him alive in his house in Norway. He then carved the blood eagle on Halfdan's back, *"Einar had his ribs cut from the spine with a sword and the lungs pulled out through the slits in his back. He dedicated the victim to Odin as a victory offering"*.

Thorfinn *Skull-Splitter*, said to be buried in the Howe of Hoxa on South Ronaldsay, became sole Earl when his brothers were killed at the Battle of Stainmore in 954. He was said to be *"a mighty chief and warlike"*, but it is not officially recorded how he came by his nickname.

Sigurd the Stout was a powerful Earl, known for his prowess in battle, his sorcery and his ability to invoke the old gods. His mother was a sorceress and made him the enchanted Raven Banner, warning *"My belief is this: that it will bring victory to the man it's carried before, but death to the one who carries it"*.

Sigurd was forcibly converted to Christianity by King Olav Tryggvesson at Osmondwall (Kirk Hope) on Hoy in Orkney

Norse bronze pins

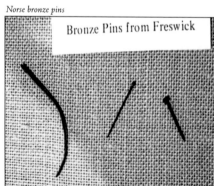

Bronze Pins from Freswick

Norse pottery

in 995, on pain of the death of his son. The whole of Orkney was said to have embraced the faith. The son, Hvelp, died soon after, so Sigurd renounced Christianity and refused to recognise King Olaf.

He was killed in 1014 at the Battle of Clontarf when he himself took up the Raven Banner, after many had fallen carrying it, *"There was no man who would bear the raven-standard and the earl bore it himself, and fell there."*

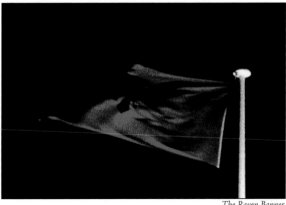

The Raven Banner

Sigurd's son and successor, **Thorfinn the Mighty**, presided over the period of maximum power and extension of the Orkney Earldom. Thorfinn was a close relative of Macbeth and the Scottish author, Dorothy Dunnet, has even suggested that they may have been the same person. He was brought up in the Scottish Court by his grandfather, Malcolm II, who granted him the Earldom of Caithness and Sutherland.

His foster father and mentor **Thorkel Fostri** played an important part in his power struggle to become sole Earl. His main opponent was **Rognvald Brusison** who had the support of the Norwegian King. Eventually after several spectacular battles, house burnings and escapades, Rognvald was cornered on Papa Stronsay at Yule 1046 and killed by Thorkel Fostri.

By this time Thorfinn was said to control nine Earldoms from his base in Birsay where he presided over a lavish household. He was to rule his earl-

doms peacefully for another 18 years, during which he made a pilgrimage to Rome in 1049-50, after which the first Bishop of Orkney, **Bishop Thorolf**, was appointed.

The Norse Earls were always in as close touch with Scottish rulers as they were with their Norse superiors, frequently marrying the daughters of other noblemen, or of the Scottish or Norwegian King. Their divided loyalties often caused problems, which eventually led to the end of the Earldom.

In the later 10th century Norse power in the west was at its peak, with the conquest of

Pot lids

Normandy, the discovery of America by Leif Erikson and Norse migrations to northern and eastern England. Many hoards of valuables were hidden either by locals fearing Viking attack, or by Vikings themselves for safekeeping. Some of these caches have since been found, but more may yet be hidden.

In addition, the climate was considerably better than today, greatly facilitating sea voyages in open boats. The tradition was that after the crops were sown a spring cruise was made, while later on after harvest a second autumn cruise followed.

Norse Tortoise brooch

Swiney Castle south of Lybster

LATE NORSE TIMES By 1066 the Viking Age was nearly over as the power of kingdoms grew. Scandinavians settled in many places in Britain, as revealed by the placenames derived from Old Norse. A number of churches date from this time, a few of which remain standing, or are incorporated into later buildings.

The 12th century saw the martyrdom of Earl Magnus, followed by a pilgrimage to the Holy Land by his cousin, Earl Haakon Paulson, the instigator of his death. He was succeeded by his son Paul in 1123, who in turn was succeeded in 1135 by Earl Rognvald Kolson, nephew of Magnus during whose time the Orkney Earldom continued to flourish.

St Magnus Cathedral, founded in 1137 by Earl Rognvald, in memory of his martyred uncle Magnus, is the most spectacular Norse structure in Scotland. There are several Norse churches in Caithness, such as St Mary's Kirk at Forse and the early parts of St Peter's in Wick.

With the death of *The Ultimate Viking*, Sweyn Asleifson, at Dublin on a raid in 1171, the independent power of the Earldom of Orkney was coming to a close. In 1193 a fleet manned by the *Island Beardies*, many of the leading men from Orkney, Shetland and Caithness invaded Norway with the support of the Earl. They were roundly defeated at the **Battle of Florvag** in 1194 near Bergen by King Sverre Sigurdsson.

The estates of those involved were taken by the Norwegian Crown, and a Royal *Sysselman* appointed to collect taxes and administer the sequestrated estates on behalf of the King. More seriously, Shetland was from now administered directly from Norway, while the Earl, Harald Maddadson had to give an oath of fealty to Sverre. Thus, the Orkney Earldom became less independent of Norway.

The situation was further complicated when the Scottish King, William the Lion, took advantage of the situation by invading Caithness. Scrabster Castle was demolished in the process. The result was that the Earldom's Scottish lands were now held under the Scottish Crown rather than directly and the Earl had to submit to the King of Scots as well as the King of Norway.

On the death of Harald Maddadson, himself three-quarters Scottish, in 1206, Norse power was on the wane. The first Scottish Earl, albeit with strong Norse connections, was Magnus II, in c.1233. In 1262 Norway annexed Iceland

Lambaborg or Bucholie Castle, south of Freswick

and Greenland, then, in late Summer 1263, King Haakon Haakonson arrived in Orkney with a large fleet of over 100 ships intent on re-asserting Norse power in the west of Scotland and the Hebrides. The fleet mustered at Elwick Bay in Shapinsay before heading out into the Pentland Firth bound for the Clyde.

There was an indecisive skirmish, now called the Battle of Largs, but the main factor was the arrival of a sudden and severe gale during which the fleet was scattered and some vessels damaged. Haakon retreated to Orkney to regroup, but became ill and died in the Bishop's Palace at Yule. He was temporarily buried in St Magnus Cathedral before being returned to Bergen in 1264. By the Treaty of Perth in 1266, Norway resigned all of the Hebrides and the Isle of Man, but only on condition that Norway retained Orkney and Shetland. The agreement was that the Scots would purchase the Hebrides for 4,000 merks

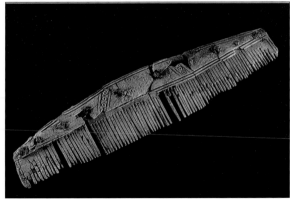

Norse comb made from Reindeer antler

plus an annual payment thereafter in perpetuity of 100 merks. This *Annual of Norway* was to be handed over in St Magnus Cathedral each year.

Norwegian- Scottish connections were strengthened by the marriage of Alexander III's daughter to King Erik of Norway. The accidental death of the former and the sad death of their daughter, the Maid of Norway, on her way to become Queen of Scotland was a severe setback, compounded by the death soon after her mother. Eventually, the success of Robert

the Bruce and the marriage of his sister, Isabella, to King Erik would greatly settle relations for some time.

The Scottish Earls continued to have strong ties with Norway. During the 14th century they gradually lost power and influence as the nation states of Norway and Scotland grew. Increasing Scots influence and an influx of lowland Scots during the 15th century gradually eroded Udal Law and the Norn language, the last known official Norse document being dated 1425. With the takeover of

Fish bones found at Freswick

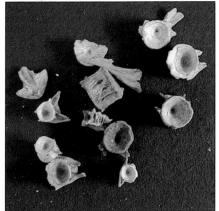

Norse bangle

Sea Stallion is a replica longship which sailed to Dublin and back in 2007-2008

Norway by Denmark, the Norse interest in the North further reduced, particularly as the connection had always been with Western Norway, rather than with Denmark.

When the daughter of the Danish King was to marry the Scottish King in 1468, the Danes had no compunction about using Orkney, which had been Norway's closest colony, as a guarantee for the dowry. It is interesting that this has never been repaid. Thus ended ignominiously over 600 years of Norse rule of the islands.

Relatively few excavations have been made at Viking sites in the North Highlands. Sadly, so far, only a few of the recently excavated artefacts are on display and even fewer of these sites are open to visitors.

Worse still, much earlier work was poorly recorded and has never been reported on. Many artefacts found in the 19th century simply disappeared, or are of unknown provenance. Despite this lack of tangible evidence, the wealth of Old Norse language in the placenames is a constant reminder of Norse heritage.

Norse Castles Perhaps the best example of a 12th century Norse castle is the Castle of Old Wick, just south of Wick. This small square stone keep may have been built by Earl Harald Maddadson. Similar strongholds are mentioned in the *Orkneyinga Saga*, perhaps the most interesting being Lambaborg, or Bucholie Castle north of Freswick, which belonged to Sweyn Asleifson, the *Ultimate Viking*. Other sites include Swiney Castle, Castle Gunn, Halberry Castle and Scrabster Castle. The last was destroyed by King William the Lion.

Bishop's Palace When the Diocese of Caithness was estab-

Steatite pestle and mortar from Freswick   *Pot lids from Freswick*

lished in 1145 a Bishop's Palace was erected soon after near Scrabster. Later Gilbert de Moravia built a new residence shortly after being appointed in 1222. This palace was in ruins by the early 18th century and only a few grassy mounds remain.

Old Wick Castle today

Freswick today is a quiet sandy bay backed by extensive sand dunes and machair. It was the site of a large Norse settlement and farm during the 11th to 13th centuries. Fishing was a major activity here and also at Robertshaven on the north coast. Cod, Saithe and Ling were caught, some of which were up to 2m long.

Oats and Barley were grown and cattle, sheep and pigs were raised. Limpets were used for fish bait and large numbers of domestic artefacts were found.

Hog-backed Tombstones were a fashion from the 10th century onwards and may have originated in the north of England. None of the elaborately carved rooflike examples found elsewhere are present in the North Highlands. There are a number of examples of simple long oval carved stones including in Tain and at St Drostan's cemetery at Westfield in Caithness, which could date from Norse times.

Old Wick Castle in 1821 by William Daniell

Possible Norse tombstone at Tain

NORSE AGE TIME-LINE

AD	
795	Iona first attacked
995	Sigurd the Strong baptised by force
c1000	Sigurd makes Earl Gilli Governor
1014	Battle of Clontarf, Isles under Kingdom of Man
1066	Stamford Bridge
1098	King Magnus Barelegs' expedition
1156	Loss of Southern Hebrides
1263	"Battle" of Largs
1266	Treaty of Perth

SITES TO VISIT

St Mary's Chapel
Scrabster
Old St Peter's, Wick
Freswick
Lambaborg/Bucholie Castle
Old Wick Castle
Swiney Castle
Ciderhall
Dingwall

Old St Peter's Church at Balnakeil Bay, Durness dates from 1619

CHRISTIAN CHAPELS were established by the 6th century and probably earlier at several places in the North Highlands. These were founded by clerics from Whithorn, Northumbria and Ireland. By the late 600s monasteries were founded at Portmahomack, Rosemarkie, Dunbeath and Applecross.

St Ninian is reputed to have preached at Navidale, north of Helmsdale, in c.390AD and indeed traces of an ancient chapel are evident in the old kirkyard there. The nearby parish of Kildonan is an early dedication and this suggests that a St Donan's chapel stood here once.

Pictish Period These monasteries were centres of Pictish craftsmanship where beautifully carved cross-slabs were created. Vellum and parchment were made to produce books, while bronze, silver, gold and glass were all worked. Farming was also practised on a substantial scale.

In about 800AD the Portmahomack monastery was burnt down, perhaps by the Vikings, though there is no evidence for this. The Tarbat Discovery Centre has displays from excavations here. Groam House Museum in Rosemarkie has much to see relating to this period.

Norse Period Although the Vikings may have arrived as marauders, they soon settled down as farmers and traders. In 995 Earl Sigurd the Stout was forcibly converted to Christianity by King Olav Tryggvesson. After this the whole of Orkney, Caithness and the rest of his people are said to have embraced the faith.

Pictish carving, Portmahomack

Tarbat Discovery Centre, Portmahomack

Although there are no records of stone chapels dating from the 10ᵗʰ century in the North Highlands, there are many sites which could originate from this period. With the creation of the Diocese of Caithness in 1145 more substantial churches were built, including St Peter's in Wick, St Mary's near Forse and the original Cathedral at Halkirk, now gone.

St Mary's Chapel, Crosskirk, near Forse

St Magnus Hospice (ND158549) dates from the 12ᵗʰ century, when the cult of the saint was very strong. It gives its name to nearby Spittal, on the A9 Cassiemyre Road south of Thurso. All that can be seen now is the gable end of a small chapel, but doubtless a quite substantial structure once stood here to accommodate pilgrims on their way north and south.

Old St Peter's Kirk, Wick

Dunnet Kirk

St Drostan's Kirk, Canisbay

12ᵗʰ Century Churches Dunnet Church and St Drostan's at Canisbay both date from the 12ᵗʰ century. They have been extensively modified over the centuries. The present buildings both date from the 17ᵗʰ century. So far no evidence has been found of an ancient chapel at Thurso, but undoubtedly there would have been one near the Bishop's Palace.

St Mary's Chapel (ND024700) is roofless, but otherwise intact. Originally it probably had a thatched roof. It has a small nave and a little square chancel. This design is unique to Caithness in the Highlands, but also is common in the Northern Isles. There are similar ruinous examples at Skinnet (ND130620) and Watten (ND233524).

History & Culture

Dornoch Cathedral

Dornoch Cathedral was established by Bishop Gilbert de Moravia in 1224 at the southern end of his diocese. It was built at his own expense. Despite the roof being burnt in 1570 during a clan feud and being restored in the 19th century, this old kirk retains a special feeling of beauty and sanctuary quite out of proportion to its size.

St Duthac's Collegiate Church in Tain was built in c.1370, near the site of a much older chapel. This was one of the most popular pilgrimage places in Scotland partly because James IV and V both regularly visited it.

Fearn Abbey was founded in 1221 on the site of a much earlier chapel, but moved in 1238 to its present site. Although the monastery was dissolved at the reformation it continues in use as the parish church. Nearby the Nigg Old Church dates from 1626, but undoubtedly replaced a much more ancient building.

Fortrose Cathedral was built in the 13th century as the cathedral of the Diocese of Ross. The seat of the bishop was originally at Rosemarkie, but Bishop Robert moved it to Fortrose in the early 13th century. Today only the south aisle, chapel and chapter house remain standing.

Enough survives to show that this building was once the most impressive church in the North Highlands. Sadly it was a victim of the Reformation, the roof was removed and sold in 1572. Thereafter the walls were used as a quarry to build the town and perhaps by Cromwell to build his fort at Inverness. The foundations of the main church are visible which gives an idea of its former glory.

Dornoch Cathedral

Reformation After 1560 many of the larger churches fell into disuse. Some were used for their stones, or burned down by accident. Many were also modified in line with presbyterian forms of worship. Instead of the celebration of mass, services took the form of preaching the Word of God.

Pulpits were built on the south wall, and interior furniture (where it existed) was changed to suit. Generally a long communion table ran down the church from east to west and the congregation took their own stools to sit on. Aisles were added to many churches to increase the space for congregations, often with an upper laird's loft.

Old St Peter's Church at Balnakeil Bay, Durness dates from 1619 and is roofless, but illustrates the style of the time. Many charming old churches from the 18ᵗʰ century can be visited, including those at Cromarty, Golspie, Reay and Tongue.

Fortrose Cathedral

Nigg Old Parish Kirk

Old gravestone at Tain

Aumbry at Tain Collegiate Church

Fearn Abbey

OLD CHURCHES TIMELINE

AD	
5ᵗʰ or 6ᵗʰ cent	Mid Fearn & Tarbat
673	Applecross founded
8ᵗʰ cent	Oldest Tarbat church
9ᵗʰ cent	St Duthac at Tain
1150	Halkirk
1220	St Peter's, Wick
1224	Dornoch Cathedral
1238	Fearn Abbey
1240	Fortrose Abbey

SITES TO VISIT

Caithness	St Mary's, Reay
	St Peter's, Wick
	Dunnet
	Canisbay
	Halkirk
Sutherland	Balnakeil
	Dornoch
Ross-shire	Fortrose
	Fearn Abbey
	Tain
	Portmahomack
	Edderton
	Nigg
	Applecross

Sinclair & Girnigoe Castle is spectacularly sited on cliffs near Noss Head, northeast of Wick

CASTLES were built in the North Highlands since Norse times. From the 13th century onwards the typical castle was a tower-house. Many are situated in dramatic coastal positions with natural defences such as on rocky headlands. Others are in equally strategic positions on lochs or commanding narrows where boats must pass to enter rivers or sea lochs.

The basic design had one room per floor, enclosed by massive stone built walls. The ground level was usually vaulted and access was by removeable wooden stairs to the hall above. Above that would have been one or more bedrooms, and all were reached by a spiral staircase within the wall.

Defence was largely passive, just as with the earlier brochs, but arrows could be fired from slit windows or from a parapet below the roof. Generally, these keeps were protected by curtain walls, ramparts and ditches.

Domestic buildings such as storehouses, kitchens, stables, byres, barns and accommodation blocks would also have been enclosed within the curtain wall. Later, defence became secondary to appear-

Ardvreck Castle, is on Loch Assynt, Sutherland

Skelbo Castle

Castle of Mey, the Caithness home of HRH, the Queen Mother

ance. Extra wings were added, towers became more elaborate and corbelled windows were incorporated.

Scottish Crown   As the power of the Crown grew in the 13th and 14th centuries, castles were built either by the King or by loyal nobles to consolidate control. Few of these remain today. As they fell into disuse they were either used as convenient sources of stone or re-developed over the years. As a result many remaining castles incorporate ancient sections within their fabric.

Visits   All of the ruined castles mentioned in the book can be visited, but it should be noted that some are in a dangerous state and should not be entered. The Castles of Mey, Dunrobin and Eilean Donan are all open to the public in the summer. Others (or their grounds) are occasionally open to visitors for a few days in the year.

Eilean Donan is perhaps the most iconic castle in the North Highlands

Old Keiss Castle is perched on the edge of cliffs north of Wick

OLD CASTLES TIME-LINE

AD	
1266	Treaty of Perth
	Girnigoe oldest
c.1300	Eilean Donan
c.1400	Ardvreck Castle
c.1600	Old Keiss Castle

SITES TO VISIT

CAITHNESS
Dounreay
Mey
Sinclair & Girnigoe
Old Wick
Swiney
Old Keiss
Bucholie
Dunbeath
SUTHERLAND
Dunrobin
Dornoch
Ardvreck
Tongue

ROSS-SHIRE
Strome
Eilean Donan
Skelbo

HISTORY AND CULTURE

Fortrose Cathedral, a quarry for Cromwell and others

JAMES VI officially came to the Scottish throne in 1578. In 1603 he became King of England and Ireland on the death of Elizabeth I. He was in many ways the first modern ruler of Scotland, though he never had much interest in the Highlands, and had no Gaelic.

The Union of the Crowns changed attitudes to the Highlands, which went from being half of a small country to being a peripheral part of a much larger Kingdom. Ever since the forfeiture of the Lord of the Isles in 1493 the Scottish Crown had been trying to assert control over its northern and western regions.

The Statutes of Iona in 1608 were one means by which James reeled in the powers of the clan chiefs. This ultimately allowed the survival of the clans and their heads, albeit in a vastly different form.

The North Highlands were even more peripheral and largely escaped the carnage of the Civil War (1625-1660) and the restoration and revolutionary times that lasted until 1692.

Jacobite Rebellions in 1715, 1719, and 1745 made a strong impact on the whole of the Highlands. Apart from the general mayhem and slaughter by Government troops after

the Battle of Culloden in 1746, the main effect was to draw the North Highlands closer to the Lowlands. The Highland chiefs were stripped of their powers and their dependents became tenants.

Forfeited Estates As part of the suppression of the Highlands, many landowners who had supported the Jacobite cause had their lands confiscated after 1746.

General Wade was appointed to build a network of military roads in 1724. He and his successors built over 1,000 miles of roads and many bridges, some of which were north of Inverness. However, by 1800 many were in disrepair due to lack of maintenance.

Emigration to North America increased enormously after these reprisals. In 1760-1775 at least 40,000 people left for the New World. People from the Highlands and Islands had always gone south in search of work, but never in such numbers or so far.

The Highland Society was founded in London in 1784 by 25 Scottish gentlemen. Its aims were to foster cultural and economic development in the Highlands. The first president was the popular 5th Duke of Atholl, while its members were landowners and men of letters.

Papers on agricultural improvement, livestock and

The picturesque old Oykel Bridge

new crops were published. They also investigated the controversy surrounding the authenticity of *Ossian, Fragments of Ancient Poetry*, which were presented by James MacPherson. These were claimed to be translations of ancient Gaelic poems composed by the bard, Ossian. This furore, created by MacPherson, enhanced interest in the Highlands, which became a new cultural vogue. During this time a Gaelic dictionary and New testament were published.

Agricultural Development had been proceeding apace further south and the first sheep farm to reach Ross-shire was around 1777. In 1792 two Cameron brothers from Lochaber evicted 37 families from their land at Kildermorie. Soon sheep-rearing was in competition with the traditional way of life in the Highlands.

In Easter Ross and the Black Isle, farms had always been bigger and produced large quantities of grain for export. This was stored in girnels, such as at Storehouse of Foulis and Portmahomack, before shipment to Europe.

Further north and to the west the tenants were smallholders who continually divided up their already small plots of land. They had no security of tenure over their holdings. The pressure on landlords to increase the revenue from their land was becoming more

Blackface Sheep

acute, and from then on clearances of people from their traditional lands in favour of the short-term benefits of sheep farming became irresistible to many.

The sheep did well on the ancient croftland for a time until the land was exhausted.

During nearly 30 years of wars against the French, demand for mutton, wool and sheepskins had soared. The coming of peace in 1815 meant that Britain turned to empire-building and industrialization which in turn required food and other agricultural products.

Girnels at Portmahomack

Bernera Barracks, Glenelg

History and Culture

Cape Wrath lighthouse was first lit in 1830

The 19th Century was to see the North Highlands finally, though somewhat reluctantly, become part of industrialized of Britain. The Industrial Revolution brought great improvements in transport everywhere, including to the far north.

Transport Infrastructure
The Commission for Highland Roads and Bridges was created in 1803 and Thomas Telford was appointed to oversee the work. Ultimately this included many harbours, piers, churches and manses, as well as the Caledonian Canal.

Much of the road network remains in use today, and examples of his bridges can be seen at Helmsdale, Ousdale and Golspie. His cast-iron bridge at Bonar Bridge was replaced by a new one, but many of his harbour works remain in use today.

Steamships were introduced from the 1830s and immediately transformed the reliability and safety of sea transport. Export of grain, cattle, sheep, flagstone and whisky allowed these industries to thrive as never before. The first regular Pentland Firth steamship service started in 1856.

West coast services were started in 1851 by the forerunner of the company that eventually became today's Calmac, but services only reached as far as Skye and Kyle of Lochalsh. In 1855 services began from Kyle to Lewis. The ferry terminal for Stornoway was moved to Ullapool in 1973, with the introduction of ro-ro services.

Harbours were developed and enlarged in response to the introduction of larger and larger ships, increased trade and fish landings. Apart from the harbours built during the Herring Boom, major deep water ports were constructed at Scrabster and Invergordon.

While Scrabster's success has always been as a ferry and freight handling harbour, Invergordon was from the first a military port. The Royal Navy built a coaling station here in the mid 1800s and continued to use the base for over 100 years thereafter.

Railways The Far North Line runs from Inverness to Wick and Thurso. It was built in stages, reaching Invergordon in 1863, Helmsdale in 1871 and finally Thurso in 1874, and was largely financed by local landowners such as the 3rd Duke of Sutherland.

This line runs along the coast for much of its route but takes two great loops inland. The first was designed to avoid having to bridge the Dornoch Firth and to encourage the development of Lairg. The northern loop runs inland from Helmsdale via Forsinard

Telford Bridge across the River Helmsdale

and the Flow Country, then northeast to the coast.

The Kyle of Lochalsh Line goes from there to Dingwall. It was also opened in stages, reaching Stromeferry in 1870, from where ferries operated to Kyle, Skye and the Outer Hebrides. This scenic line only reached Kyle in 1897 and has been threatened with closure many times.

Lighthouses The Commissioners of Northern Lighthouses was established by Parliament in 1786. The first lighthouses in the North Highlands were installed on the notorious Pentland Skerries in 1794. Due to the French Wars, shipping was increasingly using the northabout route around Britain. Many were lost due to the numerous hazards.

In typical 19ᵗʰ century style the Board set about building lighthouses all around the coast. Eventually over 20 major and minor lights were built around the coast of the North Highlands. Several others cover the approaches to the Pentland Firth. Most are still operational and all are remotely controlled by the NLB from Edinburgh.

Caithness Flagstone has been used as a building material ever since the first people settled there. The beds of Old Red Sandstone split into convenient sized pieces, which can be further trimmed or cut as desired. Shipments are said to have been first made in 1793.

Telford's Bonar Bridge was built of iron in 1812 but has since been replaced

Cities all over the world, including Edinburgh, London, New York, Boston, Bombay and Melbourne have Caithness flagstone pavements.

For over 100 years from 1825, when James Traill shipped his first full cargo from Castlehill on the west side of Dunnet Bay, hundreds of thousands of tons of flagstone were shipped far and wide. Quarries were opened, at Castletown, as well as west of Holborn Head, at

Modern train at Helmsdale which the railway reached in 1871

St Ola I at Scrabster, her long service lasted from 1892 until 1951

The Duke of Sutherland failed to clear the very fertile Durness Estate

Spittal and elsewhere.

The flags were worked by hand, bed by bed, without explosives, to avoid shattering the stone. Water and wind power were used to pump water and drive saws. Steam power was introduced in 1861 which led to a much higher output of finished stone.

Finally, competition from locally mixed concrete made Caithness flagstone too expensive. There has been a recent revival in demand for building projects where natural stone has been preferred. It also has the advantage of being maintenance free and virtually indestructible, as well as being impervious to water and extremes of heat.

The Clearances, or *coercive depopulation* as they have been described, took place from the 1790s until the 1880s arousing conflicting and strong emotions. This great exodus of people from the Highlands, whether voluntary or not remains a contentious subject.

During this period articles started to appear in newspapers such as *The Times*. The harrowing reports of whole valleys, such as Strathnaver, being brutally cleared of their indigenous people for economic reasons aroused much indignation and concern as far south as London.

Some landowners were reluctant to evict their tenants. Of those displaced, many emigrated to North America, New Zealand or Australia with or without assistance, to the great advantage of their chosen new homelands. However, others lacked financial and spiritual resources to leave.

Failures It should be noted that the landlords did not always succeed in evictions, even when they resorted to the use of police and military force. In 1882 the Battle of the Braes took place near Portree, where Lord MacDonald failed to evict his tenants despite the use of 50 Glasgow policemen. Press reports of this battle shocked public opinion.

The Cromartie Estate made several attempts to evict tenants from Achiltibuie in 1882 and 1883. On each occasion the Sheriff Officer was met by the local women, stripped, and the legal papers burnt in the boat which had taken him from Ullapool. The Marquis of Stafford asked for a military escort, but this was refused and the evictions failed.

In 1841 at Durness the women made the Sheriff Officer hold his hand over a fire, so that he dropped the papers, which were burnt. A few days later the Procurator Fiscal arrived with 14 special constables and other officials.

Caithness flagstone at Achanarras Quarry

A group of 40 Durness men tried to negotiate with the Sheriff Officer, but he refused. The men then attacked the Durine Inn, disarmed the constables and escorted the party to the parish boundary. The riot had been well reported in the newspapers and an official enquiry was held. Military intervention was called for, but this request was not met.

Although the Ceannabeinne people to the east of Durness were nevertheless evicted in 1842, the strongly negative publicity forced the Duke of Sutherland to order his Factor to desist from any attempt to clear tenants of the Durness Estate. Their descendants still hold and maintain those crofts on the fertile land of Sangomore and Durine.

The Crofters Act was passed in 1886 as a result of the Napier Report. This was the result of a Royal Commission headed by Lord Napier, which toured the Highlands in 1883 and heard witnesses from every crofting area. The report, of over 5,000 pages, is a remarkable historic document. Perhaps its one of most telling comments states, *"The opinion was often expressed before us that the small tenantry have inherited an inalienable right to security of tenure in their possession while rent and service are duly rendered, an impression indigenous to the country though it has never been sanctioned by legal recognition, and has long been repudiated by the actions of the proprietor."*

Napier had many innovative solutions, but most were too far ahead of their time to meet official sanction. A compromise solution, whereby the main content of the Irish Land Act of 1881 was re-used to grant tenants guaranteed tenure, fair rents and the right to inherit land holdings.

The result was that while crofters had gained many rights, in fact the Act ossified Highland society in its 1886 state and inhibited development and progress. The landless remained so and grievances between landowners and tenants continued in a sterile, unproductive way.

Education and Gaelic Ever since the Statutes of Iona in 1609 the position of Gaelic in Scotland was ambivalent. The Church of Scotland for long resisted the use of the *"Language of Eden"* in its services. Church schools only taught in English. This slowly changed, especially after the Disruption of the Church of Scotland in 1843, when many ministers and their flocks left to form the Free Church of Scotland.

Even the 1882 Education Act made no provision for the teaching and use of the language in schools. It was not until 1918 that this was generally permitted. Today the language is positively encouraged, even to the extent of the Highland Council putting up confusing Gaelic signposts in places where nobody has spoken the language for centuries.

19ᵗʰ CENTURY TIMELINE	
c.1760	Sheep farming
	Start of Improvements
	Many emigrate
c.1780	Crofting system introduced
1786	Northern Lighthouse Board
1794	Pentland Skerries lights
1803	Telford's masterplan
1825	First shipments of flags
1830	Steamships arrive
	Cape Wrath lighthouse
1843	Disruption in the Kirk
1855-1856	Regular ferry services
1790-1880	Many evictions
1872	Education Act
1874	Railway to Thurso & Wick
1884	Napier Commission
1886	Crofters Act
1897	Railway reaches Kyle

Rispol, Achiltibuie

Making kippers - Wick Heritage Museum

Several possible ports were identified, including Ullapool and Wick, both of which were successfully developed by the Society. Many other smaller harbours were built by landowners and merchants. Examples include Helmsdale, Lybster and Cromarty.

Local fishermen in smaller numbers were already using *Great Boats*, of about 10m keel for fishing and carrying cargoes. Markets were soon created, and by 1814 many more people were being attracted to the fast-developing industry. Fishing required skilled seamen to man the boats, but also required a great deal of shoreside labour to process and pack the catches.

Soon hundreds of boats were participating in the fishery. Due to the migratory behaviour of Herring, the boats and associated shore workers followed the shoals, basing themselves accordingly. The shoals change their patterns of movement depending on the season, weather, availability of prey and other factors.

By the later 19th century, Wick had become the Herring Capital of Europe. Its peak year was 1862, when 1,122 boats were based here during the Herring season. Over 10,000 fishermen, shore workers, ships' crews and others swelled the population of Wick and Pulteneytown dramatically for a few weeks.

Exploitation of stocks on this

Herring Fishing As early as the 10th century, Fife fishermen were catching and salting Herring (*Silver Darlings*) on the east coast of Scotland. By the late 12th century the Dutch were also fishing for them off Scotland and were using northern harbours. Harbour dues were already a useful source of income to the local economy.

Zulu heads to the fishing grounds

From the start they used bigger boats than the Scots and preserved their catches in salt, whilst still at sea. In the early 17th century they had about 2,000 boats at work, consisting of *Herring Busses* of 60-120 tons and smaller *Doggers*. As a result of the heavy losses at the Battle of Kilsyth in 1645, Scottish east coast fishing activity was much reduced until the 1830s.

British Fisheries Society The Dutch had been involved in the Herring Fishery for centuries but this industry remained undeveloped in the north of Scotland. In 1786 the British Fisheries Society was incorporated to develop the industry. Fishing villages and harbours were to be built in the north and west of Scotland and markets encouraged for the catches.

scale could not last and the fishery effectively ended by 1937. Changes in vessels and, in particular, the use of Klondyker factory ships after World War II, meant that the local industry did not revive. Today a small number of huge Shetland based purse-netters still catch large numbers of Herring.

Processing Herring at the harbour

Whitefish People had fished offshore since at least Neolithic times. Inshore **Cod** (*Stockfish*) fishing was however carried out on a large scale in the 19th century until steam trawlers fished out the grounds. **Dog Fish** (*Hoes*) were also popular. They followed the shoals of Herring in large numbers and their livers were especially prized.

Coal Fish (*Saithe*) were also caught in huge quantities for fertiliser as well as for food. They are not particularly tasty when fresh, but when lightly salted and dried outside, followed by gentle smoking in peat smoke they can be quite delicious. The multiplicity of local names for these fish

species shows how important a resource they were to the inhabitants.

Shellfish Fishing for crabs and lobsters has probably always been popular for the local market. By 1775 live Lobsters were being shipped to London on well-smacks and soon large numbers were exported annually.

Molluscs have also featured strongly in the diet for millennia. Fermented Limpets make excellent bait, while Cockles, Whelks, Razorfish and Mussels are seasonally abundant, tasty and easy to cook.

Salmon Fishing was practised on a large scale for hundreds of

years at the mouths of rivers such as the Naver, Halladale, Thurso, Helmsdale, Brora and Shin. Now just the ice houses used to store winter ice to pack fish for export remain. The skills of the fishermen and shore workers no doubt were very useful when the Herring fishery was being developed.

FISHING TIMELINE
c.1600 Avoch established
1775 Lobsters shipped to London
1786 British Fisheries Society
1803 Thomas Telford's masterplan
1810 Wooden pier at Lybster
1814 Helmsdale village & harbour
1838 Lybster had 101 boats
1862 Peak Herring year at Wick
1900 Steam drifters introduced
     Smaller ports abandoned
1937 End of Herring Boom

SITES TO VISIT
CAITHNESS
Wick
Whaligoe
Lybster
Dunbeath
SUTHERLAND
Lochinver
Kinlochbervie
Bettyhill
Portskerra
Helmsdale
Bonar Bridge
ROSS-SHIRE
Ullapool
Gairloch
Lochcarron
Avoch
Cromarty
Shandwick

Steam drifters in harbour

The spherical housing of the Dounreay Fast Reactor

The 20ᵗʰ century saw major changes in some parts of the North Highlands, but most of the area escaped the blight of developers and town planners. Outside agencies, this time mostly of national or local government, tried various possibilities to develop the economy, but with only limited success.

Wartime During both WWI and WWII the Far North Line carried many thousands of servicemen the 717 miles from London Euston to Thurso. They were travelling to Orkney, where Scapa Flow was the base of the Royal Navy's Home Fleet in both wars. The Jellicoe train was named after a WWI British admiral and journey time was at least 22 hours.

Invergordon was too vulnerable to air attack in WWII for use as a major naval base, but was used for re-fuelling as was Loch Ewe in the west. The Cromarty Firth was host to flying boat bases in both wars, while there were fighter and training bases in Caithness and near Tain.

Dounreay The Dounreay Nuclear Power Development Establishment was built on a WWII airfield 9 miles west of Thurso, starting in 1955. The purpose was to develop fast breeder reactor technology. It was operated by the United Kingdom Atomic Energy Authority, which constructed three nuclear reactors there.

The Dounreay Fast Reactor came on line in 1959 and produced 14MW between 1962 and 1977. It was used to test coolant systems using liquid Sodium and Potassium, fuels and materials. It was enclosed in the distinctive white sphere which is to be retained.

The Prototype Fast Reactor was cooled by liquid sodium and powered by mixed oxide (MOX) fuel. This contains both Uranium and Plutonium oxides which can be used in normal fission reactors, but is much more efficiently burnt in fast breeders which utilize neutron induced fission. This reactor operated from 1975 to 1994 and produced 250MW to the National Grid.

The site is now being decommissioned, which will take at least until 2036. Dounreay still employs a large number of

WWII anti-aircraft site at Aultbea, Loch Ewe, Wester Ross

Russian Convoy memorial, Loch Ewe

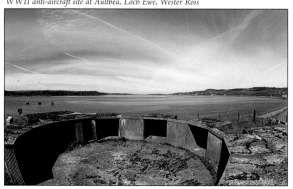

highly skilled people and will thus remain an important part of the Caithness economy for decades to come.

Vulcan NRTE is a Ministry of Defence facility which develops and tests nuclear propulsion plants for Royal Navy submarines. It is operated by Rolls-Royce and remains operational. Part of the site called *HMS Vulcan* was used to test safety systems to protect reactors in the event of coolant loss.

Industry Highlands and Islands Development Board was formed in 1965, to distribute government grants for economic and cultural development. It became Highlands and Islands Enterprise in 1991. Initially grandiose plans such as an aluminium smelter at Invergordon and other major industrial projects were in favour. Eventually it was realized that the North Highlands is unsuited to such developments and nowadays HIE concentrates on smaller scale projects which are more likely to succeed and be sustainable.

Infrastructure One of the main long term benefits has been the investment in transport infrastructure north of Inverness. This has greatly improved access to Easter Ross and the Black Isle as well as the far west and north. Road improvements continue at a slower pace throughout the North Highlands, but sadly the main access roads from the south, the A9 from Perth, A82 from Fort William and the A96 from Aberdeen remain in serious need of major investment.

Inverness Airport has had a great deal of investment in recent years. Flights are operated by several airlines to a large variety of UK destinations. Invergordon, Scrabster, Kinlochbervie, Lochinver and Ullapool harbours have also been expanded for ferries, fish landings and cruise liners.

North Sea Oil was first discovered in 1996 and the North Highlands have had some benefits. The Beatrice Field lies 15 miles east of Dunbeath. Its platforms were put in place in 1975 and 1983, from where oil and gas are piped to the oil terminal at Nigg on the Cromarty Firth.

Oil fabrication yards were established at Nigg in 1972-2000 and Kishorn in 1975-1987 to build platforms for the oil and gas industry. Both

The Beryl Oil Platform lies 15 miles east of Dunbeath, Caithness

The opening of the Kessock Bridge from Inverness to North Kessock on the Black Isle in 1982 transformed access to the north

Fabricating offshore wind turbines at Nigg, Cromarty Firth

numbers, especially in Caithness, but also in East Sutherland and parts of Wester Ross.

provided work for thousands of workers until demand for these huge structures for the North Sea was fulfilled. The huge graving docks at both yards may yet find a use in the de-commissioning of oil rigs, fabrication of offshore aero-generators, or even ship building.

Oil pipelines ten miles in length have been constructed at Reiss in Caithness on a 5 mile double rail track. The sections were shipped in by train to Georgemas Junction. Once complete the units were floated to their final site and joined up. During recent times Invergordon has become a centre for the repair and maintenance of oil rigs. Sometimes they are lined up here when demand for them is low.

Primary Industries Despite all of the many attempts to develop new industries in the North Highlands, the often derided primary industries - farming, fishing and tourism remain an integral part of the local economy.

Agriculture is concentrated in the east. Easter Ross and the Black Isle have been large grain producers for hundreds of years and continue to be so. Beef cattle are reared in large

Sheep numbers everywhere have declined greatly due to changes in farm subsidies and, they are no longer quite the hazard on remote single track roads that they used to be. Many farms and most crofts still keep small flocks of Cheviot, Blackface and, increasingly, Texels.

In the north and west Highland Cattle remain popular due to their hardiness. The calves are especially cute, but as always care should be taken not to approach cows and calves too closely.

Fishing also remains a substantial industry, despite consistent lack of interest by the authorities. Scrabster has become one of the largest white-fish landing ports in the country with Scottish, Faroese, Icelandic and other boats taking advantage of its northerly location. Landings at Kinlochbervie, Lochinver and Ullapool have, however, fallen.

All around the coast crabs and lobsters are fished by inshore boats, while the west coast lochs and The Minch have fertile prawn grounds. Fish farming, mainly of Salmon, but also Sea Trout, is a substantial industry on the west coast, with cages in many of the sea lochs. Species such as Halibut and Cod have also

Oil Rigs at Invergordon, Cromarty Firth

been tried, but so far not with much commercial success.

Tourism has been important to the North Highlands since the 19th century when all things Scottish were in vogue. George IV came to Edinburgh in 1822, the first visit to Scotland by a reigning monarch since the 1600s. Sir Walter Scott stage managed a splendid Highland pageant, with a Grand Highland Ball, where gentlemen, unless in uniform, had to dress in the *ancient Highland costume*.

The result was an increase in goodwill and a renewed Scottish national identity which took in Highlanders and Lowlanders. The pride of the Clan chieftains and members alike in their shared heritage was reinvigorated, not least by the iconic symbolism of kilts and tartans.

Hunting and shooting became popular among the wealthy and villages such as Strathpeffer developed to take advantage of natural assets, in this case its spa waters. With

Highland calf near Drumbeg, West Sutherland

the coming of the railways, roads and steamers, the North Highlands became accessible to more and more people.

After WWII increasing car ownership and better public transport led to a steady growth in visitors to the far north. It is the enduring appeal of the landscape which continues to attract people to this area. The North Highlands is one of the last remaining parts of Britain where nature has been left largely untouched.

In recent years quality standards have improved dramatically as have services for visi-

tors. Many accommodation providers are open all year. Visitor attractions, museums, interesting shops, cafes and restaurants are on the increase, but many are still shut out of season.

The widespread availability of local produce not only enhances the menus but helps sustain the economy. The closure of many rural filling stations means that motorists should take care not to run out of fuel miles from the nearest one. Although things are changing, many places are closed or have limited hours on Sundays.

Plockton Prawns

Ullapool Haddock and Chips

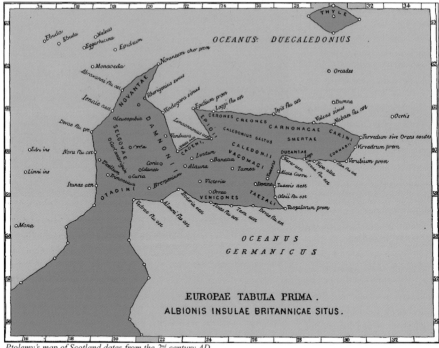

Ptolemy's map of Scotland dates from the 2nd century AD

Ancient Placenames The placenames of the Highlands reflect the complex ebb and flow of people over millennia. The earliest recorded visit was by Pytheas in c.325 BC when he circumnavigated Britain and took many sun sights to determine his latitude.

Ptolemy's *Geographica* was written c.150AD and contains a large number of co-ordinates, placenames and the names of indigenous tribes. He described his land positions using latitudes and longitudes derived from celestial sightings and though the names quoted are Latinized, they doubtless represent an approximation of those used by local people at the time. In Britain, Celtic languages were

current which were well-known to the Romans.

Headlands, rivers and sea features predominate, suggesting that most of the survey work was done by ship. While latitudes are probably fairly accurate, longitudes are more problematic. The placenames have been interpreted variously by scholars but remain fascinating as a link to the people of the ancient past.

Celtic languages are thought to have been spoken throughout Britain from at least the Iron Age. The original language of the Neolithic Age may well have persisted in remoter areas. A few of the oldest placenames possibly date from this period.

River names such as the Farrar (*Varar*) now called the River Beauly, the Ila (*Ilae*), the River Ullie or Helmsdale and the Rive Naver (*Nabari*) are ancient. Others, such as Loyal, Broom, Carron, Conon Glass, Oykel, Shin and Tain may also be very old.

Pictish placenames have survived in small numbers, especially in Easter Ross and the Black Isle. The Picts spoke a Brittonic Celtic language and the most common survival is *pit* or *pett*, meaning a "piece of land". The distribution of these names follows that of class II Pictish symbol stones.

Scottish Gaelic is in fact a derivative of Irish Gaelic and was imported by the Scotti

118

who came over from Ulster in the 5th and 6th centuries to found Dal Riada (what is now Argyll). In 843 Kenneth macAlpin became the first King of Scotland, uniting the Scots and Picts. Gaelic replaced Pictish in the west and in the Highlands.

Gaelic only survives today as a native tongue in the Western Isles and in the northwest of the Highlands. Its legacy is the huge number and variety of placenames in the language which can be seen on the map today. Even before it reached its peak, Gaelic was already under attack from Norse all around the coast and from Early English from the south and east.

Norse influence came from the Vikings who raided extensively before settling. Caithness, Sutherland, and most of Easter Ross were all part of the Norse Orkney Earldom and there is extensive placename evidence of this. Coastal features (Cape Wrath, Noss Head, Eriboll), parts of the sea (Pentland Firth,) settlements (Dingwall, Helmsdale, Wick, Durness, Ullapool), farms (Scrabster, Thurdistoft, Ham) and mountains (Suilven, Assynt, Arkle, Hope) are all examples.

The Old Norse words *dalr* (valley), *toft* (farm), *setr* (upland farm), *stadir* and *bolstadir* (settlement or farm) all occur where the Norse settles. Farms and settlements are often named after a person, as in Ullapool, or a purpose as in

Cape Wrath was called "Hvarf", or Turning Point, by the Vikings

Dingwall, the site of law making assemblies.

Old English, or Anglian, was used less in the north. After the Norman conquest, as the church and state became anglicized, Latin was replaced by English which was increasingly spoken. Easter Ross, the Black Isle, East Sutherland and Caithness were the most strongly affected.

Throughout all of these periods it seems likely that new variations on placenames were often translations of, or additions to, existing words rather than direct replacements. In this way ancient roots may be preserved. Old Celtic, Pictish, Gaelic, Norse, Anglian and English are all inter-related with roots in Greek and Latin.

This fascinating spectrum of placenames adds colour as well as life to the archaeology and history of the region. Throughout this book suggested derivations are given, from Pictish (P), Gaelic (G) and Old Norse (ON). Some are certain, others speculative and a few are cryptic.

POSSIBLE LOCATIONS ON PTOLEMY'S MAP	
Scitis Insulae	Isle of Skye.
Volsas Sinus	Loch Broom or Loch Eriboll?
Nabari Fl. Ostia	River Naver
Tarvedum	Cape Wrath
Cape Orcas	Cape Wrath
Virvedrum Pr	Dunnet Head
Orcades	Orkney
Verubium Pr	Duncansby Head
Ilae Fl. Ostia	River Ila, Helmsdale or River Ullie
Ripa Alta	River Oykel (Loch Fleet, River Shin)
Loxae flu	Dornoch Firth
Varrar Aest	River Farrar, now Beauly River & Firth

119

CAITHNESS

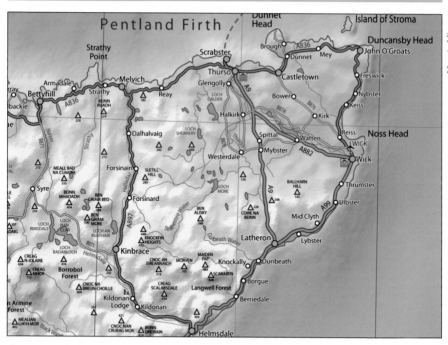

CAITHNESS (ON *Katanes*, Headland of the Cats, a Pictish tribe; G *Gallaibh*, Land of Foreigners) is the northeast extremity of Scotland. The landscape is in contrast to that of most of the rest of the North Highlands. East of a line running from Reay in the northwest to Berriedale in the southeast, the underlying rock is Old Red Sandstone, so that the topography resembles that of Orkney and parts of Easter Ross. To the west, the sandstone gives way to the impermeable Moine rocks of the Flow Country.

Dunnet Head (100m) is made of Upper Old Red Sandstone

Much of the coastline is made up of cliffs, in places quite high, without any sea lochs. There are several large bays with wonderful sandy beaches, backed by dunes and machair. The rolling countryside is generally given over to beef cattle farming, though sheep are also reared. Silage and barley are grown in large quantities for winter feed.

Archaeology Caithness has a wealth of archaeological sites to visit, although very few are formally managed. These range from Neolithic chambered cairns and standing stones, Bronze Age houses, burnt mounds and cists to Iron Age roundhouses and many brochs.

122

The Stacks of Duncansby in 1821 by William Daniell

Pictish symbol stones, Norse settlements, keeps and churches as well as medieval castles, all give a fascinating insight into the past.

Wildlife With a wide range of habitats ranging from its varied coastline, farmland, moorland, rivers, lochs, bogs, and hills, Caithness is home to a wide variety of birds, plants and animals. Although the Flow Country is indeed special, the rest of the county has many treats in store, such as *Primula scotica* and other unusual plants on coastal maritime heath.

Heritage Caithness is culturally distinct from the rest of Scotland, sharing some place-names, surnames and dialect words with Orkney and Shetland. It was part of the Orkney Earldom for hundreds of years and retains a sense of its Norse heritage today. A few Pictish names have survived while to the west and inland Gaelic place-names predominate.

Primula scotica

The Round Cairn of Camster near Lybster

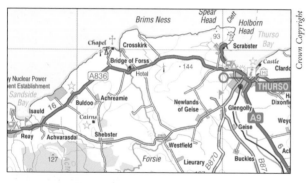

Reay from Drum Hollistan looking eastwards

REAY (ON *Ra*, Boundary Mark) is the first Caithness settlement east of Melvich. The border was created by Charles I. It runs from Drum Hollistan in the north from where there are fine views over the Pentland Firth, Reay and western Caithness to the Ord, north of Helmsdale. The village overlooks Sandside Bay and its links.

Sandside harbour

Reay Parish Church dates from 1739. It has a fine tower at the east end, accessed by an external stair, and a north aisle. It retains its 18th century layout with the original pulpit on the south wall, long communion table and seating.

The west window was installed in 1933, and the building was fully renovated in 1989 to celebrate its 250th anniversary. On the southeast corner a louping stone was used to help people on and off their horses, while next to the door is an iron loop for attaching the jougs. People who had committed some misdemeanor were fixed here with chains and fetters to be publicly disgraced.

Market Cross Reay has an attractive centre with a village green surrounded by stone cottages. The Market Cross is said to have come from Old Reay which lay to the west of the burn, but is now buried under sand dunes.

Shurrery Pictish Stone was found next to an ancient ruined chapel at Shurrery. It is built into a dyke at Sandside House. The **Sandside Pictish Stone** was found in the Reay Links in 1860 and is also now at Sandside House. Both may be viewed by appointment only.

Reay cross-slab is in the Old Reay Cemetery in the Bighouse Mausoleum, which is kept padlocked. It was re-

Dounreay Nuclear Site and Sandside Bay

used in the 18th century on the grave of one Robert McKay. Another cross-slab used to be set into the wall of the church but has since been removed to the National Museum.

Sandside Bay is a fine wide sandy beach, backed by extensive sand dunes overlooked by the nearby Dounreay Nuclear Power Development Site. Signs indicate possible danger yet, despite this, local people still walk on the beach.

The pretty harbour was built about 1830 but suffers from silting up with sand so is only used by small boats. The attractive cottages, storehouse and high quality masonry work all enhance the appeal.

New Year Shinty As in Durness and other places, a game of Shinty or Knotty was formerly played on the Sandside Links on Old New Year's Day, the 12th of January. Large numbers of men and boys played on each side, watched by an enthusiastic crowd. A dance and much celebration followed.

Norse burials Several Viking burials have been discovered around Reay, including a female who was interred with a pony and a variety of objects. A Viking warrior was found in 1926 together with his axe, shield and other items. Further Norse finds in the area have included pottery, but no settlement site has so far been discovered.

Girls braving Sandside Beach

Reay Church interior

Reay Church exterior

Dounreay Nuclear Site

Dounreay Nuclear Power Development Establishment Work started here on the site of a WWII airfield in 1955. The purpose was to develop Fast Breeder Reactors. Nuclear powered electricity generation ceased in 1994 and the focus is now on decommissioning which is expected to take well into the 2030s. Dounreay still employs about a third of the Caithness workforce.

Dounreay Castle dates from the 16th century and is a former hunting lodge of the Earls of Reay. This L-shaped house had three floors with 1 metre thick walls but is now ruinous.

It lies on the coast outside the licensed site perimeter fence and can be visited. In the 1950s it was contaminated during some experiments with radioactive liquids, but it has been extensively cleaned up.

Cnoc Freiceadain (G Watch Hill) has two long chambered cairns on the top of the Hill of Shebster (ND012653). The south cairn is known as *Na Tri Shean* (The Three Fairy Mounds), is about 70m long and has a higher mound at each end, with "horned" forecourts. The northern one has a round mound and a forecourt at its south end.

There are fine views over

Reay, Dounreay and the Pentland Firth from here. Nearby there are several other chambered cairns as well as stone rows.

Broubster is a collection of 19th century longhouses with many interesting features. The domestic accommodation was at one end and the byre at the other. Roofs were held up with cruck trusses. A barn also survives and the narrow strips cultivated by the tenants can also be made out.

Beinn Freiceadain (ND558060, 238m) lies to the south of Loch Calder, and east of Loch Shurrery. A large Iron Age hillfort covers an area about 300m x 150m on its summit. A substantial 3m-thick rampart encloses the west and south sides, but not the steep north and east slopes. This is the most northerly such fort in the UK. There is a chambered cairn within the fort, as well as others on the lower slopes.

Cnoc Freiceadain chambered cairns with Dounreay in the background

Westfield St Drostan's Kirkyard at Westfield (ND067642) has two ancient hog-back tombstones, which could date from Norse times. There is a fascinating collection of 19th century headstones and monuments here. Nearby the name of *Priest Hillock* suggests an early chapel site, which would explain the ancient kirkyard.

St Mary's Chapel, Crosskirk, is probably 12th century. It is without a roof but otherwise complete with a small nave and a small square chancel. The east and west doors are original with jambs inclined inwards at the top. The south door is more recent. Nearby St Mary's Well can still be made out. The chapel can be reached via a side road just east of Forse House Hotel.

Forse Mill is a particularly fine 19th century grain mill in a lovely situation overlooking waterfalls and surrounded by Beech trees. The Highland Buildings Preservation Trust has converted the mill to housing, but has retained much of the mill workings. A

Brims lies west of Thurso and is the site of a ruined castle and small harbour

path runs down the east side of the river to Crosskirk.

Brims Castle is a ruinous 16th century tower house with three storeys. The main entrance to the courtyard is an archway of carved sandstone. The abandoned house next to it may date from about 1800.

The fields here have particularly fine drystone dykes and flagstone slab fences. Port of Brims is a small and exposed harbour, while there is an ancient ruined chapel on Brims Ness. There are fine views across the Pentland Firth to Orkney from here.

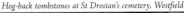

Forse Mill has been tastefully renovated into apartments

Forse windfarm

Hog-back tombstones at St Drostan's cemetery, Westfield

Thurso beach from the Esplanade

THURSO (ON *Thors* or *Thiorrs A*, Thor's or Bull River) was already an important settlement in Norse times as it is mentioned frequently in the *Orkneyinga Saga*. Both the Earl and the Bishop had castles here. The site of the former keep is unknown, but it is said to have been slighted by King William the Lion in about 1197 after the mutilation of Bishop William. Part of the Bishop's Palace can be seen near the Coastguard hut on the road to Scrabster.

With a population of just under 9,000, Thurso is the largest town in Caithness and the most northerly in mainland Britain. It has a distinctive aspect, facing north to the Pentland Firth and Orkney. The town grew rapidly in the 19th century due to the success of the flagstone industry and, again in the latter half of the 20th century with the development of Dounreay.

The original village was on the west side of the river and, until recently, was known as *Fishers'*

Biggings . Many of the houses here date from the 17th and 18th centuries, and have been tastefully renovated rather than demolished. Sir John Sinclair of Ulbster laid out the new town in 1798 to provide homes *"for all sorts and conditions of men"*.

The regular layout of wide parallel streets, attractive and varied houses with gardens to the rear and narrow lanes gives the town a somewhat refined air. Janet Street faces the River Thurso and has some particularly fine Georgian-style buildings.

Old St Peter's Kirk dates from the 13th century, or earlier, with 16th and 17th century additions. It is said to have been founded by Gilbert de Moravia, who was appointed Bishop in 1222, most probably on the site of a much more ancient chapel. The Diocese of Caithness was founded in 1145 and Bishop Andrew

Thurso River and the bridge looking upstream

Thurso is twinned with Brilon, Germany

The area around Shore Street is the oldest part of Thurso

served for 40 years as the first Bishop of Caithness. The present church may well have been founded by him.

The chancel is in the east end and has a second floor, reached via a stair in the tower. The fine window on the west aisle was inserted in about 1630 during the time of Charles I and is said to be

Sir John's Square is colourful in summer

Thurso pedestrian precinct - Rotterdam Street

Small boats in Thurso Harbour

THURSO
Origin of the name

The name Thurso may indeed derive from the Norse god Thor, but it is more likely to come from a much more ancient river name, represented by *Thiorsa* in Norse but probably very much older and reflected in Ptolemy's supposed name for Holborn Head *Tarvedum* or Bull Head from the Celtic roots *tarv*, bull and *dun*, fort. The headland has a series of ramparts defending its landward approaches. River names seem to be most highly conserved of all placenames, often surviving multiple language changes.

Old St Peter's Kirk dates in part from the 13th century or earlier

carved from a single stone slab. The west window of Dornoch Cathedral is very similar in style.

Unusually, the tower is set at an angle to the rest of the building between the east and south aisles. This may reflect the layout of an earlier building. The graveyard has many interesting old memorials but sadly access is often blocked by locked gates. A runic stone

cross was found here in the 19th century and can be seen in the new museum.

Unfortunately, the church was abandoned in 1832 with the opening of the new St Peter's and St Andrew's.

Thurso Castle is now a derelict ruin. It may well be the site of Thurso's missing Iron Age broch and, of a Norse fortification. However,

any traces were obliterated by the building of a new castle in the 1660s by George Sinclair, Earl of Caithness. From 1872 Sir Tollemache Sinclair completely remodelled the castle to his own design.

During WWII an anti-shipping mine came ashore below the castle and exploded. As a result the building, said to never have been very structurally stable anyway, was mostly demolished in 1952 and left in its present unfortunate state.

Thurso River arises on the northern watershed of Cnoc Cromuillt and flows through Loch More before meandering across Caithness' central valley to the sea. It is famous for its Salmon angling today. In former times there was a large fishery at the river mouth.

The present bridge was built

Thurso Castle in 1821

in 1887 to replace an early 19th century one. The former toll-house is now an art gallery. There are fine walks along the river banks upstream of the bridge. The river is a good place to observe migrating waders and waterfowl in spring and autumn.

Surfing has become a popular sport in Thurso. In certain wind and tidal conditions very large waves build up and break on the east side of Thurso Bay. The Pentland Firth is famous for its strong tides and ferocious seas, which are responsible for the waves that so please surfers.

Esplanade and Beach The Esplanade was first built in 1882. It is a good viewpoint for observing the impressive waves which break here in certain conditions. The sandy beach has fine views over Thurso Bay and the Pentland Firth to the Orkney Island of Hoy.

Thurso has many elegant 18th and 19th century buildings - Janet Street

Surfing on the east side of Thurso Bay

Fossil fish in the Museum

CAITHNESS HORIZONS, THURSO

Ulbster Pictish symbol stone

"Caithness is steeped in outstanding archaeology, history, wildlife and ecology, with a pioneering industrial past. Yet with so much to discover, where do you begin to uncover the secrets and intricate treasures of this northerly county?

Caithness Horizons is a major new visitor attraction which celebrates and raises awareness of this rugged and beautiful region in the far north of Scotland. The Centre is the hub for the area, acting as a signpost for attractions and facilities in Caithness.

Located at the magnificently refurbished Thurso Town Hall and adjacent Carnegie Library, Caithness Horizons is a vision that has been six years in the making. The result is an impressive, state-of-the-art attraction incorporating a museum, interactive exhibitions and displays, lecture and audio-visual presentation facilities, a tourist information centre and café. Designed to meet the needs of both the local community and visitors to the county, the Centre is based around the permanent exhibition. Here, the exciting story of mankind's past and present interaction with the environment of North East Scotland, the geology, archaeology, history and ecology of the area is revealed. A series of themed rooms uncover the stories and people of Caithness's past.

Learn about the well-preserved Stone Age sites, the standing stones, cairns and brochs, or follow the incredible adventures of the Norse invaders and settlers and onwards to Mediaeval times, visiting the main castle sites, such as Castle of Mey and Castle Sinclair Girnigoe.

The Caithness landscape, which has long been renowned for its great natural beauty, is also home to a wealth of geological and stone treasures. The Stone and Geology room displays a collection of stone items and explains how this important resource has had a powerful impact shaping the area's economy over the millennia.

An area has been specially dedicated to Thurso's famous geologist and botanist, Robert Dick, which showcases artifacts and personal items and pays a fascinating tribute to the life's work of this enthusiastic naturalist.

In the Flow Country, wander through displays of birds, track bird migration routes and see specimens preserved in the area's bogs. You can also explore Coastal Caithness to appreciate the wealth of ecology and seabird habitats of this rugged and beautiful area.

Finally there is Dounreay, a vital part of the UK's scientific and industrial history and a major element in the solio-economic heritage of Caithness. You can hear the story of its development, the activities that took place on the site over a period of more than 40 years, its environmental impact and its continuing influence on the North Highland Community.

The exhibition moves on to the present day, where it uncovers the impact man has had on the planet. Here visitors are challenged to explore ways in which our environment can be preserved for future generations to enjoy.

Caithness Horizons offers a truly remarkable journey delving into all that Caithness has to offer. Thought provoking, informative, and visually stunning, this is a fascinating attraction and a first class venue for locals and visitors alike."

Open all year
Free admission
Caithness Horizons, Town Hall, High Street, Thurso, Caithness, KW14 8AJ

aithness
Horizons

Revealing the past and signposting the future

ourney beyond the huge skies and sweeping
andscapes and discover some of the intricate treasures
hat are being revealed in the very north of Scotland

aithness Horizons – the carefully restored Thurso Town
all and Carnegie Library – is a fascinating museum and
xhibition which tells the story of mankind's past and present
nteraction with the environment of North East Scotland

Caithness Horizons guides visitors through:

- the archaeology and history of the area
- the geology and ecology
- the changing seasons
- the wildlife, flowers and fauna
- our need for fuel and energy and a sustainable future

Welcome to Caithness Horizons

www.caithnesshorizons.co.uk

info@caithnesshorizons.co.uk

Scrabster Harbour and MV Hamnavoe

SCRABSTER (ON *Skara Bolstadir*, Steading on the Edge) nestles in the shelter of Holborn Head on the west side of Thurso Bay. It was formerly a small fishing village as shown by the icehouse, now The Captain's Galley restaurant.

Scrabster Harbour Trust was established in 1841 and, by 1855,

a regular steamship ferry service to Stromness in Orkney had commenced. Holborn Head lighthouse was first lit in 1862, but is now redundant. The harbour has grown steadily over the years to cope with the demands of the ferries, commercial and leisure craft. The port has also become one of the busiest fish landing ports in the UK, due to its northerly position.

Orkney Ferries The first regular Scrabster to Stromness steamship was the *Royal Mail*, commencing in 1855. Several other vessels operated the route, until the first *St Ola* commenced its long period of service in 1892. Thus started the long association with what is now P&O Ferries on this route.

St Ola I ran for 59 years until replaced in 1951. Ro ro services started in 1974 with *St Ola III*, which was in turn replaced with the much larger *St Ola IV* in 1992. In 2002 the *Hamnavoe*, a completely new and still larger ship operated by NorthLink took over the route.

MV Hamnavoe leaving Scrabster

Scrabster Harbour

Thurso Lifeboat was first based here in 1860. Eleven vessels have so far served here, and there have been many heroic services involving the rescue of over 600 people. In 1956 the lifeboat shed and the brand new lifeboat *Dunnet Head* were destroyed by fire.

Holborn Head is exposed to the full fury of the Pentland Firth. The Old Red Sandstone cliffs have been eroded into a dramatic series of caves, geos, gloups, blowholes, stacks and natural arches. In summer the maritime heath is covered with wild flowers, including Spring Squill, Thrift, Maritime Plantain Grass of Parnassus, Mountain Everlasting, Primula scotica and Sea Campion. Seabirds breed on the cliffs and waders around the small lochs inland.

The disused flagstone quarry at Ness of Litter about 2 miles west of Holborn Head was worked without explosives, bed by bed. A small part of a fish-bearing bed is exposed in the southeast part of the quarry. Fish fossils are found in a dark siltstone stratum here which is about 25cm thick.

The headland itself is protected by large geos on each side, and by ramparts built across the narrow part. Although sometimes described as a "fort" this exposed location is much more likely to have been a spiritual rather than a military site.

Vikings The *Orkneyinga Saga* says that there was a *borg* above the mouth of the Wolf Burn. In about 1196 the Norse Orkney Earl Harald Maddadarson reasserted

Scrabster and Thurso in 1821

his authority over Caithness here, only to have the Scots march north and destroy the fort. Gilbert de Moravia subsequently built a residence on this site after his appointment in 1222.

Witches According to folklore, in 1529, a Scrabster carpenter called Hugh Montgomery had a problem with cats getting into his cellar and drinking his ale. He caught three, killed two and cut the leg off a third. Two old women died shortly after this, and a third had taken to bed with a broken leg. She was taken to the prison and tortured into confessing she was a witch. She admitted to the charge of changing into a cat and to other things supernatural. Before she could be tarred and burnt she died due to her injuries.

Holborn Head, Scrabster has a series of ancient ramparts on the landward side

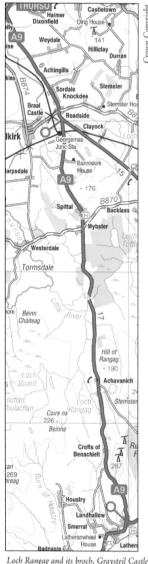

The Cassiemyre Road (or Causewaymyre) is literally a causeway across the peatbog between Lybster and Spittal. It was largely built by Sir John Sinclair who called out the statute labour of the district. In the late 18th century there were few roads and, by law, tenants were made to provide six days work on the roads.

In the early 19th century the Parliamentary Commissioners paid for half the cost of road-building and landed proprietors the rest. The result was the building of 137 miles of roads in Caithness, which greatly improved communications with the south.

There are fine views over the moors to the hills beyond as well as several interesting side roads to explore. The many ancient sites include the Guidebest and Achavanich stone settings, several isolated standing stones, chambered cairns, settlement sites and brochs. Abandoned 19th century farmsteads litter the landscape.

Loch Rangag (G *Rannach*, peninsula) has a broch, Graysteil Castle, in a lovely setting on its east shore. It has been partially excavated, so that remains of walls and a chamber can be seen. Divers may be observed on the loch, or heard flying over, while several species of wader nest here in early summer. There are many other good places to stop and take in the landscape.

Windfarms have been installed in several places in Caithness. The one on the Cassiemyre has very few habitations nearby. Visitors have to make up their own minds about the capacity of the open landscape for massive developments.

Achanarras Hill (ND150545) has a disused flagstone quarry where fossil fish may be found among the piles of discarded waste stone. Recently a unique type of fossil aquatic scorpion was found here.

It is about a mile west of Spittal, where a large quarry still produces Caithness flags. Modern equipment makes the continued output of the famous paving stone viable. It continues to be a popular and natural alternative to concrete or tarmac.

Loch Rangag and its broch, Graysteil Castle

Southwest over the Flow Country to the Caithness hills

Spittal takes its name from the medieval St Magnus Hospice. Little remains but for a fragment of a chapel gable end. (ND158549). The oldest reference is from 1476, but it likely dates from the 12th century when the cult of the saint was very strong. No doubt pilgrims on their way to and from Orkney stopped here.

View towards Morven

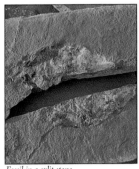

Fossil in a split stone

Discarded piles of stones at Achanarras Quarry

Windfarm on the Cassiemyre Road

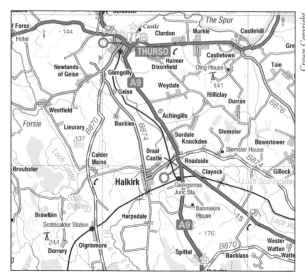

HALKIRK (ON *Ha Kirke*, High Church) is a 19th century village planned by Sir John Sinclair in a grid layout, with 55 plots, each of one acre. The bridge across the River Thurso was built about 100 years earlier with money left by his grandfather. The village hall, or Ross Institute, was opened in 1911, with the first public electric clock in Scotland. It is named after John Ross, who emigrated to New Zealand in 1861 and became very successful there.

Braal Castle is a ruinous keep among old woodlands on the north bank of the river. It was for long a residence of the Earl of Caithness and in 1222 the scene of an incident taken out of the Norse sagas. Bishop Adam had unilaterally decided to double the tax, payable in butter, due to him.

A large crowd arrived here to complain to Earl John, who is said to have advised them, "*To go and boil the bishop in his butter.*" The greedy cleric was indeed burnt in a house, a common Viking practice. King Alexander II marched north with his army to punish those involved.

The Earl denied any part in the affair but up to 80 men had hands or feet amputated and their sons were castrated. The new bishop, Gilbert de Moravia, was from a very politically astute and wealthy family and moved his main residence to Dornoch.

Distilleries Gerston, just west of Halkirk, was the site of whisky making for many years. It was first established in 1796, became legal in 1825, and operated until it was sold in 1872. The new owners opened their modern Ben Morven distillery in 1886, but the whisky was never as suc-

River Thurso and the old kirk at Halkirk

Halkirk from the east

View southwest from Sordale towards Halkirk

cessful as the old Gerston malt and it closed in 1911. Only the stillhouse remains.

Westerdale is an attractive place for a riverside walk and picnic. A fine stone bridge crosses the river, which cascades over flat rocks. Salmon can be seen on their way upstream. There are many brochs and other mounds in this area. Stone rows by the river at Dirlot are laid out in a sectored grid similar to that at Mid Clyth.

Dirlot Castle dates from the 13th century and is built on a high rock in a small ravine. It seems a bizarre place to build a castle, but the site is worth visiting for its unique wild beauty. The river plunges into a deep pool which is said to harbour a pot of gold.

Loch Calder is now the water supply for Caithness people. The plant here replaced 11 separate sites. There are chambered cairns, standing stones and brochs as well as lovely views towards the west. Many ducks and geese overwinter here.

Westerdale Mill on River Thurso

Braal Castle, Halkirk

Loch Calder, Whins and a flagstone fence

139

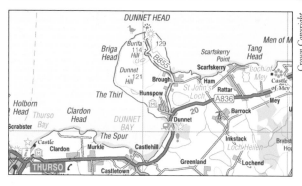

Crown Copyright

DUNNET BAY has a fine 2 mile stretch of sand, backed by high dunes and extensive links. When the sea is up, massive waves break here which is attractive to surfers. The beach is popular for walking, sand yachting and other pursuits. Dunnet Ranger Visitor Centre, at the caravan site, has displays about the various species of birds and plants here.

Dunnet Forest was planted by the Forestry Commission in the 1950s as an experiment. It is managed by Dunnet Forestry Trust as a community woodland. A number of paths and trails for walkers, horses and mountain bikes have been developed and the forest is managed to encourage wildlife.

Dunnet Kirk probably dates from the 12th century, though most of the building is 16th century. Timothy Pont was minister here from 1602 to 1610. He previously surveyed Scotland for Blaue's famous *Atlas Novus* of 1654.

The church has the traditional layout of pews and the pulpit on the south wall. The distinctive tower was added about 1700 and overlooks a graveyard packed with interesting monuments. The north aisle was added in 1837, completing the finely balanced building of today.

Castlehill Harbour was built in the 19th century to export Caithness flagstone

Windmill base, Castlehill

Dunnet Bay from the east - one of the finest sandy beaches in the north

Castlehill, the old name for Castletown, may have taken its name from the broch just north of the village, which developed as a result of the growth of the Flagstone Industry. In 1825 James Traill shipped his first cargo of paving stones from Castlehill Harbour. During the next 100 or so years over 400,000 tons of stone were shipped all over the world.

Dunnet Forest is now community maintained

Castlehill Flagstone Trail follows the story starting at the quarry. The windmill powered water pumps to empty the quarry and the dam drove a waterwheel to power saws which cut the flags. In 1861 steam power was introduced which allowed for a higher production rate. The nearby mill was used to thresh and mill grain as well as to mill flax. Castletown retains many pretty houses from this period.

Olrig There are fine panoramic views from Olrig Hill (ND175657, 119m). Olrig Kirk (St Trothan's) is roofless today. It has a stone with a date of 1633, but is undoubtedly much older in part. It is the site of one of the Selkie Woman legends. A baby was found wrapped in a sealskin, but when she grew up she was accused of devil worship and thrown out of the kirk. She later died in childbirth and was buried in the churchyard. A hollow in her headstone is reputed never to dry out.

Dunnet Sands are used for many forms of recreation

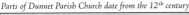
Parts of Dunnet Parish Church date from the 12th century

Dunnet Head lighthouse overlooks the Pentland Firth

Dunnet Head and lighthouse from the ferry

WWII saw the installation of a Chain Home Low radar station on Dunnet Head. Burifa Hill was also the site of the Master Station of the Northern GEE Chain which helped bombers to navigate accurately on their missions.

Mary-Ann's Cottage is a 19th century crofthouse at West Dunnet on the way to Dunnet Head. It was home of Mary-Ann Calder until 1990 when she was 93. It was built by her grandfather, John Young, in 1850. His son William took over, followed by Mary-Ann and her husband, James Calder.

The croft is not a museum, rather an authentic *social document*. The buildings, rooms, fittings, artifacts, tools and implements are all original. Except that it has electricity and running water, it provides a window into a quite recent past.

Dwarwick has a small and rather utilitarian concrete pier often used by the Royal Family when they were visiting the Queen Mother at

DUNNET HEAD (127m) is the most northerly point in mainland Britain. The lighthouse was built in 1831 by Robert Stevenson. and stands atop the imposing 90m cliffs of Easter Head. The viewpoint offers fine vistas in all directions over the Pentland Firth to Orkney and Stroma.

In summer it is home to breeding Puffins, Guillemots, Razorbills, Kittiwakes, Fulmars, Shags and Cormorants. The site is now managed by the RSPB. The clifftops are carpeted with wild flowers in early summer, while inland habitats include moorland, wetlands lochs and heathland.

St John's Loch, Dunnet

Ham has a large girnel and a small harbour

Castle of Mey. Nearby Dwarwick Head offers fine views over Dunnet Bay.

Ham has a large girnel and small harbour built by James Traill to store and export grain. A nearby mound may be an Iron Age souterrain.

Scarfskerry (ON *Skarf,* Cormorant), further east, has a small harbour, The Haven. The coastline here is low and rocky but pretty with many chambered cairns, a broch and a chapel site. Further east at Harrow there is another exposed jetty in Wester Haven.

St John's Loch takes its name from the ruined chapel at its eastern end. On the northwest shore a bird hide overlooks St John's Pool. More than 200 species have been seen here and a visit is recommended especially during the breeding season and migration times.

Brough has a slipway formerly used to land stores for the lighthouse. A large stack, Little Clett, shelters the bay. The view east goes all the way to Duncansby Head.

Scarfskerry and Dunnet Head from the east

Mary-Ann's Cottage living room

Mary-Ann's Cottage barn

Mary-Ann's Cottage, Dunnet

Five miles west of the Castle of Mey, and overlooking Dunnet Bay, this historic croft shows how successive generations of one family lived. Visitors are given a guided tour of the croft, which has been restored as near as possible to the state when last worked by Mary-Ann and James Calder

Open June-September daily except Mondays 2-4:30pm

143

CAITHNESS - THE CASTLE OF MEY

The Queen Mother with one of her Corgis at the Castle of Mey

THE CASTLE OF MEY

was originally built between 1566 and 1572 by George Sinclair, Earl of Caithness. It was renamed Barrogill Castle in the 18th century and extensive additions were made in the 19th century. By the early 1950s it had fallen into severe disrepair.

In 1952, during a visit to friends after the death of King George VI, the Queen Mother found out that the castle was for sale. It was in very poor condition, but she bought and restored it. When she took over there was neither electricity nor running water. She also changed the name back to the original.

The Queen Mother created a comfortable and welcoming northern home. Most of the interior fittings and furnishings were obtained locally. The castle is very much the product of her own taste and acquired many items from shops such as the *Ship's Wheel*

and *Miss Miller Calder's Shop* in Thurso.

In 1996 she formed The Queen Elizabeth Castle of Mey Trust and endowed it with the castle, farm and estate. The interior remains set out very much as she had it. Knowledgable guides do everything to make visits interesting and enjoyable with anecdotes and explanations.

The Tour takes in the front hall, designed in 1819, the drawing room which was remodelled in 1736, the equerry's office and the library. Upstairs the bedroom floor includes the Queen Mother's bedroom and other rooms, including one for Princess Margaret, who never did stay here.

The dining room is the most elaborately furnished room in the castle. It has several impressive artworks, gifts and treasured possessions. The adjacent butler's pantry was used to serve food and drinks prepared in the well equipped kitchen below.

The Gardens are protected by the *Great Wall of Mey* which is

The Animal Centre is based in the Old Granary

Aberdeen Angus cattle and the Castle of Mey

12 feet high. The Queen Mother was very proud of her garden here and today it is full of colour all summer. Herbaceous borders, shrub roses and other flowers are sheltered by hedges. The kitchen garden supplied all manner of fruit and vegetables in season.

Two cannons on the front lawn probably came from the Mey battery; they have a bore of 6½ inches and a barrel length of 94 inches. Their identification numbers are covered with paint, but the west one carries a George IV mark and a date of c.1820. The Mey Company of Artillery Volunteers was formed in 1866, with its drill hall in the village and battery near the shore.

The Castle of Mey in 1821 by William Daniell

The Castle of Mey from the south

The visitor centre includes a well stocked shop, which sells a variety of interesting gifts and local produce from the Mey Selection. The tearoom serves tasty homemade meals and snacks throughout the day.

The Animal Centre is in the old granary and includes a variety of interesting hens, ducks and geese. Rare breeds of sheep, goats and pigs can be seen. In spring children can feed the lambs and also see newly hatched chicks in a brooder.

Mey Selections In 2005 HRH Prince Charles, Duke of Rothesay launched the North Highland Initiative to promote economic development of the area. Mey Selections is the brand name of North Highlands Products Ltd, formed by Caithness farmers to market luxury food products. Customers can therefore support sustainable farming, fishing and other food production in the North.

Castle of Mey dining room

Castle of Mey drawing room

Castle of Mey Trust

Castle of Mey Trust

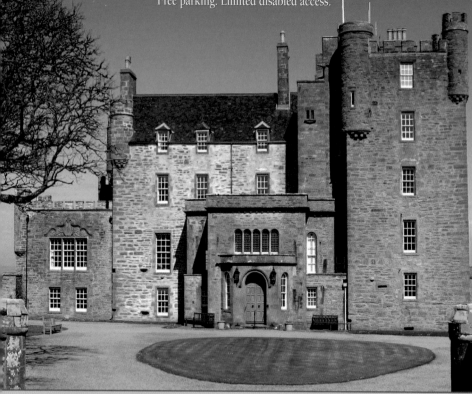

MEY SELECTIONS

Castle of Mey from the walled garden

© Copyright A.G.Carrick 2002

CAPTURING THE TASTE OF AN UNSPOILT LAND

*All Mey Selections products deliver sustainable
natural goodness from the North Highlands -
rewarding to local producers and customers alike.*

www.mey-selections.com

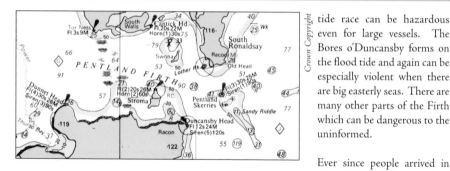

THE PENTLAND FIRTH

(ON *Pettaland Fjordur*, Pictland Firth), together with the islands and parishes on both sides, is frequently mentioned in the *OrkneyInga Saga*. This *Wild and Open Sea*, as it has been described, separates Orkney from Caithness.

The distance from Burwick to John o'Groats is about 6 miles. At the meeting point of the North Sea and the Atlantic Ocean, the strong tides of 10 knots or more are impeded by islands, skerries, the sea bed and weather, all of which combine to create complex eddies and, sometimes, dangerous seas.

The Merry Men of Mey forms from St John's Point to Torness in Hoy on the ebb tide. With a westerly sea this

The Merry Men of Mey can extend from St John's Point to Brims on Hoy

MV Pentalina at St Margarets Hope

tide race can be hazardous even for large vessels. The Bores o'Duncansby forms on the flood tide and again can be especially violent when there are big easterly seas. There are many other parts of the Firth which can be dangerous to the uninformed.

Ever since people arrived in Caithness and Orkney they have exploited the sea for transport, food and materials. We know that the Vikings were legendary seafarers, but so were their forebearers, as shown by the presence of Neolithic and Iron Age remains on some of the small islands as well as abundant evidence of fishing activity.

Traditionally, the ferry ran from John o'Groats to Burwick but there was also a ferry from Scarfskerry to Brims in south Hoy and on to the Mainland. The first recorded ferryman was Jan de Groot, appointed by James IV about 1496, to ensure communications with his recently acquired islands. Presumably there had been a ferry for thousands of years before this, but unrecorded. Large numbers of cattle were once shipped by this route.

The short sea crossing from John o'Groats to Burwick is run in the summer months by the *Pentland Venture* which carries up to 250 passengers, while Pentland Ferries operate the new catamaran *Pentalina* between St Margaret's Hope and Gills Bay all year.

STROMA (ON *Straumey*, Stream Island) lies 1.5 miles off Canisbay on the south side of the Pentland Firth and has always been part of Caithness. It has been uninhabited since 1962, although 375 people had lived here in 1901. A new harbour was completed in 1956 but this came too late to stem emigration.

Tide race off Stroma

The Stroma males had a reputation for being exceptional seamen and had an almost innate knowledge of the tides. They fished mainly for Lobsters, Cod and Herring, depending on the season.

The Stroma Yole is a traditional clinker built boat of about 20ft in length. The last one built on the island was in 1913, but several examples can be seen at John o'Groats and other harbours. They are well suited to the conditions of the Pentland Firth with a broad-beam and full ends.

For centuries the Firth has been used by cargo and naval ships and apart from fishing, pilotage was a major source of income for Swona and Stroma men. A dangerous occupa-

tion, they sometimes ended up coming home via America!

Lighthouse In 1896 a minor light was established at Swilkie Point on the north end of the island. It was upgraded to paraffin burning soon after, to electric power in 1972 and was automated in 1997.

The Swilkie Off the Northern point of Stroma, the Swilkie (ON *Svegr*, whirlpool) is the most dangerous whirlpool in the Pentland Firth, at the meeting of several strong contrary tides. In Norse legend it is where the salt of the oceans is ground in a giant quern, stolen from King Frodi by a sea-king

Stroma lighthouse from Duncansby Head

The Harbour, Stroma - from St John's Point

Abandoned houses on Stroma

Stroma Yoles at John o'Groats Harbour

named Mysing. Mysing's longship foundered off Stroma under the weight of the millstones, it is said that he still grinds salt beneath the sea. The tides can yet be heard roaring through the ancient quernstones.

Shipwrecks were, historically, a source of wood, iron and all sorts of supplies. Even the minister might intervene, "*Oh Lord, if it will be thy will to send us a wreck, send us a good one*". As recently as 1994 the brand new Danish coaster *Bettina Danica* (1,354 tonnes) went ashore on the flat rocks of Mell Head at the south east of Stroma and was a total loss.

THE PENTLAND SKERRIES, 4 miles northeast of Duncansby is another hazardous place for shipping, with very strong tides, dangerous eddies and many unmarked dangers. The Skerries consist of **Muckle Skerry** and a long shoal running northeast from **Little Skerry** to **Clettack Skerry**. Many ships have foundered here in the past, especially in foggy weather. Sailing ships were particularly prone to be grounded on calm days with poor visibility.

Lighthouses The first lighthouses were erected here in 1794, with two towers to distinguish them from North

Ronaldsay lighthouse in Orkney. One was 24m high, the other 18m, and a total of 66 catoptric reflectors were used in the two sets of optics.

In the 1820s it was decided to heighten the towers and the higher lighthouse was increased to 35m. The catoptric (reflecting) lamps were replaced in 1848 with dioptric (refracting) lamps of higher efficiency, while in 1895 the lower light was discontinued and finally replaced by a foghorn in 1909. The lighthouse was automated in 1994, nearly 200 years after first being lit.

Wildlife The Pentland Firth has an abundance of wildlife, which is best seen from one of the ferry crossings, a specialist wildlife boat tour or whilst on a trip to one of the islands. Boat trips are available from John o'Groats but access to Swona or the Pentland Skerries is difficult and often dangerous, ensuring that the wildlife is mostly undisturbed.

Arctic Terns, Guillemots, Razorbills, Puffins, Great Skuas, Arctic Skuas, Kittiwakes and other gulls, Fulmars and Shags all breed in the area. Gannets are frequently seen on passage during migration times but may be seen plunge diving at any season.

Cetaceans are also often seen. These include Minke Whales, Killer Whales, White-sided and other Dolphins and

The Bettina Danica was wrecked on Stroma in 1994

A large school of dolphins in the eastern Pentland Firth

Gannets are frequently seen from the ferries

Puffins on Muckle Skerry

Porpoises, with always the possibility of rarer species. Basking Sharks are also now occasionally spotted during the summer months.

Many Grey Seals come ashore to pup in autumn, especially on the Pentland Skerries. Otters frequent the shorelines and may be glimpsed from time to time.

Pentland Skerries lighthouses

A tranquil Pentland Firth from the Bay of Sannick, Duncansby

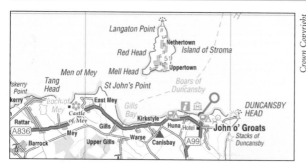

JOHN o'GROATS is 876 miles from Lands End, the furthest distance apart of any two places on the UK mainland. Ever since the American Elihu Buritt completed the walk in 1865 there have been all manner of record breaking and charity fund raising traverses of Britain.

Along the A99 from the south, there is a panoramic view over the Pentland Firth to Orkney from Warth Hill (ND371699, 124m), which is well worth the short walk from a nearby old quarry. John o'Groats itself has a VIC and a selection of shops selling crafts and souvenirs as well as a good cafe. Sadly, the hotel is closed.

St Drostan's Kirk, Canisbay

The harbour is home to a variety of creel boats, as well as John o'Groats Ferries summer passenger ferry to Burwick in South Ronaldsay. There are also wildlife cruises on offer to see Puffins and other seabirds on Duncansby Head.

St John's Point is named for the ruined chapel which lies inside a rampart and ditch which defends the headland. Whether this was in a military

St John's Point has an Iron Age fort and an ancient chapel site

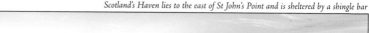

Scotland's Haven lies to the east of St John's Point and is sheltered by a shingle bar

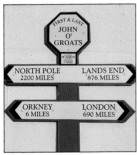

John o'Groats mile marker

Stroma yoles and John o'Groats hotel in the mist

John o'Groats Harbour

or spiritual sense is unknown. In 1919 a cross-slab was found which had been re-used in a stone lined grave. The famous and dangerous tide race first forms on the ebb tide off the Men of Mey rocks.

Scotland's Haven is just east of St John's Point. It is a bay sheltered by a shingle covered skerry at low tide, and as such is not easily accessed by boat. It is a favourite haul out place for Grey Seals, especially in autumn when they come ashore to pup.

Gills Bay (ON *Gil*, ravine) is named for the many small clefts in the low banks above the shore. It is now the terminal for the Pentland Ferries service to St Margaret's Hope.

Canisbay Kirk is dedicated to St Drostan and is built on top of a prehistoric mound, perhaps a broch. It is first mentioned in 1222 but the present building mostly dates from the 17th century. The tower is said to have replaced an earlier circular one. St Drostan was a 6th century missionary to Pictland.

Jan de Groot Stone, Canisbay Kirk

JOHN o'GROATS
Origin of the name

A mound near the pier marks where Jan de Groot, a Dutchman, had his house in the reign of James IV (1488-1513). His 7 sons disagreed about precedence and Jan de Groot solved this by building an octagonal house with 8 doors, and an 8-sided table so that no one had the head of the table. He ran a ferry to Orkney and charged 2p a trip. This coin became known as the *'groat'*. He is buried in Canisbay churchyard where his tombstone stands in the porch. Locally he became known as John o'Groats, and the area took on his nickname.

DUNCANSBY

The Stacks of Duncansby are very impressive, in early summer the clifftops are carpeted by wild flowers

DUNCANSBY HEAD (ON *Dungal's Boer*, Dungal's Estate) is called *Veruvium Promantarium*, or Clear-cut Cape on Ptolemy's map, which well describes it. Many people drive to the car park, take a look and leave, which is a pity as the coastal walk south from the lighthouse is a delight which should not be missed.

To the north of the car park, the Glupe has a large natural arch which is best viewed from the landward end. South from the lighthouse the Long Geo of Sclaites is a collapsed cave, while the Knee is a stack where Puffins may be seen. The shore can be accessed with care at Queenie Cliff for a fine view of the Thirle Door, another natural arch.

The finest views of the Duncansby Stacks are from the vantage points on the path, south from above the Thirle Door, and north from Hill of Crogdale. This walk is perhaps best on an early summer's morning with the sun on the cliffs and carpets of wild flowers. However the scene on a stormy winter's morning is equally impressive.

In winter easterly seas can be especially spectacular

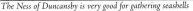
The Ness of Duncansby is very good for gathering seashells

Groatie Buckies at the Ness of Duncansby

The Duncansby cliffs offer excellent views of breeding seabirds in early summer, whether from the clifftops or, from a wildlife cruise boat. From May to July there is a sea of colour from the carpets of wild flowers which change as the various species come into bloom.

Primula scotica can be found in this area

Spring Squill

Duncansby lighthouse was established in 1924. In common with other newer designs its tower is square rather than round. It was automated in 1997. Despite modern aids to navigation it remains an important seamark to the southeast entrance of the Pentland Firth.

Duncansby lighthouse on a summer's evening

Duncansby Head from the east

The Ness of Duncansby is one of the best beaches in the North Highlands for those wishing to collect shells, especially *Groatie Buckies* or Cowrie Shells. There is a very good walk along the shore from John o'Groats to the Bay of Sannick. The fine views, mixture of sandy beaches, Old Red Sandstone boulders, fossiliferous rocks and flower-covered links is quite sublime on a summer's evening.

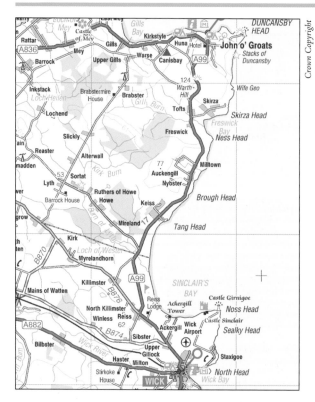

Keiss Harbour

bly started life as a Viking castle. It was enlarged in the 17th century and later. It has variously been called both a castle and a manor.

Lambaborg, or Bucholie Castle (ND383658) at Kingans Geo is built on a large rock which sticks out into the sea. It was the site of one of Sweyn Asleifson's many exploits detailed in the *Orkneyinga Saga* where he escaped from Earl Rognvald by means of swimming and a small boat. It was re-named

Freswick (ON *Tres Vik*, Tree Bay, in the sense of driftwood) is an attractive bay about 4 miles south of John o'Groats. The long sandy beach is backed by sand dunes and machair. The area has been occupied for at least 2,500 years, as shown by the presence of four brochs. Remains of an extensive Norse settlement which was involved in large-scale fishing have been excavated in the links.

The house of Freswick proba-

Sinclair's Bay has a three-mile sandy beach backed by impressive sand dunes and links

Pipeline fabrication at Reiss

Bucholie by the Mowat family in the 15th century.

Nybster broch was excavated in the 19th century and has a rather naive folly built into it. Despite this, the site is worth a visit, if only to enjoy the attractive shoreline walk.

Freswick is the site of an extensive Norse settlement

Keiss has a fine harbour built in about 1831 by James Bremner. A fine fishing store and a small icehouse add to the pretty scene. The harbour is reached from the main part of the village by passing an attractive terrace of cottages.

Old Keiss Castle is a romantic 16th century ruin which can be reached from the harbour. It is perched on the edge of low cliffs and is slowly disintegrating. Keiss and Whitegate Brochs are passed along the way.

Bucholie Castle is the Lambaborg of the Orkneyinga Saga

Sinclair's Bay has a three mile stretch of sand, again backed by extensive dunes and machair links. It can be accessed via car parks south of Keiss and at Reiss. Ackergill Tower dates from the 15th century but was extensively altered in the 19th century. The nearby lifeboat house at Ackergillshore was built in 1878, when a lifeboat was established here. It is the oldest in Scotland, while the concrete slipway dates from 1910.

Oil Recently long pipelines have been fabricated at Reiss on a five mile double rail track. They were then towed out to be laid offshore.

Keiss Castle is a romantic ruin

Keiss Castle and Herring boats in 1821 by William Daniell

Castle Sinclair Girnigoe from the northeast

CASTLE SINCLAIR GIRNIGOE is located 900m west of Noss Head lighthouse, 5 miles from Wick by road. It is spectacularly sited atop 20m cliffs on a promontory. It is protected on the landward side by a large geo (ON *gja*, narrow sea inlet)

Recent archaeological investigations have shown that it was built as one castle in the 14th century. It was developed over the years until it was ransacked and partially demolished by George Sinclair of Keiss in about 1680. Cromwells' troops occupied it in the 1650s and may well have done much damage here as elsewhere.

Stairs to the Sally Port

The castle was protected by a deep ditch, drawbridge and barbican on its west side. It is internally divided by another dry moat into an inner and outer bailey. The entrance to the latter is by means of a 14th century vaulted passage which leads to a courtyard.

A second drawbridge then led to the three storey tower house and ranges of outbuildings which extend to the end of the promontory. From here a stairway descends to a doorway giving access to the shore.

The castle is built from Caithness flagstone, with red sandstone decorations and facings. It was lime washed at one time, and must once have been an extremely prominent and impressive structure. Its purpose was less military and more symbolic of prestige and power.

Quote from the Clan Sinclair Trust website, *"It seems that the appearance of the site helped to give rise to the idea that there were two, rather than one castle, as the ruins are separated by a dry moat in addition to the larger moat around the property. The main structure is the Tower House, and this became known as 'Castle Girnigoe'. All that remains of the West Gate House is the structure around the chimney stack, and the construction and appearance gave rise to the idea that this was 'Castle Sinclair'. 'Castle Girnigoe' was deemed to have been built for strength and 'Castle Sinclair' for beauty, reminiscent of that other well known Sinclair edifice, Rosslyn Chapel, and its famous pillars."*

Sally Port to the shore

The first written reference to the castle was made by Rev John Brand in 1700, when it was already ruinous. He said, *"... Upon the south side of the bay next to Wick have been two strong Castles joined to one another by a Draw Bridge, called Castle Sinclair and Girnigoe, the former heath been the strongest House, but the latter they ordinarily had their dwelling in; their situation is upon a rock disjoined from the Land, environed for the most part with the Sea, to which Castles from the Land, they passed also by a Bridge which was drawn up every night, whence there was no access to them. I found the year of God upon the Lintel of a window in Castle Sinclair to be 1607; which hath been the year wherein this castle was built or at least repaired. Some account these two Castles to be but one, because of their vicinity."*

The Clan Sinclair Trust owns the ruined castle as well as the Noss Head lighthouse

Castle Sinclair Girnigoe from the east in 1821 by William Daniell

buildings and about 35 acres of surrounding land. The trust is continuing archeological surveys and renovation work on the site. The Clan Sinclair Study Centre at Noss Head holds a large number of books, documents and genealogical material.

Noss Head (ON *Snos*, nose) lighthouse was established in 1849, the engineer being Alan Stevenson. A new style of lantern with diagonal instead of vertical framing was first used by Stevenson here.

Stronger and less liable to intercept light in any particular direction, it was adopted as the standard pattern for the service.

The original lamp from Noss Head is now in the museum at Wick. The lens which is approximately 6ft in diameter rotates by clockwork machinery around a mercury vapour lamp. The road from Wick was built by the unemployed poor of the area who were paid 3/6d per day.

Noss Head lighthouse

Castle Sinclair Girnigoe from the east today

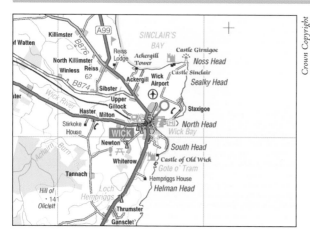

Crown Copyright

Lighthouse on South Pier

WICK (ON *Vik*, Bay) The town developed along the north bank of the Wick River, which is tidal until well upstream of the present Bridge Street. This would have afforded Vikings, Picts and earlier navigators a safe haven on a hard coast. The earliest harbour would have consisted of small jetties and wharfs along the river.

The town was became a Royal Burgh in 1589, but it was not until the early 19th century that Wick's dramatic development as a town

and harbour began. Up until then Staxigoe was preferred as a harbour, but it could only cope with small vessels in good conditions. Yet, by 1800, there were already about 200 boats working from the north side of the river. There were also sixteen firms processing and packing Herring into barrels.

The centre of Wick has a large selection of 19th century architecture, especially on Bridge Street. The Royal Bank of Scotland and the Town Hall date from about

1830, while the Sheriff Court is from the 1860s. The ornate Victorian style is in stark contrast to modern utility. Caithness flagstone was used apart from sandstone ornamentation.

The world's shortest street is Ebenezer Place. At 2.06m it has only one door and one address, Mackay's Hotel's No 1 Bistro. It was officially declared a street in 1887 and entered the Guinness *Book of Records* in 2006. The menu is highly recommended.

Wick River and the Wick Bridge from the southeast at high tide

Wick River has been bridged at least three times. The first, wooden, bridge was replaced by a Telford designed one in 1805. This was in turn removed in favour of the present Wick Bridge, opened in 1877.

Wick Harbour developed hugely throughout the 19ᵗʰ century, causing engineers such as Telford, Bremner and even the Stevensons many problems, due to its exposed location. Thomas Telford identified Wick as a prime site to develop a major fishing station. Through Sir William Pulteney the British Fisheries Society was persuaded to purchase 390 acres south of the river to develop a harbour and housing.

Pulteneytown was designed by Thomas Telford as a new town for fishermen and people involved in the fishing industry. The residential upper part was laid out in a grid fashion of streets around Argyll Square on the higher ground. The harbour area was developed to provide curing sheds, cooperages, boatyards and all manner of other services necessary for a large fishing fleet.

Sir William Pulteney was Telford's patron and had changed his name on marriage to the Earl of Bath's heir. Many of the streets here are named after directors of the British Fisheries Society. Pulteneytown and Wick did well all through the 19th century, but were also bitter rivals, and only became administratively joined in 1902.

Old Pulteney Distillery was established in 1826. It produces a Highland single malt Scotch

Wick Fountain dates from 1904

The shortest street in the world

Bridge Street is lined with Victorian buildings

Old Pulteney Distillery

Houses in Pulteneytown

Wick Bay from the south in 1821 by William Daniell

which reputedly gains its characteristic nose due to exposure to the sea air. The water comes from the Mill Lade, a burn flowing from Loch Hempriggs. There is a visitor centre in Huddart Street.

The distillery is now owned by Inver House Distillers Limited, which also owns the Speyburn-Glenlivet, Knockdhu, Balblair and Balmenach Distilleries.

Wick Heritage Museum was opened by the Wick Society in 1981. Situated in Bank Row, it has a huge variety of interesting displays, which include a 1920s dwelling house, with rooms typical of the period, a herring curing yard and a cooperage. Many artifacts, documents and photographs pertaining to Wick and Caithness can be viewed. The story of Caithness Glass, the original lighthouse workings from Noss Head, and the story of Herring Fishing at Wick as well as a host of interesting machines, tools and objects are all on display.

Isabella Fortuna was built in 1890 at Arbroath for the Smith family, who worked her until 1986. She was acquired by the Wick Society in 1997 and has since been fully restored. She is berthed in Wick Harbour in the summer and is used to promote the heritage of Wick's fishing industry.

Herring Fishing was a boom industry during the 19th and early 20th centuries and Caithness led the way for a long time. Technology improved steadily and sometimes at great speed, allowing much greater catching effort. Inevitably this eventually led to overfishing with, at first a decline, and, later, a failure in catches.

The peak year for Wick was 1862, when 1,122 boats were based here during the season. The fishermen, shore workers, ships' crews and other workers expanded the population by well over 10,000 during this time. It was said that when a really good catch was landed no less than 500 gallons of whisky would be drunk in a single day. There were said to be 22 pubs in Wick and 45 in Pulteneytown.

The Wick people were early to

Wick Heritage Museum - longlines

Wick Heritage Museum - kippers

Wick Harbour from the south

embrace innovations. As catches from near waters fell, steam drifters and, later, seine netters were adopted. These innovations only accelerated the demise of the vast shoals of Herring that once swam here and by 1937 the local industry was finished. Today only a tiny fleet of seine netters and small lobster boats is based at Wick.

Wick Lifeboat was established in 1848

Isabella Fortuna

Wick Heritage Museum - Stroma yole

The Old Fish Market dates from 1890

Wick Harbour

Several small fishing boats still work out of Wick

Pilot House presented by Sir Arthur Bignold MP 1908

The Old Fish Market on Harbour Quay was built about 1890. Prior to this catches were auctioned straight from the boats, but increasing landings meant that a mart had to be set up. It has recently been renovated.

Staxigoe and Broadhaven are two of several small bays north of Wick which were much used as landing places until Wick Harbour was developed. Staxigoe was used to export grain, salt fish, salt beef, hides and tallow to the continent. The presence of two Iron Age brochs nearby suggests that these small harbours were important as early as 2,000 years ago.

Old Wick Castle, known to seamen as the *Old Man of Wick*, is on a peninsula between two deep geos a mile south of Wick. The castle probably dates from the 12th century, when Caithness was ruled by the Norse Earls of Orkney. It has a rock-cut ditch on the landward side defended by a rampart and gatehouse and is defended on the other three sides by steep cliffs.

The keep had four floors set on scarcements which can be seen within the tower. There is no evidence of stairways or chimneys, so access must have been by ladders and heating by open fires. Access

Broadhaven and Papigoe

from outside was by ladder to the first floor. On the seaward side a range of buildings extends to a small courtyard. These would have included a kitchen, a bakery, stables and other outhouses.

In Norse times the castle belonged to the Earl of Caithness. From the 14th century on it was held by various Scottish families including de Cheynes, Sutherlands and Dunbars and was abandoned in the 18th century. It is the best preserved of many similar structures in Caithness, and the only one in the care of Historic Scotland.

Wick Airport is the most northerly on mainland UK and is operated by Highlands and Islands Airports Ltd. Eastern Airways operates flights to Aberdeen and Flybe to Edinburgh from here. The airport was established by Highland Airways in the 1930s and was taken over by the RAF in 1939. It was very busy throughout WWII mostly with Coastal Command squadrons, but was also an important Met Flight base.

Old Wick Castle

Old Pulteney logo at the Distillery

Old Wick Castle from the north

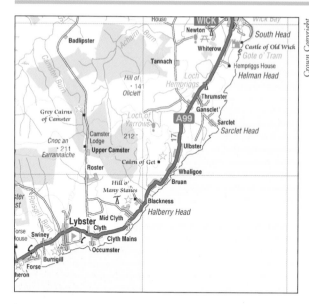

Crown Copyright

Sarclet Haven and village were developed in the early 1800s. There were salt pans here in former times. Today all that remains is a fish curing shed and an old windlass. The Haven is a very pleasant place for a picnic and is a good starting point for coastal walks to the north or south. In summer, nesting seabirds throng the cliffs whose tops are awash with colourful wild flowers.

Ires Geo is about 1.5 miles to the north and is one of several such features along this coast. It has a stack which is still attached to the cliff.

The A99 to the south of Wick passes through farming countryside on the way to Lybster. The coast consists of low cliffs with many geos and stacks. Lots of these inlets have been used for centuries to keep boats and land fish. During the early years of the Herring Boom these tiny harbours were to see a huge increase in landings. However as the boats got larger, landings were increasingly made at Wick.

Whaligoe and its steps (ND322403) were first mentioned by Rev Pope of Reay around 1769, *"In this parish (Wick) there is a haven for fishing boats, called Whaligoe, which is a creek betwixt two high rocks. Though the height of*

Whaligoe Steps, Ulbster

The Whaligoe Steps cling to the cliff as they wind to the top

one of these rocks is surprising, yet the country people have made steps by which they go up and down, carrying heavy burdens on their back; which a stranger, without seeing would scarcely believe. This is a fine fishing coast."

The 330 steps lead down to a large geo with deep water which was used to land and ship Herring, Salmon, whitefish and shellfish. The curing house at the top dates from 1813, and replaced a much older *corfhouse*, where Salmon was processed.

Clythness lighthouse was established in 1916

Incredibly, schooners used to dock here to collect barrels of Herring and probably also salt Cod. They dropped anchor outside and were warped into the cove stern first. Whaligoe continued to be busy with fishing for a long time. By 1855 there were 35 boats here, with 140 fishermen. In 1928 there were only 8 boats and 16 fishermen.

Ires Geo has a fine stack still joined to the land

Great care should be taken when visiting Whaligoe as the steps can be treacherous if wet. There is a good viewpoint from the south side clifftop. Wester Whale Geo is also worth a visit.

The Haven, Sarclet

Scene at Hempriggs by William Daniell 1821

Clythness lighthouse sits below the road north of Lybster and was established in 1916, the engineer being David A Stevenson. It was automated in 1964 and the cottage is a private house.

Camster Long Cairn silhouetted against the sky

Archaeology Caithness has an abundance of archaeological sites from many periods. No more so than the route from Wick to Latheron, near which are many of the most impressive and accessible monuments in the county.

The Grey Cairns of Camster (ND260440) are 5 miles north of Lybster. They are among the best preserved Neolithic chambered cairns in Britain. Both have intact chambers and passages with rooflights so that no torches are needed. They should not be missed and are accessed from the road by boardwalks.

Camster Round is about 20m in diameter and 4m high. The east-facing entrance has an impressive facade and leads to a passage about 6m long. The chamber has a nearly intact corbelled roof. It is divided by 3 pairs of upright slabs. The roof is made of one large monolith and is over 3m above the floor.

Camster Long is a huge extended pile of stones over 60m long. There are horns at each end and a large forecourt at the north end. The retaining wall has been repaired to represent the original appearance. The monument

Camster Round Cairn

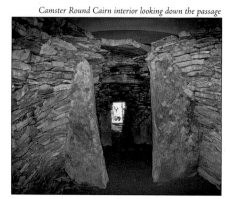

Camster Round Cairn interior looking down the passage

Camster Round Cairn interior showing the monolithic stalls

Achavanich U-shaped stone setting overlooking Loch Stemster

started off as two separate round cairns which were subsequently joined and extended southwards.

The north chamber is lined with vertical slabs, while the south one resembles that of Camster Round. Both entrance passages face eastwards. The chamber roofs are not original as they were destroyed in the 19th century, but they retain a strong sense of grandeur.

Achavanich Stone Setting (G The Monk's Field, ND187417) is about 5 miles north of Lybster near Loch Rangag on the Cassiemyre Road. The standing stones form a U-shape with their narrow faces aligned inwards. About 40 stones remain about of a probable 54. They vary in height between 1m and 2m. The setting is thought to date from before 2,500BC. The small mound to the southeast is a Neolithic chambered cairn.

Hill o'Many Stanes, Mid Clyth (ND295384) about 3 miles north of Lybster is the best-preserved of a type of stone setting only seen in Caithness and Sutherland. Over 200 stones are arranged in 22 or more rows on the south side of a hill. They run north to south in a fan shape with their broad faces aligned with the rows. The stones are less than 1m high.

The site may once have had 600 stones and was possibly an ancient lunar observatory. Forty-five metres west a fallen standing stone could have been part of this. Though assumed to have been laid out about 2,000BC, this is purely conjecture.

Chambered cairn, Achavanich

Hill o'Many Stanes, Mid Clyth

Broch of South Yarrows

Cairn of Get or Garrywhin (ND313411) is signposted off the main road at Ulbster opposite Whaligoe. It is a small, short horned Neolithic chambered cairn. The roof has gone but the passage and chamber are otherwise intact.

On excavation in 1866 the walls were still over 2.5m high. A 0.5m layer of ashes, burnt wood and bones covered the chamber floor. Large amount of flints and pottery shards were also present. A number of skeletons were placed on top of this layer, with skulls along the east wall.

There are several other sites of interest here, including Kenny's Cairn (ND310408), several brochs and a 19th century dam to supply Whaligoe Mill. Probably the most interesting is **Fort of Garrywhin** (ND313412). A stone built rampart about 150m long surrounds a steep sided hill. The north entrance is faced by large upright stones, suggest-ing that in its day the fort must have been quite impressive. There is also a south entrance and remains of ruined buildings within the fort.

Yarrows Archaeology Trail is signposted off the A99 near Thrumster. From the car park (ND306435) a circular walk takes in a variety of interesting sites spanning at least 3,000 years. There are three long and two round Neolithic chambered cairns. All are in a

Cairn of Get or Garrywhin

Cairn of Get or Garrywhin

ruinous state, but the layout can still be discerned.

To the south of the loch there are circular ruins of several Bronze Age huts. The piles of stones around them would have been cleared from the land during cultivation of crops. The nearby broken standing stone may also date from this period.

South Yarrows chambered cairn

Broch of South Yarrows is one of the best in Caithness and sits on the edge of the loch, partially flooded. The walls survive to over 2m in places, with parts of intramural stairs and passages still visible. The entrance has a guard cell and lintel still in place.

Long cairn at South Yarrows

The broch has banks and ruined remains of aisled buildings which may be Pictish houses. In Caithness these are called *wags* (G uaimhach, little cave). They are partially sunk into the ground and the roofs were held up on large upright stones. Most are found in the Latheron area.

The Wag of Forse (ND204351) is just off the A9 a mile north of Latheron. Here, the aisled stone pillars are obvious in a long structure with small cells which lies beside the remains of a broch.

Broch of South Yarrows from the south showing remains of the wag

Conspicuous broch mound and ramparts at Bruan, south of Ulbster

There are many other broch mounds in this area, some of which are prominent and retain ramparts and outside settlements.

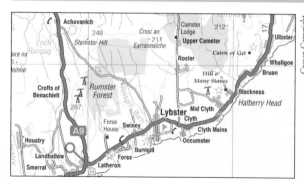

9th century Norse farm. The beach is reached by a steep track at the south end of the street.

LYBSTER (ON *Hlith Bolstadir*, Slope Farm) developed as a Herring station in the 19th century. The local Sinclair landowners built a wooden pier in 1810 and over the next 80 years harbour improvements continued. In 1808 there were 8 boats but by 1838 Lybster had 101 boats working from the harbour and was the third biggest Herring port in Scotland.

The Reisgill Burn (ON *Hris Gil*, Brushwood Ravine) enters the sea here through a deep ravine. There was clearly a large river here after the Ice Age. The Norse called the bay Haligeo, suggesting a possible early monastic settlement.

Shaligoe is a delightful small sandy cove to the northeast of the harbour. It is overlooked by Skaill, the probable site of a

The village was planned by the landowner, Patrick Sinclair and was developed from 1802. He had been in the army in Canada and retired as a Lieutenant General. The wide Main Street was his idea as was the name "Quatre Bras" after a battle in which his sons served in 1815.

Main Street was planned to be 50ft wide, 24ft to be carriageway and 6ft on each side foot pathway, to be flagged with stone, all to be financed and maintained by the feuars.

The harbour continued to be developed right through the Herring Boom, and the lighthouse was built in 1884, by which time the fishery was in decline. Today a small number of boats fish for lobsters and crabs from here. Lybster also welcomes many yachts every year, either cruising or during races.

Waterlines Visitor Centre is in the restored building above the harbour. It has an exhibi-

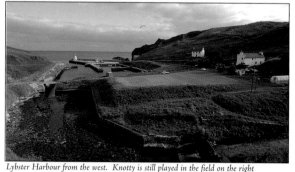

Lybster Harbour from the west. Knotty is still played in the field on the right

Main Street is 50 feet wide

The lighthouse was built in 1884

Debby Snook

The Waterlines Visitor Centre overlooks Lybster Harbour which is still busy with small boats

tion on Lybster Harbour's history and natural heritage. There are also demonstrations of traditional boatbuilding, and other regular events. As well as a coffee shop there are facilities for visiting yachts.

Knotty is a type of shinty which was played by large numbers on both sides at Old New Year. The game is still very popular, but more regulated nowadays.

Lybster Show attracts many fine cattle

175

Whalebone arch, Latheronwheel

LATHERON (ON *Hlith-tun*, cultivated slopes) is at the south end of the Cassiemyre road, where the A99 and the A9 meet. In former times a castle stood here, perhaps of Norse origin. By tradition there was a monastic site near the old church. Pictish symbol stones have been found in the area suggesting that there may be some truth in this.

The Clan Gunn Centre is situated in Latheron Old Parish Church which dates from 1734. It tells the story of the clan from Norse times against the background of the history of the north of Scotland. It also contains a substantial Clan archive and shop.

Archaeology The area around Latheron has a profusion of Bronze Age standing stones, burnt mounds and hut circles. There are also several Iron Age brochs and wags to be seen. The detached bell tower just north of the road junction is 17th century and was so placed because the church bell was difficult to hear in the parish.

Clan Gunn Museum in the Old Parish Church at Latheron

Swiney Castle in 1821 by William Danielle

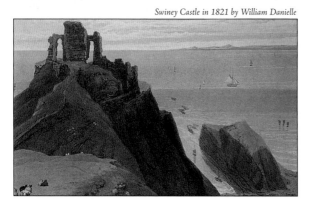

Swiney and Halberry Castles were originally Clan Gunn properties and go back to Norse times. Substantial remains of the former survive at Acastleshore (ND232338), but almost nothing remains of Halberry (ND307387) which is at Mid Clyth.

View northeastwards along the Caithness coast from south of Latheron

Latheronwheel (ON *Vathill*, ford) was planned by the laird, Captain Dunbar as another Herring harbour. The hotel was the first building and is universally known as "The Blends" since the 1890s when the then proprietor did his own whisky blending. Incoming tenants were allocated 2 acres of ground and the right to fish from the small harbour.

Latheronwheel Harbour entrance

Over 50 boats once fished from the attractive but exposed little harbour. The old road followed the coast more closely, crossing a fine old bridge which may date from 1726, no doubt replacing the ford across the Latheronwheel Burn.

Oil An onshore drilling rig north of Latheron belongs to Caithness Oil. Recent technological advances allowing drilling from the land using extended reach systems can go two or more miles to the well offshore.

Latheronwheel Burn, old bridge and harbour

Onshore oil drilling near Lybster

This allows the use of much cheaper and more environmentally friendly drilling rigs. Thus small fields such as this will be economically viable and exploitable.

Latheronwheel Valley from Guidebest looking southwest

Interesting valleys A short detour to explore the valleys of the Latheronwheel and Houstry Burns is well worthwhile. Apart from the expansive views over a landscape which has been farmed for 5,000 years, there are chambered cairns, standing stones, brochs and even a charming stone circle.

They can be accessed from the Cassiemyre Road, from Latheronwheel and from Dunbeath and make for a pleasant change from the busy A9 if you have time to spare on a fine day.

Guidebest Stone Circle close to the Burn of Latheronwheel (ND183351) is 57 x 52m in diameter. Along with several other similar Caithness rings this is among the 20 largest such monuments in the UK. Eight stones and several stumps remain, the highest being 1.5m. There is a cairn on the south side of the circle.

Houstry Standing Stone is a fine isolated megalith (ND155344) set in an open landscape. One can only speculate on whether there are sighting lines to the hills to the southwest. Nearby Cnoc na Maranaich above Dunbeath Water also has a standing stone and a scattering of chambered cairns.

Houstry Chambered Cairn (ND153331) is just west of the Burn of Houstry across a small bridge. Although ruinous, the layout of the cairn can be made out. The passage has gone but two large upright slabs mark its inner

The stone circle at Guidebest has over a dozen small monoliths

Guidebest stone circle on the Burn of Latheronwheel

end. Four more uprights can also be seen as well as the massive back-slab, showing that the chamber is over 5m long.

Brochs juxtapose the small farms of today. This is a landscape showing continuous habitation for at least 5,000 years. All of the broch mounds are worth a look, but only the one on the Dunbeath Heritage Trail is excavated (ND155306).

Windfarms are proliferating in Caithness as elsewhere. The Buolfruich Wind Farm at Houstry has an output of 9MW from 15 wind turbines. Their somewhat lonely aspect ironically symbolizes a continuation of human presence.

Neolithic chambered cairn overlooking the Burn of Houstry

Standing stone above the Burn of Houstry

Broch at Houstry

19th century croft, 20th century forest, 21st century windmills

Scaraben (626m), Maiden Pap (484m) and Morven (706m) from the viewpoint north of Smerral

Dunbeath Harbour is in the estuary of Dunbeath Water and was built in the 19ᵗʰ century

DUNBEATH (G *Dun Beithe*, Fort of the Birches) is named after the broch at the confluence of Dunbeath Water and the Burn of Houstry. The surrounding woodland is indeed mostly knarled old Birches, covered in interesting mosses and lichens.

Dunbeath street dates from the 1840s and 1850s

Ken and the Salmon statue at the harbour near the fishermens' store

Dunbeath Harbour developed from the 1790s, when Herring fishing started here. Over 80 families were cleared from Dunbeath Strath by the landowners in an early example of monetarism. Many settled at the mouth of the river and became involved in fisheries for Salmon and Herring.

The main street dates from the 1840s and the old bridge was built by Thomas Telford in 1810, now replaced by the large curving concrete viaduct. By the 1840s up to 100 boats worked out of Dunbeath. The attractive harbour remains, but few boats fish from here now.

Dunbeath Heritage Centre is situated in the old school to the south of the river. It has much to offer the visitor, including displays , archives, exhibitions and lectures. There is an excellent little shop. The Centre is a very fine place to start a tour of Caithness.

Neil M Gunn (1891-1973) was born and raised in Dunbeath. He is one of Scotland's most acclaimed 20th century novelists. *"Highland River"* and *"The Silver Darlings"* are two of his most acclaimed works.

The Ballachly Stone was found when a 19th century farm building near Chapel Hill was demolished. It may date from the 7th century and is part of an upright cross-slab with the top of a cross. An early symbol of Christ was the fish and the Salmon facing the centre of the cross may therefore reflect this. The Salmon was also a common Pictish symbol, perhaps related.

7th century Ballachly stone found on the nearby early monastic site

Fragments of another cross-slab have been found nearby. They may be 8th century and the suggestion is of a high-status monastic settlement here. There used to be a cemetery at Chapel Hill but it got washed away in the 1860s.

Dunbeath Castle dates from the 13th century. It started as a Norse tower and over the centuries has been extended and developed. The castle stands on the edge of the cliffs south of Dunbeath. The gardens are occasionally open to visitors.

The novelist Neil Gunn was born here

Dunbeath Castle

The Trail starts at a car park next to Dunbeath watermill

Looking east over the monastic site from Dunbeath broch

Dunbeath Strath Heritage Trail starts at the car park beside the Meal Mill, built in 1850 and operated until 1950. The path follows the river upstream past Chapel Hill and across a footbridge.

Dunbeath Broch sits prominently above the confluence of the Houstry Burn and Dunbeath Water. It is surrounded by trees and a wall. The entrance with its guard cell and a corbelled cell in the opposite wall can be seen. The highest part is still over 3m high. The site is best visited in winter when the vegetation has died back. There are excellent views over the Strath from a vantage point next to the broch.

Woodlands The trail continues up the north side of the river through Hazel, Birch, Rowan and Cherry trees. In autumn Hazel nuts are abundant here. The woodland is sheltered in all seasons and is home to many birds. Dippers hunt for prey under water in the river while Buzzards often patrol overhead. Roe Deer and Badgers are present here and are occasionally seen

Prisoner's Leap is a deep glacial ravine. Tradition says that Ian McCormack Gunn was being held in Forse Castle by the Keiths, who wished to kill him. He came from Braemore on the south side of the river and claimed he could jump the gorge. Sure that he would he fall to his death the Keiths agreed that he would be freed

Dunbeath broch is still over three metres high on the west side

The woods have many lovely lichens

Prisoner's Leap, which Ian McCormack Gunn is said to have leapt to gain freedom

if he succeeded, which of course he did. He was said to have been an orphan and weaned on hind's milk, which gave him the ability to jump so far.

Chambered cairns litter the hillsides further up the Strath, clearly showing how this lovely valley was inhabited 5,000 years ago. Today there are only the sounds of the river and of the birds. A standing stone on Cnoc na Maranaich (172m) aligns (nearly) with a notch in the hills to the west to indicate midsummer. In 2000BC this alignment would have been accurate.

Corbelled cell in the broch wall

Braemore is reached by a small side road south of Dunbeath. Hut circles and ruined crofts can be seen at several places. Braemore is a pleasant little settlement beside Berriedale Water.

A track leads across the moor to the foot of Maiden Pap (484m). Morven (706m) is a three mile hike across boggy moorland. Buzzards, Golden Eagles, Greenshanks and divers may all be seen here.

The interior of Dunbeath broch is well preserved on the west side, with an intact cell, scarcement, and the remains of intra-mural stairs

The Ord of Caithness forms the border with Sutherland. In spring and early summer the Whins (Gorse) are resplendent

BERRIEDALE (ON Bergi dalr, Cliff Dale) and its steep Braes is at the mouth of the Berriedale and Langwell Waters, where the old bridge was built by Thomas Telford in 1813. Nearby the Old Smithy has a large number of antlers mounted on the exteri-or walls. A small road leads along the river to a range of cottages set on a raised beach. Further old cottages line the shore on the north side over a small suspension bridge.

This little harbour is protect-ed from the east by a large rock. The presence of at least five brochs shows that this was once a thriving area. In the 19th century Langwell Farm was created to graze sheep. Paths lead up both rivers and among the woods.

Berriedale Castle, the *Brevik* of the *Orkneyinga Saga*, may date from the 12th century, but all that remains is some rub-ble. The *Duke's Candlesticks*, two towers looking like giant chessmen, were built in the 19th century as leading lights to the harbour, financed by the Duke of Portland.

Laidhay Croft Museum, north of Dunbeath is a 19th century croft, comprising a dwelling house, byre and barn in one long-house. The fur-nishings are typical of the late 19th and early 20th century with box beds, cupboards, tables and chairs. The ben end was the sitting room and the kitchen would have been where most activity went on.

The byre leads directly off the kitchen, while the barn has

Berriedale from below the grave yard looking south towards the site of the castle

Berriedale in 1821 by William Daniell - not much has changed

multi-timbered cruck frames holding up the roof. There are interesting displays of old tools and implements.

Ousdale Broch (ON *Austr dalr*, East Dale, ND071188)) is on the south bank of the Ousdale Burn in a prime defensive position over 100m above the sea. There is a panoramic view from here, the broch being situated on a small steep promontory.

Laidhay is typical of 19th century Caithness crofthouses

The walls are 5m thick and enclose an interior 8m in diameter. The entrance passage still has lintels and guard cells on both sides of the doorway. An intramural stair leads upwards from a small cell and a scarcement runs around the interior about 2.5m above the floor. Stone lined water tanks, a central hearth and a drain to the burn outside complete a very interesting visit.

The "but" end of Laidhay

Badbea (ND488200), south of Berriedale is the sad remnant of a village formed by 28 families evicted from nearby Langwell. The steep, poor ground above precipitous cliffs made the settlement untenable. A memorial put up in 1912 does nothing to alleviate the sadness.

The ruins of Badbea clearance village north of Ousdale

Ousdale Broch is about a mile north of the Ord of Caithness

The Ord of Caithness (G *Aird*, steep headland) is on the border between Caithness and Sutherland. This area of high moorland is beautiful with flowering Whins in spring, can be foggy at any time of year, and is often blocked by snow in winter.

SUTHERLAND - THE EAST COAST

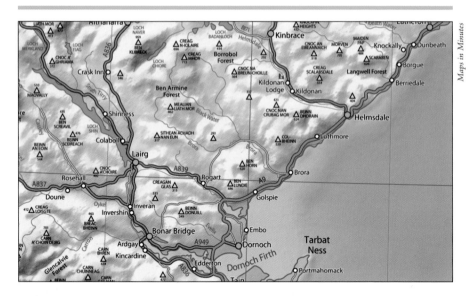

SUTHERLAND (ON *Sudrland*, South Land) covers 5,252km² with a population in 2001 of only 13,466, most of whom live on the fertile east coast. In the Gaelic language the south-east part is called *Cataibh*, referring to the *Cat* people who inhabited Caithness and Sutherland.

Helmsdale

Brora Beach

The east coast is mostly composed of Old Red Sandstone, but there are also Jurassic rocks exposed along the coast between Helmsdale and Golspie. In contrast to much of Caithness south of Wick, the shores are gentle and low, with expansive sandy beaches backed by links.

Loch Fleet and the Dornoch Firth are large inlets from the sea with many sand and mudbanks. They are both fed by river systems running from the watershed far to the west. Waders and waterfowl feed and roost in large numbers, especially in winter.

The county town of Dornoch is an ancient settlement and a Royal Burgh with the only cathedral in the area. It is also home to the Royal Dornoch, one of the best and oldest golf courses in the world. Most of the other settlements are also on the coast and include

Golspie and Ben Braggie

Dornoch Cathedral

Golspie, Brora and Helmsdale. Bonar Bridge at the Kyle of Sutherland and Lairg at the head of Loch Shin are at strategic crossroads.

Inland there is much evidence of former settlement. The Straths of Kildonan, Fleet and Oykel, as well as most of the remainder of the area was cleared of a large number of its indigenous people in the 19th century during the notorious clearances. In recent times people have started to return but the remoter locations remain largely unpopulated.

There are many interesting places to stop and explore, seek out ancient sites, watch birds or enjoy spectacular scenery.

Debby Snook

Loch Shin at Lairg

Strath Fleet

Loch Fleet from the Mound

Bonar Bridge

189

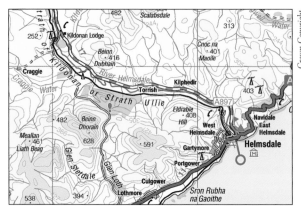

Helmsdale already had a long established Salmon fishery made this a natural option.

The fine old Telford Bridge was built in 1813 to carry the new road north. By 1819 this was completed over the Ord of Caithness. Communications were further improved by the arrival of the railway in 1871.

The harbour was developed in several stages from about 1818 coinciding with the development of Herring fishing. It was greatly enlarged again in the 1890s, but by the early 1900s the harbour and its curing sheds lay abandoned.

During the season over 200 boats packed the basin. However, the advent of larger boats and then steam drifters in 1900 meant that catches were landed at bigger ports.

Helmsdale in 1821 by William Daniell with the Telford bridge and ruined castle

HELMSDALE (ON Hjalmundur's Dale) is a pretty little village at the Mouth of the River Helmsdale. For centuries it was an isolated salmon fishing and curing station. In 1814 building of a new planned village and har-bour was commenced by the Sutherland Estate to accommodate some of the families who had been displaced. The idea was that some would work small holdings near the village, while others would go to the fishing. That

Today a few inshore vessels fish for lobsters, crabs, prawns and shellfish. The riverside and harbour area is a very pleasant place for a stroll.

The Emigrants Statue overlooks the river and harbour

Helmsdale from the south side of the river with the old and new bridges

Helmsdale harbour

Emigrants Statue

from the south side. This haunting sculpture commemorates the tens of thousands of people who were displaced from the Highlands during the 19th century. The stone was commissioned by Dennis MacLeod, a local who became rich through gold mining in South Africa.

Angling The River Helmsdale is renowned for its Salmon and Sea Trout. The Salmon run starts in early spring and lasts until May or June, while Sea Trout and Grilse are best in June and July. There is an excellent tackle shop in Dunrobin Street.

Helmsdale Castle may well have originally been the site of a broch or a Norse stronghold.

The building in the Daniell print dated from the 14th century. Its ignominious place in history was made in 1567, when Isobel Sinclair devised a plan to murder her nephew, the 11th Earl of Sutherland, his wife and son, so that her own son would inherit the estate. They were invited for dinner and served drinks laced with poison. However, her plot

backfired and it was her own son who drank the poisoned wine and died. She then committed suicide to escape execution. The remains of the castle were demolished in the 1970s when the new bridge was built.

Early Christianity. St Ninian is said to have preached at Navidale in about 390AD.

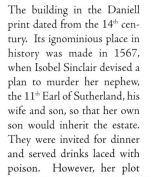

Pretty cottages line the shore of the harbour

Helmsdale ice house with the war memorial clock tower in the background

Broom and Whins in flower at Navidale, north of Helmsdale

Timespan geological garden and the Telford Bridge

There are faint ruins of a chapel in the old kirkyard, while the parish name, Kildonan (G *Cill*, cell or chapel, dedicated to St Donan) suggests the presence of an early chapel.

Timespan is a newly refurbished museum near the Telford Bridge. It has a permanent collection and changing exhibitions, an art gallery, a riverside café, and shop. Beside the river there are gardens featuring Scottish herbs, flowers and local geology.

It provides insight into the history of Helmsdale and the surrounding area. The multifaceted collection illustrates many aspects of past ways of life with re-creations of a

Old Salmon coble next to the river

croft, byre, smithy, and shop. Other displays present the area's archaeology, geology and natural history.

The gallery holds exhibitions of the work of local, national and international artists. They often feature original works produced here by artists who have spent time in residence in the gallery.

The Ice House dates from the 1780s and is sited across the old bridge from Timespan, below the War Memorial. Ice was gathered from a pond nearby and the chamber was filled via a chute. The structure was well insulated, so that the ice was available all through the Salmon season. There are good views of the river and village from the bridge and from the elaborate war memorial.

Beach and Fossils. The coastline south of Helmsdale is an excellent place to seek Jurassic fossils. The boulder beds on the foreshore are rich in reptilian, coral and fish remains. Some Ammonites and molluscs may also be found. Exposures of Jurassic and Kimmeridgean rocks continue from here to Golspie.

This coastline has excellent examples of raised beaches. These were formed when the level of the sea was higher than today, during and after the Ice Ages. Since then the land has risen, leaving these raised beaches well above the current shoreline.

Timespan Museum - replica shop from the early 20th century

Timespan Museum - agricultural tools

Fossil coral at the Timespan Museum

St Andrew's Well

SUTHERLAND - THE EAST COAST

Strath Kildonan from the Glen Loth road

Kildonan Gold Rush. In 1818 a gold nugget was found in the River Helmsdale and made into a ring for the Sutherland family. In 1868, Robert Gilchrist, a local who had prospected for gold in Australia, got permission to pan the river.

He struck gold in the Kildonan and Surgical Burns. Soon, over 600 hopefuls had arrived in Strath Kildonan, but this number fell to about 50. Most of the prospectors lived in huts at *Baile an Or* (G, Township of Gold). The gold rush was over by January 1870 when the Duke of Sutherland decided that other interests, including sheep grazing, hunting and fishing were more economically viable.

Today panning is permitted as a recreation. People still find grains of gold, and information is available in Helmsdale. Many find the practice relaxing and strangely addictive, returning year after year.

Archaeology Like other areas, the Strath of Kildonan or Strath Ullie was cleared of its inhabitants for sheep farming in the 19th century. Evidence of settlement over thousands of years includes chambered cairns, hut circles, standing stones, brochs and the ruined homesteads which line the valley.

Kildonan Burn

None are formally presented for visitors, but the most spectacular are the brochs, especially the those at Kilphedir (NC994189), Borrobol Broch (NC889253) and Surgical (NC899250).

Glen Loth A narrow and winding road runs north from Lothbeg to meet up with the main Strath Kildonan Road at Dal-Langal. It follows the Loth Burn through a remote and beautiful landscape. Carn Bran (NC942122) is a ruinous broch near the south end of the road.

Clach Mhic Mhios (NC941151), stands on the moor overlooking the valley. At 3.3m high this is the largest and most spectacular standing stone in Sutherland. It may be a marker for the winter solstice as it aligns with a notch in the hill to the southwest on

Kildonan Gold Rush

Borrobol Broch

Raised beach between Portgower and Helmsdale

Contorted mixed rocks

an azimuth of 214° - that of the midwinter sunset.

The **Glen Loth** road should not be attempted in snowy or icy conditions and is unsuitable for caravans or large vehicles. It is a very pleasant detour, but is narrow and windy with few passing places.

Portgower is a small village on the A9 just south of Helmsdale which is worth stopping at to visit the beach, with its dramatic Fallen Stack of Portgower. Boulder beds are mixed with Kimmeridgean shales and set in a sandy rock. The contorted and confused rocks with many pools are aesthetically appealing, but the terrain is difficult to walk on.

Ammonites, molluscs, fish, coral and plant fossils can be found here. The shore south from Helmsdale is a good example of raised beaches. Be careful when crossing the railway line. The village itself was built as a result of the 19th century clearances. Park near the track which leads down to the beach taking care not to block any entrances. There are fine walks along the shore here.

The Fallen Stack of Portgower

Carn Bran Broch, Glen Loth

Clach Mhic Mhios

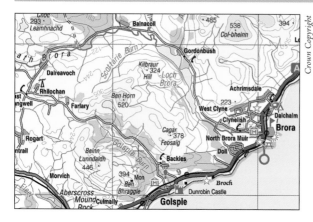

Crown Copyright

BRORA (ON *Brua A*, Bridge River) in the parish of Clyne (G *cleonadh*, sloping) lies at the mouth of the River Brora. There is ample evidence for prehistoric settlement including chambered cairns, hut circles, field systems, brochs, and a substantial hillfort.

These early inhabitants would have been attracted by the fertile land of the coastal plain and fishing for Salmon and Sea Trout in the river. The long sandy beach stretches for nearly two miles and is backed by dunes and machair.

Jurassic Rocks are exposed on the coast and river around Brora. There are interesting exposures on the low cliffs to the south of the village and on the cliffs along the river. Fossilised plants and molluscs are easy to find.

Coal Mining. Although most British coal dates from the Carboniferous Period, some was laid down in the Jurassic. There are several outcrops on the coast near Inverbrora, which were no doubt worked for many centuries. In about 1529 open cast quarrying was started near the coast. By the 17th century shafts were sunk and the coal was used to fire salt pans.

During the 19th century mining was expanded further. A brewery, brickworks and a distillery, all using local coal, were established. The mining was constantly plagued with spontaneous fires caused by pyrites in some of the coal layers. Operations ceased in 1975, but large reserves remain.

The Electric City Brora became the first town north of Inverness to have electricity, when in 1913 Brora Electric Supply Co was established.

Brora Golf Course was designed in 1923 by the great James Braid as his most northerly Scottish course. Golfers share their space with friendly cows on these attractive links, which in summer are covered by a sea of colourful wild flowers.

Brora has miles of lovely beaches to the north and south

Jurassic rocks on the beach

Brora Harbour at the mouth of River Brora

Strath Brora The country-side around the village is perfect for walkers and those interested in wild flowers, birds or archaeology. In a relatively small area there is a diverse range of habitats. These range from the gentle coast, the river and its estuary, to farmland and woodland, Loch Brora and the bleak moors above.

Loch Brora and Strath Brora

Archaeology Of the many prehistoric remains around Brora perhaps the most dramatically sited is the hillfort on Duchary Rock (NC850848), with its expansive views. Again, none of the monuments are signposted or officially presented, but seeking them out enhances the sense of discovery.

Brora icehouse at the harbour - formerly used to preserve fish

Clynelish Distillery was set up in 1819

Capaldi's Ice Cream

In 1929 Bernardo Capaldi and his son Alfredo from Lazio in Italy opened their ice cream parlour, and ever since it has been an essential stopping place for families on the way north and south. Today, *Capaldi's Ice Cream by Harry Gow* is still produced from local fresh ingredients to the traditional recipe.

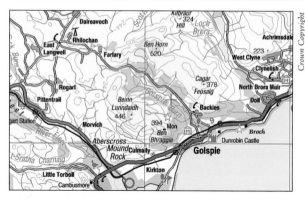

Golspie from the pier looking north

GOLSPIE (ON *Golls Baer*, Goll's Farm) is situated on the narrow coastal plain below Ben Bhraggie. The village is sheltered from the west and faces south to the Dornoch Firth. With an award winning and lovely sandy beach, nearby woodland and links, it is a very

Ben Bhraggie winter sunset from the north

pleasant place to stop.

St Andrew's Church was rebuilt in 1737 on the site of a much older medieval chapel. Fixed seating was installed in 1738 for the first time. By 1750 the building was already in disrepair and was needing a

great deal of maintenance. The south aisle may have been added about this time. The kirkyard has many intriguing tombstones.

Golspie Mill is one of the few water mills still in operation in Scotland. It was built in 1863, renovated in 1992 and is powered by the Big Burn. The mill produces peasemeal, beremeal, wholemeal flour, rye flour, and oatmeal, all of which may be bought locally.

Ben Bhraggie (394m) and its statue of the 1st Duke of Sutherland is a prominent landmark. The summit can be reached by a path leading from the centre of the village. There are fine panoramic views along the coast. The return route follows Dunrobin Glen and the Big Burn past a waterfall and small gorge.

Carn Liath (G Grey Cairn) is a well preserved broch about 2 miles north of Golspie on the A9 and has walls nearly 4m high. For access, park as indicated and take the signposted path. It was cleared out in the 1800s and a variety of items found, some of which are in Dunrobin Museum.

The entrance, complete with side cell, intramural stairs and lower scarcement can all be seen. A small settlement, which was in use until about 400AD, surrounds the broch.

The Orcadian Stone Co has a fascinating collection of, mainly, local fossils and miner-

Golspie has attractive stone cottages and shops

Carn Liath and surrounding buildings

als built up over many years by Don Shelley. It can be found at the north end of the village and certainly warrants a visit. Fossils can be found at low tide among the Jurassic rocks below Dunrobin Castle.

Balblair Wood was replanted with Scots Pine in 1905 after a violent storm. It lies to the south of Golspie past the golf course. A series of nature trails though the wood offers pleasant walking in all seasons, but it is a special treat in summer. The very rare One-flowered Wintergreen (or St Olaf's Candlestick), Creeping Lady's Tresses and Twinflower are three botanical surprises to be found here in June.

Crested Tits and Scottish Crossbills, Treecreepers and Great Spotted Woodpeckers may be seen in the woods here. Red Squirrels, Pine Martens and Roe Deer are also present.

Loch Fleet There are good views from the car park over tidal mudflats and salt marsh, where waders and waterfowl congregate in migration times and in winter. High tide is

the best time to get close views.

Ferry Links is an area of coastal heathland with an interesting variety of grasses and wild flowers adapted to this environment. Several rare species of butterflies and moths feed on the nectar from the flowers. In summer, Arctic, Common and Little Terns nest here.

Golspie Golf Course was designed by James Braid and

Golspie Mill

opened in 1889. It offers a mixture of links, heathland and parkland, as well as fine views and lies just south of the village.

Golspie Beach stretches for nearly 3 miles from Carn Liath to Littleferry. Families appreciate the sheltered areas near the village, while walkers, nature lovers and, fossil hunters will all find much to interest them.

Fossil fish at Orcadian Stone Company

St Andrew's Church

Dunrobin Castle from the Gardens

DUNROBIN CASTLE

(G *Dunrobin*, Robin's Fort) stands on a bluff just north of Golspie. It has an enchanting fairytale appearance when seen from afar. Closer inspection reveals a huge multiperiod mansion house.

The oldest part of the building is a 14th century keep, but it is probably built on the site of a Norse fort, itself on an Iron Age broch.

Dunrobin Castle by William Daniell, 1821

Additions were made during the 16th century, but most of Dunrobin visible today dates from the 19th century.

In 1835 Sir Charles Barry, the architect of the Houses of Parliament, was commissioned to build what Queen Victoria called *a mixture between a Scotch castle and a French chateau.* In WW1 it was used as a naval hospital and in 1915 suffered serious fire damage.

Sir Robert Lorimer of the Arts and Crafts movement undertook major renovations in 1919 and made several major alterations in the style of the Scottish Renaissance. A grand staircase leads from the entrance to the public floor rooms, which have expansive views over the sea towards Moray and the Black Isle.

During the self-guided visit, the Dining Room, laid out as in the 1850s, the Drawing Room, saved from fire in 1915 and the Library with its 10,000 books are perhaps the highlights. There are a number of works by artists including Canaletto, Reynolds, Ramsay and Wright, as well as fine furniture and tapestries.

The gardens were laid out in French style in 1850 on the sheltered ground below the

Falconry display

Dunrobin Castle

The Gardens from the castle terrace

castle. They supply the flowers for the arrangements within the rooms and also offer particularly good views of the front of the building.

The museum was originally built in 1732 as a summer pavilion. It houses an eclectic mixture of items and trophies from around the world, but probably its collection of Pictish symbol stones is of greatest interest. There are also displays on geology, the Kildonan gold rush and coal mining at Brora.

The surrounding woods have many trails, which are open all year. There is a particularly fine circular walk from Golspie along the coast past old piers and the east gates of Dunrobin.

When the castle is open there are daily falconry displays on the lawn which feature Golden Eagles, Peregrines and other birds of prey. There are excellent opportunities to observe and photograph the birds.

Dunrobin is recorded as being a Sutherland fort in 1401 and

is still in the family today. William of Duffus was made first Earl in about 1235 when Sutherland was still a disputed Norse-Scottish territory. Today Lord Strathnaver welcomes visitors to the home of his ancestors.

The Castle has a well stocked shop and a tearoom.

Dunrobin Castle

The splendid stone staircase

Dunrobin Castle

Pictish stone in the Museum

The Drawing Room - saved from fire in 1915

The Library is home to over 10,000 books

Dunrobin Castle

Dunrobin Castle

unusual combination supports a wide range of wildlife throughout the year.

There are good vantage points on the A9 at the Mound car parks, all along the road which runs along the south side of the loch as well as from the Ferry Links and Balblair Woods.

LOCH FLEET (ON *fljotr*, flood), the tidal estuary of the River Fleet, lies between Golspie and Dornoch. It has a diverse combination of habitats including both salt and fresh-water mudflats, saltmarsh, Alderwoods, Pinewoods and sand dunes. The varied sur-roundings include farmland, woodland and moorland. The

Residents Common Seals haul out on sand banks and Otters are present, though rarely seen. Osprey breed here and are regularly seen fishing, while Buzzard are common and Sparrowhawk breed in small numbers. Curlew, Oystercatcher, Redshank, Shelduck, Widgeon, and Teal are present all of the year.

Migrants. In autumn and winter Bar-tailed Godwits, Dunlin, Turnstones, and other waders are present. Greylag and Pink-footed Geese as well as many species of duck may be seen here. Some are in transit and some linger. It is always worthwhile stopping here to scan for birds.

The Mound was built between 1814 and 1816 under Thomas Telford as part of the road to the north. It is nearly 1,000m long with a bridge at the north end. Sluice gates prevent sea water travel-ling upstream, but allow Salmon and Sea Trout to pass by on the ebb tide. The struc-ture has changed the ecology of upper Loch Fleet and a

Ospreys sometimes fish on the Reserve

Looking north from below Skelbo Castle

Littleferry

Upper Loch Fleet panoramic from the Mound

large area of willows and alders has developed due to a build up of silt in the shallow freshwater west of the causeway.

National Nature Reserve
The NNR covers over 1,000ha and is managed to sustain its wealth of wildlife. Loch Fleet is the most northerly river estuary in the northeast of Scotland

Skelbo Castle is a dramatic crumbling ruin overlooking Loch Fleet from the south. It is in a strategic position to control the crossing at Littleferry and dates from at least the 12th century, but probably much earlier. The ruined keep, curtain wall and courtyard are 13th- 15th century, while the nearby mansion house dates from c.1600.

The house deserves renovation and the ruins consolidation. Skelbo was an important strong point, perhaps the oldest reference being to Gilbert of Moravia (later Bishop of Caithness) being granted lands here in about 1211.

The dramatic ruin of Skelbo Castle overlooks Loch Fleet

Loch Fleet is an excellent place to observe wintering wildfowl

Alderwoods from the Mound

Balblair Wood is a magical place

Birds typical of coniferous forest, which may be seen or heard in these woods include Crossbill, Siskin, Redstart, Treecreeper, Great-spotted Woodpecker, Buzzard and Sparrowhawk. Crested Tit have been seen here, but may not breed. The Capercaillie was formerly resident but is no longer.

Coul Links, north of Dornoch, is a large area of dunes which is rare in having a complete transition from the shore to wood and heath in the drier parts while wet slacks and winter pools add to the range of habitats.

Ferry Links is slightly less rich in vascular plants, but includes large areas of lichen-rich and moss-rich heath. A gap in the dunes lets the sea sometimes flood part of the area, creating a large colony of Sea Milkwort.

BALBLAIR WOOD is a mature Scots Pine plantation which dates from 1905. This replaced a much older wood which was destroyed by a severe storm around 1900. Ferry Wood has more variety, with plantings dating from the early 1800s, though much of it was replanted in the 1960s.

Three rare plants typical of Pinewoods grow at Balblair, these are specifically, One-flowered Wintergreen, Creeping Lady's Tresses and Twinflower. Common Wintergreen and Lesser Twayblade may also be found. These wild flowers may indicate that Pinewoods have long been established here.

Ferry Wood and Ferry Links have especially interesting lichen-rich heath. Over 100 species have been found. The Reserve is home to over 50 species of fungi.

Twinflower

Laurie Campbell

One-flowered Wintergreen

Laurie Campbell

Wood Brown Butterfly

Ferry Links lichen-rich heath

Creeping Lady's tresses

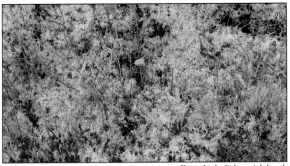

Ferry Links lichen-rich heath

Loch Fleet NNR is also very inviting. The large variety of habitats mean that there is always something to observe in every season.

Littleferry - view to southeast

Crested Tits like pinewoods

Crossbill

Laurie Campbell

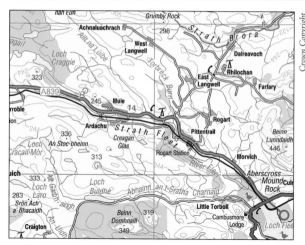

Loch Fleet sunset from the Mound

ROGART (ON Red Farm), or Pittentrail, is in the middle of Strath Fleet, which leads west from the Mound to Lairg. This valley and the surrounding area is ruggedly attractive with a scattering of farms, houses and crofts and forms part of the parish of Rogart.

St Callan's Church sits in a prominent position with expansive views to the west over croftland and moorland. The present building dates from 1777, but is undoubtedly on the site of earlier churches. The inside layout was changed around 1817. The kirkyard has many interesting tombstones.

Battle of Torran Dubh. In 1517 a ferocious battle was fought near Rogart between the Sutherland men under Alexander Sutherland and the Strathnaver men under John MacKay. Sir Robert Will Gordon says that this *"was the greatest conflict that hitherto has been fought in between the inhabitants of these countreyes, or within the diocy of Catteynes, to our knowledge."*

The **Rogart Shirt** is a large woven woollen garment found in a grave near Springhill in Rogart. This russet brown shirt may date from the 14th century and is a rare example of a type of traditional tunic.

Illegal Whisky was a common product in the Highlands and Rogart was said *"to be entirely packed and crammed with* *whisky smugglers"*. Illicit stills were hidden in peat banks and in the hills. Before the building of the road to Lairg, Rogart was a relatively remote and isolated township, however its fertile valley is perfect for growing crops.

Bere, an old fashioned type of Barley is an excellent food crop for humans and animals but is also a good source of malt for brewing and distilling. Malted Barley is much more nutritious and easier to store than fresh grain so there was undoubtedly a good supply after the harvest.

John Alexander Macdonald was the First Prime Minister of the Dominion of Canada. He served two terms and a total of 19 years. A cairn to his memory stands near Pittentrail, on the south side of the river. It is on the site of the home of his grandparents, John and Jean Macdonald. Both families came from Rogart and although Sir John was born in Glasgow, the parish is proud of its connections with him.

Old Oak tree, Rogart

Strath Fleet near Rogart

Old graveslab

16th century graveslab

St Callan's Church

St Callan's Church

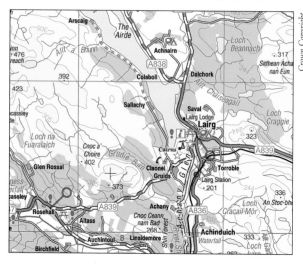

This was one of the first areas of Sutherland where, from 1807, the people were cleared from the land to be replaced by sheep runs. The first general store was opened here in 1811, followed by an inn. The main street, Rogart Road, was built by 1816 and the village slowly developed.

With the arrival of the railway in 1868 and the development of proper roads, its position changed from remote to central. The Victorian fashion for outdoor sports such as fishing and shooting gave Lairg a boost in the late 1800s.

In 1919 Lairg was bought by Sir William Edgar Horne, who invested considerably in the area. In 1924 the village had its own diesel power station, one of the first in the Highlands.

Hydro Electricity Work on the Loch Shin dam started in 1954. The power stations were fully operational in 1959 and can generate 38MW. A small turbine is enclosed in the dam, with most of the water being carried 5 miles by

Herding sheep

LAIRG (G *Lairig*, sloping hill) is the crossroads of Sutherland. Situated at the south end of Loch Shin, it is an ancient settlement site, with many Neolithic remains.

Today it is renowned for its great annual sheep sale, the largest in Scotland. At the main sale in August over 25,000 sheep may change hands.

Loch Shin looking northwest towards Ben More Assynt

Lower Loch Shin and the dam from Lairg

tunnel to Shin Power Station at Inveran. The dam is 427m wide and 12m high and raised the level of Loch Shin by about 11m. Fish lifts allow Salmon to migrate past the dam and diversion weir. The latter maintains the level of Little Loch Shin and allows water to continue to flow along the River Shin.

The Parish of Lairg formerly extended to the west coast. In a time when there were no roads, Loch Shin would have been an easy route to the northwest. It was MacKay country, like Strathnaver to the north, and the people did not take kindly to being ruled by the Earls of Sutherland, who were seen as incomers.

Tradition has it that St Maelrubha visited Lairg in the late 6th century and established a chapel. He is said to be buried at Skaill on the River Naver. There was certainly a parish church here in 1222, probably on the site of the present kirkyard.

Little Loch Shin from the lower dam

Sunset over Little Loch Shin

Lairg from the Ord

Ord Archaeological Trail starts at the Ferrycroft Countryside Centre, which has information on Sutherland's past and present. Audiovisual displays cover archaeology, history and nature conservation. Special events and activities are regu-

Achany chambered cairn

larly organised, while the local Countryside ranger can give advice on where to see wildlife and where to visit.

The trail takes in Neolithic chambered cairns as well as Bronze Age houses, cairns, and a burnt mound. There are fine views of Lairg and Loch Shin from the top of Ord Hill (NC574055). In prehistoric times this hillside was cultivated farmland very different from todays rather desolate landscape.

Ord North chambered cairn is a round cairn about 25m in diameter. It still stands to 2.5m and contains two cells.

Ord South is ruinous. The Bronze Age ruins are less impressive in summer when they become overgrown, but the colours are best in late August when the heather is in flower.

The Broch of Sallachy (NC549092) is the best preserved of several such Iron Age buildings around the Lairg area. It is accessible by following a sign posted road off the A839 southwest of the village. The broch can be reached by following a track down to the shore.

Apart from the impressive situation, the walls stand to over

Ord North chambered cairn, Lairg

Ord South chambered cairn, Lairg

Lairg, Lower Loch Shin and the dam from Sallachy

2m, surrounded by much fallen rubble. The entrance with guard cell, intramural stairways, scarcement ledge and many other features can be examined. The views across Loch Shin to Lairg from here are lovely.

Achany Glen runs south from Lairg to the falls of Shin and Invershin. Many cairns, hut circles and, burnt mounds litter both sides of the glen showing that it was well populated in the Bronze Age. There is a ruined chambered cairn at Grudie Bridge (NC571020). The chamber is visible and is surrounded by a ring of kerbstones.

Dalchork Bird Hide is approximately 2 miles north of Lairg on the A836. It offers the chance to see Ospreys fishing on Loch Shin. Red and Black-throated Divers, Greenshank, Merlin, Hen Harriers and even a White-

tailed Sea Eagle have all been spotted from here. Several pairs of Ospreys breed in this area, Buzzards are common while Golden Eagles, Deer, Pine Marten, Otters and perhaps even a Wild Cat may be seen.

Broch of Sallachy

Broch of Sallachy

Broch of Sallachy

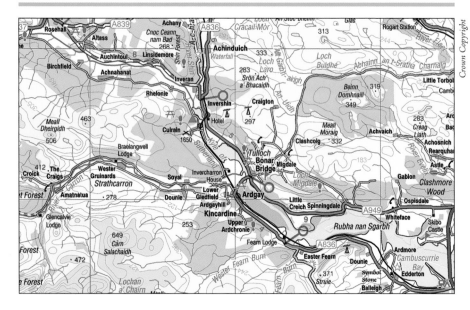

BONAR BRIDGE lies at the south end of the Kyle of Sutherland, the confluence of the Salmon rich rivers of Carron, Oykel and Shin. It was for long a ferry point, but in 1812 Thomas Telford chose it for the first of three bridges to cross here, and the village prospered until the Dornoch Bridge was opened in 1991.

Salmon were a major source of income here for centuries. They were caught in nets or traps on their way upstream and salted for export in wooden barrels until the early 19th century. Thereafter they were boiled in a brine pickle and exported in ice. Today the Salmon are only fished for sport.

Bonar Bridge

The new Bonar Bridge was built in grey steel in 1973, the third bridge to cross the Kyle of Sutherland

Carbisdale Castle and the Kyle of Sutherland from Shin railway viaduct

Carbisdale Castle overlooks the Kyle of Sutherland. It was built between 1906 and 1917 for the Duchess Blair, widow of the 3rd Duke of Sutherland. It was built in Ross-shire as she was refused land in Sutherland. In 1945 it was left to the Scottish Youth Hostels Association and since then has been their flagship hostel.

The castle was home to King Haakon VI of Norway and his family during WWII. There is a good view of the Castle and the Kyle of Sutherland from the railway station.

The Falls of Shin is one of the great Salmon Leaps in Scotland, where the fish run upstream to spawn the next generation. There is access to observe the Falls from a platform, and a nearby visitor centre has a shop, cafe and a children's playground.

The falls are most spectacular after heavy rain. Salmon run here in late spring and early summer. There are several trails in the woods, which are mostly conifers, but include Aspen, Oak, Hazel, Alder, Birch and Rowan.

Laurie Campbell

Salmon leaping the falls on their way upstream

The Falls of Shin

Lichen-covered Birch trees at the Falls of Shin

SUTHERLAND - THE EAST COAST

Oykel Bridge

Strath Oykel is on the route to the west. It is the site of a battle between Earl Sigurd of Orkney and Maelbrigte, Thane of Moray. Sigurd was victorious, but died after being infected by the protruding tooth of his opponent's severed head. The Earl is said to be buried at Ciderhall, near Dornoch.

The first Sutherland clearances happened here in 1800 , with riots in the final evictions in 1820. Today a beautiful

and fertile valley remains largely empty. The Bonar Bridge to Ledmore road (A837) is very scenic and was built during 1821-1827. On a nice day it makes for a very pleasant drive despite the narrow single track road.

The Old Oykel Bridge dates from 1825. The rapids just upriver from here can be dramatic after heavy rain and Salmon may be seen running here from May onwards as the water warms up.

Croick Kirk is 10 miles west of Ardgay at the head of Strathcarron. It is a Thomas Telford designed Parliamentary Church and was built in 1827. Though remote, this place evokes more than almost anywhere else the poignant events of the 19th century clearances.

The clearance of Glen Calvie took place on 24th May 1845, when 18 families, comprising 80 people, were forcibly evicted from their crofts. They took shelter in makeshift booths in the graveyard and several left messages scratched onto the outside of the east window of the church.

By this time public concern about the clearances was mounting, and a journalist from *The Times* was on hand to report on events. Apparently he had problems communicating with these people as they were Gaelic speakers. This raises interest-

Strath Oykel

ing questions about the graffiti on the window panes.

River Carron

Although some certainly date from 1845, others are from later years. They are all written in English in Victorian copperplate style. It also seems bizarre that the people did not shelter in the church because that would have been desecration, yet they had no inhibitions about scratching the windows.

Croick Broch

A ruined Iron Age broch lies just west of the church. It may have been a convenient source of stone and explain the siting of the building. Despite the questions, Croick Kirk remains a vivid and remarkable direct link to the brutal events of these times. Monetarism and the Market are part of the reason that these beautiful valleys are largely uninhabited today.

Strathcarron is a pretty valley which is well worthwhile visiting on its own account. There are several fine walks along tracks and through mixed woodland. Croick Kirk is open at all times to visitors.

The panes of the east window have many inscriptions some dating from May 1845

They make for a very poignant visit

Croick Kirk

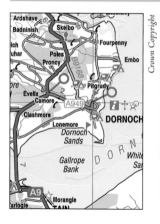

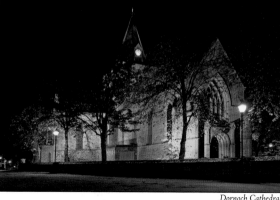

Dornoch Cathedral

DORNOCH (G *Dorn Eich*, horses hoof) is a lovely little town facing south and east across the Dornoch Firth. Major redevelopment during 1810-1815 by the Countess of Sutherland created the pretty cottages. The sandstone buildings fit in well with the ancient Cathedral, giving the town a picturesque appearance reminiscent of a Cotswolds village.

Dornoch Cathedral. Gilbert de Moravia became Bishop of Caithness in 1222, and moved the centre of the diocese from Halkirk to Dornoch. He started work on the Cathedral in 1224 at his own expense. The building was largely complete by the time of his death in Scrabster in 1245. The first service was held in 1239. Gilbert was a cousin of the 1st Earl of Sutherland.

St Barr's Church stood at the eastern end of the present kirkyard. By tradition St Barr established a chapel here in the 6th century, but the dedication could also be more recent.

Feuds during 1570 between the Earls of Caithness and Sutherland led to the MacKays from Caithness burning the Cathedral, which remained partially roofless for

Dornoch by William Daniell 1821 - note the Cathedral with its ruined nave

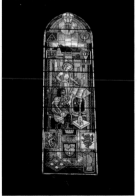

One of many stained glass windows

Dornoch Cathedral

many years. In the early 18ᵗʰ century the church was re-roofed and the spire completed.

Finally, the Countess of Sutherland had the Cathedral rebuilt in 1835-1837. The nave was reconstructed with-out pillared aisles which did not please everyone. The interior is light and welcoming with several very impressive stained glass windows. This ancient Cathedral has a special beauty and gives the whole town a stature far out of proportion to its size.

History Links Museum is a fascinating window on Dornoch's past. It has permanent exhibitions on the Cathedral, Picts and Vikings, feuding clans and the shameful burning of Janet Horne. The workshop of Donald Ross, a golfer from Dornoch

Castle Street with its delightful sandstone cottages

Dornoch's Old Jail

Intriguing signpost combination

DORN-EICH
Origin of the name

The name *Dornoch* is said to derive from an incident during a battle with the Norse just east of the town. The Earl of Sutherland fought his way to the Norse leader, but was disarmed. Undaunted he picked up the severed leg of a horse and killed his opponent, thus winning the day. A horse shoe is still used on the coat-of-arms of the burgh.

Donald Ross' workshop in the Historylinks Museum

Scotland's ancient game has been played in some form on the Dornoch Links for hundreds of years. The tradition was that monks and others from the monastery at St Andrews introduced the sport to their colleagues here. The oldest record of golf in Dornoch is 1616. Apparently the authorities frowned upon such activities as being unwarlike.

Royal Dornoch Golf Club acquired royal status in 1906. The present Championship course was laid out in 1886-1889 by Tom Morris Senior and by 1904 it was modified again to 5,960 yards. This course is said to be among the best 15 in the world.

Royal Dornoch Golf Course

who designed over 500 courses in the USA, Dornoch Light Railway and how Andrew Carnegie affected the town are also featured in this excellent little museum.

Golf Sir Robert Gordon, tutor to a young Earl of Sutherland and historian of the Earldom, wrote (1630): *"About this toun (along the sea coast) ther are the fairest and largest linkes, (or green fields), of any pairt of Scotland, fitt for archery, golfing, ryding, and all other exercise; they doe surpasse the feilds of Montrose or St Andrews."*

During WWII an airfield was built over part of the course, but it was removed after the war. A second 9 hole course, The Struie, was created and has now been extended into a full 18 holes. Tom Watson, five times Open Champion, said *'it's the most fun I've ever had on a golf course'*!

Embo was established as a fishing village during the clearances in the early 19th century. Today there is no fishing but it is a popular holiday resort due to its lovely long sandy beach. Perhaps its appeal is the chambered cairn in the car park of the caravan site. The cairn contained a number of cist graves and had two chambers, but the confusion of stone slabs to be seen now is hard to understand.

Embo chambered cairn

Dornoch Sands and the Dornoch Firth

THE DORNOCH FIRTH separates Sutherland from Ross-shire. Since 1991 there has been a bridge, which shortens the drive north, but the route round by Bonar Bridge and then over Struie Hill is much more scenic. In former times the Meikle Ferry ran across the Dornoch Firth.

The dunes of the Cuthill Links and the estuary of the River Evelix are good places for bird watching. Ospreys regularly fish near here, while the mudflats and saltmarsh are excellent for waders and roosting waterfowl especially during migration times and winter. The varied habitats, also support a diversity of wild flowers.

While crossing the bridge it is recommended to stop at one of the laybys to take in the scene. There are expansive views to the east over the sea and westwards towards the mountains of Easter Ross.

To the east of Dornoch Point, the **Gizzen Briggs** (ON *Gisnar Bryga*, leaky bridge, as in a dried-up boat) is a large sandbar, dangerous for boats, but accessible at very low tides. Seals haul out here in large numbers.

According to folklore, one may be able to glimpse fairies crossing the Firth on Cockle shells, or building a bridge of fairy gold.

The Last Witch

Janet Horne was the last person in Britain to be tried and executed for witchcraft in Britain. In 1727 she and her daughter were arrested and jailed in Dornoch. They were accused of devilish crimes, like turning the daughter into a horse, and of getting Satan himself to shoe it. The mother was said to be senile, while the daughter had a deformity to her hands and feet, which she may later have passed on to a son.

During a short trial, Captain David Ross, sheriff-depute of Sutherland, found both women guilty and condemned them to be burned to death the next day. Apparently not being able to properly recite the Lord's Prayer was part of the evidence.

The daughter was released or escaped but Janet Horne was stripped, tarred and paraded in a tar barrel through the town. When they reached the burning site, it was said that she smiled and warmed herself before her incineration.

A stone said to mark this site stands in a cottage garden in Littletown, but with the wrong date of 1722. In 1736 the Witchcraft Acts were repealed.

Dornoch Firth at low tide from the bridge causeway

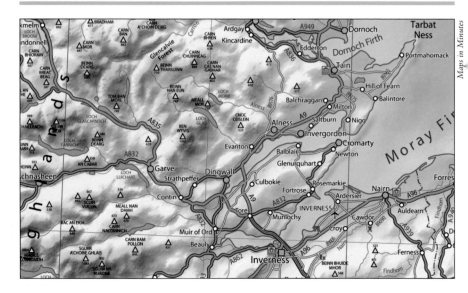

Maps in Minutes

EASTER ROSS is bounded by the Dornoch Firth to the north and the Moray Firth to the south. The hills and mountains of Mid Ross to the west shelter the fertile farmland of the east and its small towns and villages, resulting in a mild and dry climate.

There are fine views of the Dornoch Firth from the bridge, from Struie Hill and from vantage points on both shorelines. From the south after the Kessock Bridge the landscape has a much gentler aspect than that south of Inverness.

Geology The coastal plain is composed of Old Red Sandstone making for rich soils which combine with the climate to be excellent for cereal growing. The east coast is cut off by the dramatic Great Glen Fault.

Late summer colours with Ben Wyvis in the background

Iain Sarjeant

There are outcrops of fossiliferous Jurassic rocks east of Nigg and again southeast of Cromarty. The Old Red Sandstone also contains many beds of fossil fish, first revealed by Hugh Miller. To the west Moine schists with granite intrusions predominate. There are two prominent Moine Schist outcrops at the Sutors, the headlands guarding the entrance to the Cromarty Firth.

Environment Easter Ross has a huge variety of habitats in a relatively small area. A wide range of birds and mammals may be observed in all seasons while spring and summer bring wonderful displays of wild flowers.

Settlements range from small towns like Tain, Alness and Dingwall to tiny coastal villages such as Portmahomack or Cromarty. Inland there is the spa village of Strathpeffer and remote Garve. Most are ancient and have a long heritage, often dating from Pictish times or earlier.

Apart from natural and cultural heritage, there are lots of nice places to stop for a meal, or to stay a night or two. Arts and crafts are well represented, with two galleries and two potteries. In addition, many of the small towns and villages have retained interesting local shops which are a welcome change from the standard British high street.

Tain High Street - local sandstone

Debby Snook
Common Seals bask near the Cromarty Bridge

Alness has wonderful floral displays all summer

The Cromarty Firth

223

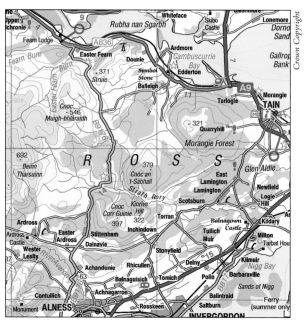

STRUIE HILL (371m) overlooks the south side of the Dornoch Firth. There are panoramic views from the viewpoint above Cagha Mor on the B9176. By taking a short walk to the top of the hill and then along the ridge a vista of the whole Firth can be taken in.

The Struie Road was a popular short cut before the Dornoch Bridge was built but is now very quiet. Sadly the remote and once very popular Altnamain Inn is now closed. There are pleasant walks along the Strathrory River. The prominent hillfort of Cnocan Duin dominates this valley about two miles downstream.

Edderton kirkyard is home to a fine Pictish cross-slab. The kirk itself dates from 1743 but is built on the site of a much older chapel. Clach Boarch (G Pointed Stone) stands in a field at Balblair Farm and may date from the Bronze Age. Later, Picts carved some of their symbols on the stone.

The Dornoch Firth from the bridge

The Million Dollar View from Struie Hill on the B9176 of the upper Dornoch Firth

Balblair Distillery was founded in 1790 by John Ross, and, from 1996, has belonged to Inver House Distillers. The original water source, the Ault Dearg Burn, is still in used in the production of this multi award winning Malt Whisky.

Nearby, **Morangie Forest** offers good trails for walking as well as some fine viewpoints from higher up. Edderton Sands and Ness of Portnaculter saltmarsh are good places to see waders and waterfowl close up at high tide. Many salt adapted plants also grow here.

Edderton cross-slab

Edderton cross-slab

A piper on Struie

Broom and the Dornoch Firth

Easter Ross

Tain was long famous for its silversmiths

TAIN claims to be the oldest Royal Burgh in Scotland, having been granted a charter by Malcolm Canmore in 1066, which proclaimed the town as a Sanctuary, known as the *Girth o'Tain*. He is also said to have granted immunity from taxes on trading to Tain residents.

St Duthac was born in Tain in the early 11th century, and was a highly venerated churchman in his own time and later. His shrine became one of the most visited pilgrimage sites in Scotland. James IV and James V visited it regularly, ensuring its continued popularity.

The Sanctuary granted in 1066 was enclosed by four crosses which marked the boundaries within which people could seek the protection of the Church. St Duthac died in Armagh and his body was buried in Tain in 1153.

In 1306 the Sanctuary was famously broken by the Earl of Ross when he and his men kidnapped Robert the Bruce's wife and daughter and handed them over to King Edward of England. In 1428 a feud between Thomas MacKay of Creich and Alexander Mowat of Freswick resulted in the former killing the latter in the chapel, which he then burnt.

Collegiate Church. The present St Duthac Kirk dates from about 1370 and was extensively renovated in the 19th century. There are two hog-backed tombstones in the kirkyard, which may be Norse. The ruins of what could be the original chapel built to hold St Duthac's remains around 1153 are near the shore to the northwest. There is another ruined chapel in the kirkyard which is probably the one burnt in 1428.

The Tolbooth dates from 1706

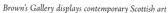

Brown's Gallery displays contemporary Scottish art

Tain through Time is housed in an old schoolhouse in the kirkyard. It describes the life and times of James IV as well as the miracles of St Duthac and the story of the Collegiate Church. The nearby small museum holds an interesting collection of local silverware. Tain was known since at least the 16ᵗʰ century for its gold and silversmiths, but especially in the 1700s when men such as Hugh Ross produced outstanding work.

Most of present day Tain dates from the 18ᵗʰ and 19ᵗʰ centuries. Building of the Tolbooth commenced in 1706. It was used as a prison and for secure storage of the town's documents and valuables. The mercat cross now stands outside the front door. Tain Through Time hires self guided audiovisual tours.

Tain is a slightly olde worldly, yet vibrant town centre, with many interesting small shops. There are a number of excellent places to eat out as well as a good selection of accommodation.

Arts and Crafts. Brown's Gallery opened in 1993 and displays a wide range of contemporary work by Scottish artists. It has a reputation for showing outstanding pieces.

Tain Pottery at Aldie, just south of the town, produces very attractive hand thrown and painted ceramics. Many of the designs reflect local nature and colours.

St Duthac Collegiate Church dates from 1370

Hog-backed graveslab

Glemorangie Distillery, just to the north of Tain, was established in 1843 and has tall gin stills instead of the usual pot stills. Today a range of finishes is available. The visitor centre runs daily tours of the distillery.

Detail on Collegiate Church

St Duthac stained glass window

TAIN
Origin of the name

The oldest record of the name is *Tene*, 1227. It may be pre-Celtic and probably derives from the eponymous river, whose Indo-European root is *ta*, to flow. There is another Tain inland from Dunnet Sands, Caithness. The areas are similar in some respects, with fertile land near a sandy bay. The name is clearly ancient but its etymology is unclear.

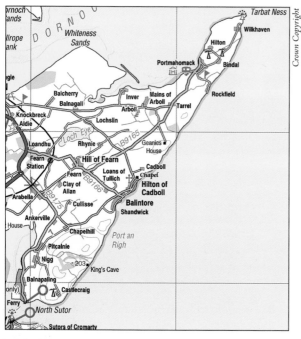

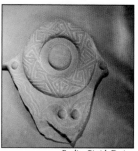

A Pictish Queen in bronze

Replica Pictish Design

PORTMAHOMACK (G *Port Mo-Cholaig*, Colman's, or Columba's Port) may claim some association with Columba. It is certainly the best harbour on the entire coast north of Burghead and has been in use as such for a very long time. The present pier was built by Thomas Telford in 1813-16.

Tarbat Ness lighthouse was first lit in 1830

Of the two warehouses or girnels, the larger was built in 1779 and the smaller by Lord Cromartie in the 17th century. They were used to store grain before shipment to Edinburgh and other southern markets. The village has many attractive 18th and 19th century houses which curve around the sandy bay. A cast iron drinking fountain celebrates the arrival of gravitation (piped) water in 1877.

Tarbat Discovery Centre in St Colman's Church tells the story of the Pictish settlement and the Pictish monastery which was established here in the 6th century and flourished until it was destroyed in the 9th century. The church has at least six phases, the earliest dating from the 8th century.

St Colman's was rebuilt in 1756 but abandoned in 1843 after the Disruption. From 1994, restoration of the church allowed extensive excavation within and around it. The oldest burials within the church date from about 560AD with others from the 8th to the 11th century.

Portmahomack has interesting girnels, old piers and cottages as well as a lovely sandy beach

Excavations to the west of the kirkyard revealed a workshop, a barn, a mill and a ditch dating from the 8th century. Over 200 fragments of sculpture were found, as well as evidence for the large scale making of parchment from cattle hides. This would probably have been used to make books akin to the Book of Kells.

Clay moulds, crucibles and glass studs were found in the workshops and show that bronze, silver, gold and glass were being worked. Many fragments of Pictish cross-slabs were also found, suggesting that several large sculpted stones may have stood here, all dating from about 800AD.

Tarbat Ness. The *Orkneyinga Saga* describes a battle at *Torfness* between Earl Thorfinn the Mighty and Karl Hundason in about 1035, where the Orkneymen won.

The lighthouse was established in 1830 and built by Robert Stevenson. The 41m tower has two wide red bands and is the third tallest in Scotland after North Ronaldsay and Skerryvore.

Tradition has it that there was a Roman camp at Brucefield Farm. Later, witches' covens were said to meet here. Mermaids may be seen offshore, however, Bottle-nosed Dolphins are more likely!

Geology The foreshore between Rockville and the lighthouse has interesting exposures of weathered Upper Old Red Sandstone as well as some Jurassic outliers.

Birds Tarbat Ness is a good place for birds during migration times, especially seabirds on passage, including Manx and Sooty Shearwaters, Arctic, Pomarine and Great Skuas and other species. Large falls of passerines from Scandinavia sometimes occur. These may include Fieldfares, Redwings, Wheatears, Pipits and other species.

TARBAT
Origin of the name

Tarbat (G *Tairbeart*, portage or isthmus) is most likely a Pictish name which has survived. It refers to a portage route between the Cromarty and Dornoch Firths via the shallows of Nigg Bay then across the low lying area to the north to Loch Eye and thence to Inver. This would avoid the strong tides and dangerous overfalls at the Sutors and Tarbat Ness.

St Colman's Church, now Tarbat Discovery Centre

Tarbat Peninsula landscape

TARBAT PENINSULA is mainly fertile farmland and has for long been known for its grain crops, first bere, then oats and barley. Nowadays a substantial amount of wheat is also grown. Alternating grazing and arable land, marshland, saltmarsh and heath make an interesting landscape.

Rockville is a small village just south of Tarbat Ness on this mostly rock bound east coast. It has a small pier built during the Herring Boom in the 1880s. Some Salmon fishing

is still done here. Ballone Castle along the coast was abandoned about 1650, but has recently been restored.

Hilton of Cadboll is famous for its Pictish cross-slab, found on the shore in 1811. At present it is in the National Museum in Edinburgh, but a recently carved replica stands next to the ruined St Mary's Chapel near the beach. The base was found in 2002 during excavations and can be seen in the Seaboard Memorial Hall in Balintore.

Shandwick (ON *Sand Vik,* Sandy Bay) is famous for Clach a'Charridh, its large cross-slab which is over 3m high. It is now protected by a glass box which fails to take away from the intricate Pictish carvings.

Fearn Abbey, *The Lamp of the North,* was founded near Edderton in 1221 by Premonstratensians from Whithorn, but moved to its present location in 1238. It continued in use as the parish church after the Reformation.

Hilton of Cadboll cross-slab

Shandwick cross-slab detail

Shandwick cross-slab detail

The beach at Wilkhaven south of Tarbat Ness

Rockville Jetty

In 1742 the flagstone roof collapsed during a service, after the church was struck by lightning, killing many of the congregation. The Minister survived, being protected by the pulpit. It was rebuilt in 1771, incorporating some of the medieval walls and remains in use as the parish church.

Geology. Apart from the fine sandy beach at Shandwick, and another smaller one at Hilton, the eastern shore of the peninsula consists of low sandstone cliffs. These run in an abrupt and straight line and, like those of the nearby Black Isle, were formed by the Great Glen Fault.

Fearn Abbey

Beach and Pier at Balintore

Fearn Abbey

Ballone Castle

231

Nigg cross-slab 8ᵗʰ century Pictish

NIGG (G 'n Eig, the Notch, or gulley), at the southern tip of the Tarbat Peninsula, is another ancient Christian site. Nigg Old Church was rebuilt in 1626. It now houses the Nigg cross-slab, an 8ᵗʰ century Pictish masterpiece.

Originally it probably stood overlooking the Cromarty Firth, one of at least four such stones on the peninsula.

The church itself is typical of Scottish kirks of the time with the

pulpit on the east wall, a laird's loft and a north wing. The kirkyard has many interesting tombstones, including the Cholera Stone, which dates from an epidemic of 1832.

Nigg Fabrication Yard is in sharp contrast to the tranquillity of the Old Kirk. In the 1970s it produced oil platforms for the production of North Sea Oil. Nowadays it is quiet except for the occasional construction of wind turbines for off-shore installation. The site has one of the largest graving docks in the world, and may well have a future in dismantling North Sea structures when they are no longer needed.

Beatrice Oil Field The nearby Oil Terminal is operated by Talisman. It is the landfall of the pipeline from the Beatrice Field. The platforms are 15 miles offshore from Dunbeath. The field was discovered in 1976 and the oil is sourced from Jurassic rocks. In 2006 two large wind turbines were installed here, each can produce 5MW. They may be the forerunners of a much larger windfarm.

Nigg Bay RSPB Reserve is a large sheltered area of saltmarsh, mudflats and wet grassland at the north head of the Cromarty Firth. The entrance to the car park for the Reserve is about a mile north of Nigg village. The nearby hide offers good views over various habitats. There are also several good vantage points along the B9175 as well as from the shore near Balintraid Pier on the west side. The road just west of Nigg Ferry terminal is a good place to watch sea ducks in winter.

The Cholera Stone

Nigg Old Church

From October to March large numbers of waders, including Bar-tailed Godwits, Knots, Curlews and other species may be seen here. In summer, Lapwings and Redshanks breed. Many ducks winter here, including Pintail. The fields in the Tarbat Peninsula are home to large numbers of Greylag and Pink-footed Geese as well as Whooper Swans. Buzzards and Sparrowhawks are present all year.

Nigg Old Church, interior

ANTA is a design and architecture firm which is based near Fearn. It makes a unique range of stoneware pottery and weaves textiles on the site. Colours and designs are inspired by the Scottish landscape and traditional styles. The shop has enticing displays of their products and the cafe serves good coffee and cakes.

Assembling wind turbines for the Beatrice Field at Nigg

Nigg from the South Sutor, Cromarty

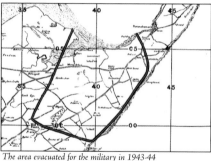

The area evacuated for the military in 1943-44

RAF Tain control tower

TAIN RANGES were developed in the 1930s to train pilots in bombing and dropping torpedoes. RAF Tain was established as a Fighter Sector Station in 1941. It was used as a forward base for bombers on several occasions, most notably by Halifaxes trying to sink the *Tirpitz* in 1942.

In 1943 Coastal Command took over the base. Beaufighters and Liberators were based here to carry out anti-submarine and anti-shipping patrols off Norway and Denmark. Some of the WWII buildings still remain.

Fearn airfield was built by the RAF in 1941, but became *HMS Owl* in 1942. Its main use was as a torpedo school for pilots of Swordfish,

Barracuda and other aircraft flown by the Fleet Air Arm.

In the 1970s Loganair had plans to use Fearn for oil-related flights, and to link to other Scottish airports, but this did not happen. Today RAF Tain is still an operational air-to-ground weapons range and is regularly used by RAF and other NATO airforces.

D-DAY landing training was carried out in 1943-44 in an area around Inver, west of RAF Tain. Nearly 15 square miles was completely cleared of more than 900 people as well as nearly 10,000 head of livestock for several months.

Tarbat was judged the most suitable place to do combined

operations training in Scotland. Beach assault, bombardment and inland tank operations were practised under realistic conditions, with intense firing of live ammunition.

Many units used the range over a period of about six months, but by mid March 1944 it had been closed down. Tarbat was ideally suited for practicing beach landings and moving inland with tanks and the training here was valuable practice for the landings at Juno and Sword beach on D-Day.

By mid 1944 the area had been cleared of ordnance and the people were allowed to return to their farms and homes.

RAF Harrier over the Dornoch Firth

Mudflats at Inver

CROMARTY FIRTH. In WWI the Royal Navy used the Cromarty Firth as a base and refuelling station. *HMS Natal*, a Duke of Edinburgh class cruiser, blew up here in December 1915, with the loss of at least 390 crew, probably because of faulty cordite, but this was never proven.

Catalinas flew from the Cromarty Firth base

In 1917 the US Navy requisitioned Dalmore Distillery as a mine store, and built the nearby to load ships to create a huge minefield in the North Sea, only to be cleared up again by them in 1919.

During the 1930s, Alness became a training base for flying boat crews. First Saro Londons and Stranraers, followed by Sunderlands and Catalinas were based here. By 1942, 22 crews were being trained each month. The base, along with Sullom Voe in Shetland, and Oban, was important in providing long range patrols over the North Sea and North Atlantic.

Extensive shore batteries were installed on the North and South Sutors in WWI and WWII. Significant remains still exist of these today and are worth exploring. A boom defence and inductive loop were also in place to protect against submarines and surface raiders. The naval base closed in 1956, but ships still refuel here.

Invergordon during WWI

Invergordon from a battleship in WWI

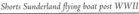

HMS Natal which blew up in 1915

H.M.S. NATAL 1905-1915

Shorts Sunderland flying boat post WWII

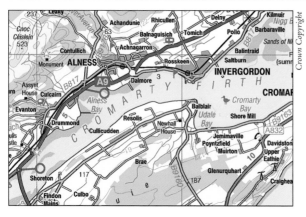

air attack in WWII and reverted almost entirely to heavily defended Scapa Flow. It did however remain in use until the 1950s, with a huge oil storage facility in the hill above the town from which ships still re-fuel.

Today many cruise liners visit the port, making use of its deep water and good facilities to provide passengers with tours of the North Highlands. Oil rigs are also often present, coming here for repairs, maintenance or de-commissioning.

In 1971, construction of a large aluminium smelter, largely financed by Highlands and Islands Development Board, was commenced by British Aluminium. At that time Government policy was the development of heavy industry. However the promise of low cost electricity from Dounreay and new hydroelectric power stations did not materialise and the facility shut in 1981.

Invergordon with cruise liners and oil rigs

INVERGORDON takes its name from Sir William Gordon, who owned land here in the 18th century. It was formerly known as Inverbreakie. The Cromarty Firth had, for a long time, been used as a safe anchorage before the Royal Navy started to see its potential in the early 1800s. In the mid-1800s it was established as a coaling station. During WWI fuel oil tanks, piers, dockyard facilities and the hospital were built.

The Navy considered Invergordon too vulnerable to

Invergordon has a wide High Street with a good selection of small shops, as well as a range of places to eat and stay. The **Naval Museum and Heritage Centre** beside the British Legion has displays of artifacts and an archive. There are several old warehouses which date from the 18th century onwards, underlining the port's importance for civil use.

ALNESS (G *Alanais*, bog, wet place or ON *A Ness*, Point of the River) has a long and

"HMS Natal" memorial garden, Invergordon

Alness is famous for its floral displays

Alness has a very pretty main street

pretty main street with a Thomas Telford bridge in the middle. The town regularly wins *Scotland in Bloom* and *Britain in Bloom* competitions due to its fine displays of floral art.

The **Fyrish Monument** on Cnoc Fyrish (NH608698, 452m), between Alness and Evanton, was built for Sir Hector Munro in 1782, who had been a General in India. It is modelled on the Gate of Negapatam which he captured in 1781. There are excellent views over the Cromarty Firth from here. It is reached by a path leading up from a minor road which is situated first on the left on the B9176 northbound after Evanton.

Dalmore Distillery was established in 1839 by Alexander Mathieson. It makes a range of award winning malts, which can be sampled in the Visitor Centre. To quote the website, *"Our esoteric, artisan approach has been passed down through generations and remains to this day."*

Dalmore Distillery

Iain Sarjeant

The Fyrish Monument was built in 1782

Large cruise liner at Invergordon Pier

Cromarty Firth and Bridge from the B817 near Alness

Alness Heritage Centre

The Alness Heritage Centre has displays of local artifacts and wartime events as well as substantial archives. Local books, crafts and knitwear are also on sale here. The genealogy unit has information for those seeking their ancestors from this area. It is situated in the main street.

Evanton is named after the

Cromarty Firth in autumn afternoon light

son of the 19th century founder of the village. It is bypassed now by the A9 and so is spared the heavy traffic that formerly clogged every little village on this route north.

Black Rock Gorge is a 36m-deep box canyon cut by glacial meltwater. The River Glass flows at the bottom of this 1,000m-long gorge. It can be

reached via a minor road which runs west from the north end of the bridge in Evanton. Recently it was used as one of the locations in the 2004 film *Harry Potter and the Goblet of Fire*.

Folklore alleges that the Lady of Balconie was enticed into the gorge by a strange man, who may have been the devil. It was said that her screams could still be heard coming from the depths, but nobody has seen her.

The Storehouse is on the A9 at Foulis Ferry just north of the Cromarty Bridge. It is a restaurant and tea-room with a farm shop which stocks a good variety of quality food products as interesting crafts, books and souvenirs.

In fine weather customers can enjoy their meals outside as well as fine views of the Black Isle across the Cromarty Firth. Clan Munro Exhibition is housed in the girnel behind the Storehouse, as well as outside on the shore. It tells the story of the Highland Clans, with particular emphasis on

Clan Munro, and the shipping of grain from this fertile area. The outside displays relate to the former Salmon industry.

Wildlife. The B817 runs along the north shore of the Cromarty Firth from Alness to Invergordon and rejoins the A9 near Milton. It offers many opportunities to observe waders, waterfowl and shoreside plants as there is little traffic and plenty of stopping places.

The shorelines below Evanton can also be reached by minor roads. High tide is generally the best time to come seeking waders, especially during migration time and in the winter, when huge flocks congregate on the foreshore, or wheel around the flight in synchronous formations.

Common Seals haul out in some places here, and Bottlenosed Dolphins occasionally take a sweep into the Firth. If you are out very early or late you might see an Otter near one of the burn mouths. Herons can often be seen standing still at the edge of the water, or gracefully flying past.

The Rivers of Balnagown, Alness and Glass together with the surrounding woodlands offer interesting walks. There is a good chance of seeing a Goosander, Dipper or Kingfisher on the rivers. Roe Deer and Badgers frequent the woods and Buzzards are frequently seen overhead.

Sundial at The Storehouse

The Storehouse

Grey Heron on Cromarty Firth

Common Seals hauled out at Ardullie

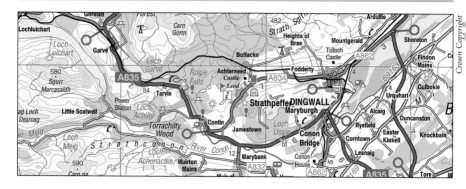

DINGWALL (ON *Thing Vollr*, Field of the Thing or Meeting Place), sits at the head of the Cromarty Firth and is sheltered from the west by hills. It was elevated to the status of a Royal Burgh in 1226 and prospered for nearly 400 years as the base of the Earl of Ross. From 1707, as one of the six northern royal burghs, the town had one vote in the general election. Dingwall town council was allegedly notorious for corruption, and used money from bribes to build its Town House in 1730.

The building of proper roads, and even more significantly, the railway made Dingwall the county town of Ross and Cromarty in terms of administration, agricultural markets, retail, and professional services. In 1907 a prominent stone tower was erected to *Fighting Mac* Major-General Sir Hector MacDonald who fought in the Boer War. Another famous son is Macbeth, said to have been born here in about 1005.

In recent times the town has suffered as the A9 now bypasses it via the Cromarty Bridge, opened in 1979. The nearby villages of Maryburgh, Conon Bridge and Muir of Ord were all on the main road north. All are quietly reviving and benefiting from a resurgent Inverness.

Pictish Stone. Just inside the kirkyard of St Clement's in Dingwall stands an unusual stone carved with various Pictish symbols on both sides, but also featuring six cup marks, from earlier times. The markings are quite hard to distinguish.

Walks There are several fine walks around Dingwall. These include one to the Heights of Brae just to the northwest of the town. There are lovely views over Dingwall and the Black Isle, especially from the ruined chambered cairn (NH514615) above the road.

Fighting Mac Memorial at cemetery

The High Street

Pictish Stone

View over Maryburgh from west of Dingwall

In 1817 a canal was built from the Cromarty Firth in an attempt to allow ships to reach Dingwall. Unfortunately the River Peffrey flowed though the canal and by 1840 it was abandoned due to silting. Today a walk along its banks is very pleasant. There are good views of the Cromarty Firth and Conon River Estuary.

Knockfarril is a vitrified stone fort with three surrounding ditches over-looking Strathpeffer to the west of Dingwall. It dates from the Iron Age and occupies a strategic position on a high ridge. It is easily reached by paths from several directions. The fort was built of stone which was interlaced with timbers. When fired , the heat was sufficient to melt the rocks.

Wildlife The Inner Cromarty Firth is an area of mudflats and saltmarsh popular with waders and waterfowl in winter. There are many vantage points from which to observe the birds, especially on the south side.

In early summer the saltmarshes are bright with wildflowers such as Thrift, Spring Squill, Ragged Robin and Sea Aster. Breeding waders and waterfowl can also be seen feeding on the mudflats, while Buzzards and Kites quarter the area.

Iain Sarjeant

Knockfarril

Conon Bridge

Inner Cromarty Firth

Partaking of the waters in the Pump Room

During WWI and WWII most of the hotels were requisitioned by the military and the Spa did not reopen in 1945. Fashions change in health as in other ways so taking of the waters was no longer popular in Britain. The village has recently undergone a renaissance with the main spa buildings all having been done up and it has a new air of confidence about it.

STRATHPEFFER is a charming and unique little village 5 miles west of Dingwall. Wells have always had supernatural powers attached to them, and those around this village are no different, except for their nature. Here there are sulphurous wells of various strengths, and also chalybeate or iron-bearing waters.

By the late 18th century people were starting to come here to partake of these waters. In 1777 the local minister wrote to the Commissioners of the Annexed Estate of Cromarty, describing the health benefits and suggesting the development of accommodation for visitors.

A number of people, including a Fortrose headmaster, a Kincardineshire tacksman and, an Aberdeen doctor all claimed near miraculous cures from partaking of and bathing in these waters.

This early tourism grew with the building of a wooden pump room in 1819. The present **Pump Room** was built in 1871, soon to be followed by **The Pavilion**, an elaborate concert hall, public gardens and a network of paths. Soon the Victorian passion for visiting spas developed into a major industry for tiny Strathpeffer, with the building of several large hotels and attractive little shops. It was all served by a branch railway line from Dingwall, which opened in 1885.

The Old Railway Station now houses the **Highland Museum of Childhood**, an interesting and different take on life in the north. It also has a good little bookshop. Next door a cafe serves tasty food and excellent coffee. A number of craft workshops are also based here.

Do not argue with this lady!

The Pump Room and a mud bath

The restored Pavilion

Viking lady

Victorian shopping precinct

The Eagle Stone (G *Clach Tiumpan*, Sounding Stone) NH485585 stands on a small hill just northeast of the village, up a path with a somewhat small sign. This Class I Pictish symbol stone has a horseshoe and an eagle on it and may date from the 7th century.

Walks There are many walks around Strathpeffer suitable for every interest. These include woodland, riverside, small hills, mountains and several great viewpoints. The mild climate and varied landscape make this area appealing in all seasons and to all ages.

Geology

In the Strathpeffer area a series of beds of foetid calcareous and bituminous shales underly the Old Red Sandstone. These rocks give off a smell of hydrogen sulphide when hammered and are the source of the famous Sulphur Waters.

The stone has been moved from its original local site lower down the strath. Tradition says this was to celebrate a clan battle in 1411 when the Munros beat the MacDonalds. The Brahan Seer, a 17th century man who made many prophesies said that if the stone were to fall for a third time bad things would happen to Dingwall.

Brahan Seer

Eagle Stone

The Old Railway Station

Confusing but politically correct signpost

EASTER ROSS

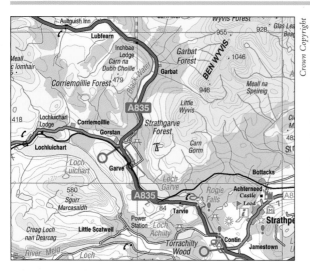

Crown Copyright

Blackwater River at Garve

The Rogie Falls (ON *Roki A, Sparkling River*) off the A835 2 miles west of Contin are well worth a visit when the rivers are in spate. A path leads from the car park to several good viewpoints over the River Blackwater including a suspension bridge near the Falls. When the Salmon are running in spring and early summer they can be seen leaping.

Strath Conon This long, lonely but beautiful valley was cleared of its inhabitants in the 19th century. In the 1950s several remaining settlements disappeared underwater due to hydro-electric schemes. This strath is a good place to seek out the many rare birds, animals and plants that flourish in the Highlands.

It reaches well into Wester Ross. From Scardroy, at its head, it is only a few miles over the moor to Glen Carron. The windy, narrow road forces a slow pace but, on a fine day, the visit can be wonderful.

Garve itself may be just a collection of houses with a railway station, but the scenery round about is lovely, especially views over **Loch Luichart** in early summer with the gorse and broom in flower, then in autumn when the trees are turning. The Blackwater River is peaceful as it flows into Loch Garve compared to its rush down the Rogie Falls a few miles downstream.

The Rogie Falls on the Blackwater River

Julia Wilmott

Salmon leaping

Laurie Campbell

244

Iain Sarjeant

Ben Wyvis on a frosty dawn

BEN WYVIS (1046m) stands in splendid isolation from the other mountains of the North Highlands. Its whaleback ridge is visible from afar. It consists of Moine schist heavily moulded by the last Ice Age. The many mounds and ridges in the lower areas are glacial as are the erratic boulders dumped as the ice retreated.

Flora Unlike most mountains in Scotland, the top of Ben Wyvis is covered with Woolly Hair Moss, a greeny-yellow plant which forms a thick and springy carpet. There are at least 170 species of plants on the mountain, including alpine flowers, rare ferns, and lichens as well as dwarf willows and birch.

Fauna Red and Roe Deer, Mountain Hare and Pine Marten may be seen. The summit ridge holds breeding Dotterel in summer, as well as Ptarmigan, Golden Plover,

Red Grouse and Ravens. Golden Eagles and Buzzards are frequently seen all over this area, the former usually at a distance but the latter often much close by.

Access. The easiest route to the summit is from the Forestry Commission car park on the A835 at Garbat. The climb to An Caber (950m) is steep but the top is gentler.

Loch Garve from the southeast

Loch Luichart from the west near Grudie

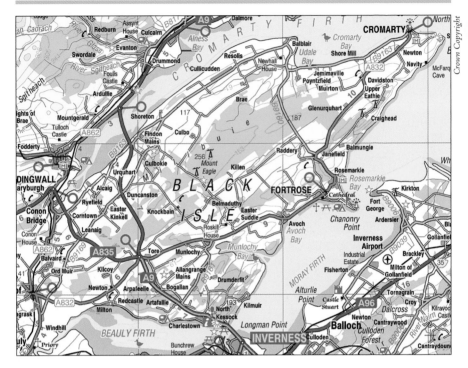

THE BLACK ISLE is neither black, nor an isle, but a long peninsula with the Cromarty Firth to the north and the Beauly and Moray Firths to the south. Conon Bridge and Muir of Ord mark the western boundary.

Before the Kessock Bridge was opened in 1982, the main road north, the A9, wound its way laboriously around the Beauly Firth to Dingwall. Thus the previously isolated Black Isle suddenly became much more accessible. A detour from the A9 on the way past is an option which will be enough to convince visitors to return and explore it at leisure.

The Cromarty Bridge from the Black Isle

Geology Most of the Black Isle is Middle Old Red Sandstone, which makes for the fertile soils and good building stone so much in evidence here. There are outcrops of Moinian schist at the South Sutor and south of Eathie, but of greatest interest are the fishbeds which outcrop at Eathie and Cromarty.

These were closely studied by Hugh Miller of Cromarty in the 19th century. Also on the foreshore at Eathie there are Jurassic shales which hold Ammonite and Belemnite fossils. The east coast runs in a straight line formed by the Great Glen Fault which runs north along the Tarbat Peninsula and south down Loch Ness.

The Black Isle has a large acreage of Wheat every year

Farming Agricultural improvement took root in the late 18th century on the Black Isle, and throughout the 19th century new breeds of stock and crops were introduced as well as innovative methods of growing them. Today's farmers are just as progressive, taking advantage of the fertile soils and benign climate to grow good crops of wheat and barley and to rear prime cattle as well as vegetables.

The Black Isle Farmer's Show, held on the first Thursday in August, is the largest such one day event in Scotland. It dates back to 1836 and is today held at Mannsfield, Muir of Ord.

This show draws people from miles around to see its fine stock, machinery, trade and entertainment stands. The events include the livestock parade with cattle, sheep, horses and ponies.

THE BLACK ISLE
Origin of the name

In Norse times The Black Isle was called *Eddirdale* (Eddir's Dale), but later *Ard Meanach*, Middle Headland). Black may originate from when most of the peninsula was moorland and oakwoods, and indeed looked black from afar, especially in winter. In Gaelic *Eilean* means both island and peninsula so the name remains an enigma.

The Upper Cromarty Firth has many mudbanks and saltmarshes

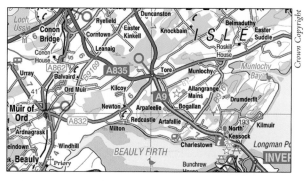

Crown Copyright

Ord Hill to the north east of North Kessock is topped by a vitrified Iron Age fort. It can be part of a circular walk from Craigton (just off the north end of the bridge on the southbound A9). Several circular routes can be followed through the woods and minor roads here, with good views over Inverness, the Beauly Firth and, the Kessock Bridge.

Beauly Firth stretches from the Kessock Narrows to Beauly at the head of the firth. The extensive mudflats, salt-marshes and sandbanks are home to many species of waterfowl and waders during the autumn and winter.

North Kessock from the old ferry pier

There are good viewpoints all along the quiet minor road from North Kessock to Milton, especially at high tide. This is an ideal place for quiet walks in the woods and lanes.

NORTH KESSOCK (St Kessoc was Pictish and died c.560) is a tranquil little village on the southern tip of the Black Isle, a backwater by-passed by the busy A9 and yet, a very good base from which to explore the area. A ferry operated to here from South Kessock since at least 1437 as part of the pilgrimage route via Fortose and Nigg to Tain.

Kessock Bridge was opened in 1982 and replaced the Kessock Ferry. This is the only cable stayed bridge in the UK and has a main span of 240m. It is similar to a bridge over the Rhine at Dusseldorf. It is designed to cope with high winds, floods and earthquakes as it straddles the Great Glen Fault. Its height allows shipping to pass.

Tore Art Gallery is in a restored 1860 church. It is a large airy space well suited to the varied displays of original artists' work from the Highlands. Paintings, pottery, silverwork, and many other items are on view.

The Kessock Bridge was opened in 1982 and transformed access to the Black Isle

Beauly Firth from Milton

Beauly Firth from North Kessock

Conon Bridge and **Muir of Ord** were formerly on the A9 road north, but like Dingwall have been by-passed so nowadays they are tranquil little villages, spared from through traffic.

Glen Ord Distillery was founded in 1838 and was originally powered by two waterwheels. It still malts its own barley and uses long fermentation and slow distillation methods. The whisky is said to be *very skillfully composed, beautifully balanced, very complex. A sophisticated all-rounder, at its best after dinner.*

The west side of the Black Isle is a large glacial outwash plain, with fertile farms and small villages. The mountains of the Highlands are close by to the south and west. They help create the special micro-climate which gives this area a special charm.

The A9 snakes rapidly north from the Kessock Bridge to the Cromarty Bridge and beyond. Visitors should resist the temptation to by-pass this intriguing area.

Tore Art Gallery

Glen Ord Distillery

Greylag Geese near Milton

Conon Bridge signpost

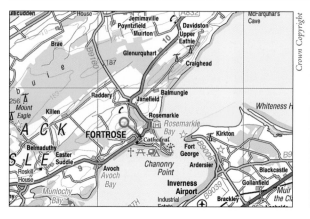

Clootie Well

Munlochy is a small settlement at the head of Munlochy Bay. It is home to the Plough Inn, one of the smallest pubs in Scotland. Workers engaged in quarrying stone for Fort George stayed here in the 1760s, which led to the growth of the village.

Munlochy Bay is a long, narrow inlet facing the Inner Moray Firth. Its large areas of sand and mudflats and surrounding saltmarshes are very attractive to birds, especially waders and waterfowl. Redshank, Oystercatcher, Ringed Plover, Dunlin, Curlew and Shelduck all breed here. Autumn sees the arrival of huge numbers of ducks, many of which overwinter. Geese and Whooper Swans pass through, but may stay for the winter, roosting on the intertidal zone and feeding on surrounding stubble and grass fields.

The Clootie Well, near Munlochy is of ancient origin. According to folklore, a gift of cloth had to be offered to its fairy before drinking the water. This ritual was supposed to restore health and give good luck. Christians took it over as St. Boniface's Well. Branches all around are covered with pieces of cloth which give a somewhat eerie feeling to the place.

Munlochy Bay

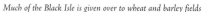

Much of the Black Isle is given over to wheat and barley fields

Black Isle Brewery was established in 1998. Its mission is to produce a range of top quality organic beers packaged in recycled materials. The barley and hops used are grown on organic farms, without artificial fertilisers or herbicides. The product can be tasted and purchased on the premises.

Chanonry Point lighthouse

Avoch (G *Obh'ch* or ON *A*, river) was established as a fishing village in the early 17th century, when it was called Seatown. The harbour was built by Thomas Telford in 1814 at the same time as the village was expanded to accommodate people displaced from the Highlands.

Avoch Harbour

The *Ochies* fished locally for part of the year for Herring but ranged as far as Caithness and Loch Broom. They were highly regarded as seamen. Avoch has attractive rows of mostly single storey cottages, separated by lanes leading down to the seashore. Ormond Hill lies to the west and, though wooded, offers fine views over the inner Moray Firth.

Fortrose is an attractive little town with fine sandstone houses surrounding its ruined 13th century cathedral. Only the south aisle and choir remain of what must once have been a very impressive building, as shown by the original outline. Although Cromwell's army is accused of its destruction, Lord Ruthven bought (or took) all of the lead off the roof in 1572. The nearby Chapter House is also 13th century.

The Brahan Seer

A stone to the Brahan Seer stands at Chanonry Point on the reputed site of his death. Coinneach Adhair was a 17th century clairvoyant who allegedly predicted many things. He was burnt here in a tar barrel as a witch in about 1660 on the orders of the Countess of Seaforth.

Apparently she wanted to know why her husband was staying so long in Paris. When the Seer informed her that the Earl was philandering with a French lady, his fate was sealed. Before his immolation Coinneach predicted that the Earl would be the last of his line, that his sons would die before him, and that one of his daughters would kill the other.

All four sons did pre-decease the father, and one daughter did die in a carriage accident while being driven by the other.

He is reputed to have made many other forecasts, such as the building of the Caledonian Canal and the Kessock Bridge.

Bottle-nose Dolphin mother and calf at Chanonry Point

THE BLACK ISLE - EASTER ROSS

Fortrose Cathedral and Chapter House

This is a very pleasant place to take a wander through the pretty streets, admire views over the Moray Firth and explore the charming sandstone harbour, which has changed little in nearly 200 years.

St Boniface Fair was formerly held on his saint's day, 16th March until about 1830. It was revived in 1978 to mark the Silver Jubilee of Queen Elizabeth II and has been held in early August ever since. The Fair is set in the 1750s

The Fairy Glen, Rosemarkie

with participants dressed in period costume. The goods and entertainments on offer are those which would have been available at the time. It is held in Cathedral Square, which becomes a hive of colourful activity for the day.

Chanonry Ness is a glacial spit which projects about a mile from the coast. St Boniface (or Cuiritan) is reputed to have come here in the 7th century and to have established the first chapel in Rosemarkie. St Moluag may

have been here even earlier. The lighthouse, by Alan Stevenson, was first lit in 1846.

A ferry once ran from the slipway near the lighthouse to Ardersier. There was formerly a large Salmon fishery here but all that remains is the ice house, which was used to store ice for the preservation and shipping of the fish being exported.

Folklore says that a wizard joined forces with the fairies to build a bridge to Ardersier. This gossamer construction was well underway when a stanger wished the fairyfolk *God speed*, after which they stopped work and returned to their homeland, some perhaps remaining in the Fairy Glen.

Rosemarkie (G *Ros*, Point, ON *Mark*, Wood, Woodburn Point) is an ancient settlement on the north side of Chanonry Ness with a fine sheltered sandy beach. The village was another Salmon station, as attested by the icehouse near the shore. There is a fine sandy beach to the north of the burn, while a more variable one of sand and pebbles stretches all the way to Chanonry Point.

Fortrose in 1821 by William Daniell

Groam House Museum is mainly dedicated to displays of the many sculpted Pictish stones which have been found in Rosemarkie. Clearly the village was an important early Christian site, along with those on the Tarbat Peninsula. The intact Rosemarkie cross-slab takes pride of place.

The Museum also houses the Bain Collection, George Bain (1881-1968) was a Caithness-born artist who made a life-long study of Celtic designs on stone, jewellery and books.

Rosemarkie from Chanonry Point

The Fairy Glen follows the Markie Burn. A path leads though these enchanted woods. In spring children would gather wild flowers and scatter the petals on one of the pools for the fairies. Wild flowers including Primroses, Bluebells and Water Avens brighten the woods in spring.

The Anderson in Fortrose has a huge collection of malt whiskies

Dippers and Grey Wagtails may be seen as well as Willow Warblers, Woodpeckers and Treecreepers. Ice from the millpond was used to replenish the Chanonry icehouse in winter. Today it is home to Herons and ducks, truly an enchanting place.

Groam House Museum, Rosemarkie

Groam House Museum, Rosemarkie

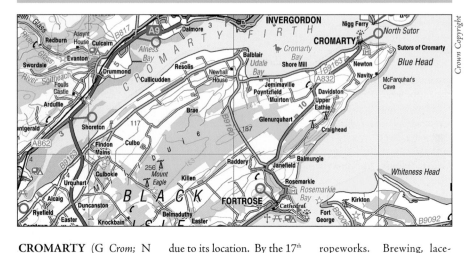

CROMARTY (G *Crom*; N *Vagr*, Bent Bay) is a delightful and unspoilt little village perched on a small headland protruding into the entrance of the Cromarty Firth. A visit here is a real treat.

The Romans called the Cromarty Firth *Portus Salutis*, and doubtless a Pictish settlement existed here, but no evidence has been found. A chapel was established here in the 6th century by St Moluag but this and any carved stones have been lost due to coastal erosion.

The town has always alternately prospered and declined

Cromarty in 1821 by William Daniell

due to its location. By the 17th century it was one of the busiest ports in Scotland, trading in grain and salt fish with the Baltic, Holland and as far as the Mediterranean. Many emigrants left here for the New World. Cromarty prospered for a long time from the Herring fishing, partly due to the Guillam Bank, five miles to the east where 1,000 barrels a day were regularly caught.

In 1772 George Ross, owner of the Cromarty Estate, redeveloped the harbour and set up a hand-weaving factory, which used hemp from Russia and which later became a large

ropeworks. Brewing, lacemaking and the manufacture of iron hand tools and nails also thrived. Many of those cleared from the land in the Highlands came here to work.

With the demise of these industries and the fishing, Cromarty declined in prosperity but in recent years many buildings have been renovated, notably by the National Trust, giving the town a new lease of life. All the same there is an air of graceful decay. Before WWII there were over forty shops, while today there remain only a few.

Hugh Miller (1802-1856) was born here. The son of a ship's captain, who was lost at sea in 1807, he trained as a stonemason and became very interested in fossils which he found in the course of his quarrying work, in nearby exposures and further afield. He wrote widely on geology and religion, his books being best sellers in their time.

Cromarty and the Cromarty Firth from the South Sutor

His collection of over 6,000 fossils is in the National Museum. He was also a leading light in setting up the Free Church in 1843 and a fundamentalist. His seeming opposing religious beliefs and scientific discoveries caused him a crisis of personal interest.

Big Vennel in the late 19th century

Hugh Miller's House is maintained by the National Trust and is well worth a visit. It was built in 1711. The sundial in the garden was carved by Miller. It retains a thatched roof and has displays related to his life and work as well as contemporary furniture.

Big Vennel today

Cromarty Courthouse dates from 1771 and has an audiovisual display of a 19th century trial and a realistic 1843

Hugh Miller's House

Hugh Miller's House

Cromarty from the west with the harbour and the North Sutor behind

prison cell complete with occupant. The old Cromartyshire administrative building houses the local museum and archives, where many original documents and facsimiles can be consulted.

Cromarty Harbour has changed little since the 1700s. Today it is home to a variety of

The Old Lighthouse

pleasure craft which use the pontoons. The basin is prone to silting due to the strong tidal currents which run through the entrance to the Cromarty Firth. The Admiralty Pier, built in 1914, is currently not in use.

Nigg to Cromarty Ferry runs seasonally between a slipway near Cromarty Harbour over to Nigg. It carries two cars plus passengers and offers an interesting itinerary to explore the Fearn Peninsula in a circular route.

Shops and Services For its size Cromarty boasts a good selection of interesting shops as well as places to eat and to stay. There are several pubs, an excellent cafe, a pottery, antique shop and, *The Emporium* to name a few.

Walks Cromarty is a village where exploration on foot is essential. Apart from the narrow streets and limited parking, the many interesting 17th century buildings, narrow streets and closes can only be seen and enjoyed at leisure.

Cromarty Court House

Cromarty Jail

There is a good sandy beach on the northeast side and a smaller one to the west. There may even be the occasional fossil left to find.

There are also several fine countryside walks in this area for example, to the South Sutor with its WWI gun emplacements. This viewpoint overlooks Cromarty and the North Sutor and offers a panoramic view of the Cromarty Firth.

Slightly to the south, Gallow Hill (156m) also offers another good view. By following the coast in a southwesterly direction several interesting features can be visited. These include, MacFarquar's Bed, a natural arch, and Marcus' Cave, one of a number along this coast. St Bennet's Well was another *clootie well*.

Eathie Burn is particularly lovely in early summer with its small waterfalls and wild flowers. It can be followed down to the shore where the remains of Eathie Fishing Station can be found.

Cromarty Harbour was once a major port

The Paye

Antique shop

Hugh Miller Institute built by Andrew Carnegie

Cafe

259

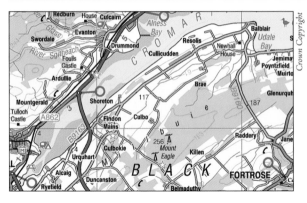

UDALE BAY has an extensive area of mudflats and sand which is exposed at low tide. This is backed by saltmarshes. This RSPB reserve is best visited from late summer to April around high tide, when large flocks of birds may be seen roosting or flying. There is a bird hide west of Jemimaville.

Waders and waterfowl arrive here in huge numbers in autumn. These include Bar-tailed Godwit, Knot, Dunlin, Widgeon, Teal, Goldeneye and Pink-footed Geese.

In summer, Lapwing, Redshank and Oystercatchers all breed along with Shelduck. Ospreys can sometimes be seen fishing offshore and Herons often patrol the shores, especially near high tide. The occasional Peregrine may spoil the party and cause great panic among flocks of small waders.

St Michael's Chapel The ruined St Michael's Kirk (NH706658) is also known as Kirkmichael Church. It overlooks Udale Bay and the Cromarty Firth, on the north coast of the Black Isle. It was the parish chapel of Kirkmichael and Cullicudden from 1662 until 1767 when a new parish church was built at Resolis. The remains of Kirkmichael include a 16th century chancel, later used as the burial aisle of the Shaw-Mackenzie's of Newhall.

Udale Bay from the east

Common Seal

Cromarty Firth autumn colours

Cromarty Firth and Dingwall from the Black Isle

Cromarty Firth The road which follows the north coast from Udale to Conon Bridge offers a variety of fine vistas across the Cromarty Firth. There are lots of good places to view the Firth, always dominated by Ben Wyvis in the background. The mudflats and saltmarshes are home to many breeding and overwintering birds.

Common Seals haul out at several locations here. Otters are also present but rarely seen. The quiet side road along the south side of the Firth is well worth a detour. Apart from the wildlife these quiet lanes offer opportunities to take in seasonal landscapes away from the constantly busy A9 trunk road.

Gordonsmill Burn runs through saltmarsh into Udale Bay

St Michael's Kirk, Udale

Sea Aster grows on saltmarshes

Mist over the Cromarty Firth

Laurie Campbell

Bottle-nosed Dolphins

BLACK ISLE WILDLIFE

Despite the intensity of farming, the Black Isle remains an ideal place to observe birds, animals and find wild flowers. There are many patches of woodland, but very little wetland. The long coastline is varied, with large areas of mudflats and saltmarsh, long stretches of low cliffs, raised beaches, glacial headlands and one good sandy beach. This wide range of habitats ensures that there are species to seek out in every season.

Bottle-nosed Dolphins are often seen in the Moray Firth which has a resident population of about 130. The best places to see them are from North Kessock, Chanonry Point and around Cromarty. They are most commonly seen in the summer when Salmon are running, or when shoals of Mackerel or Herring have come inshore.

Harbour Porpoises are also commonly seen, but Minke Whales and White-beaked Dolphins may only occasionally be present. Dolphin watching cruises are run from several locations, including Avoch and Cromarty.

Red Kites were reintroduced to the Black Isle in 1989 by the RSPB. From the original six birds, a population of over 30 breeding pairs has become established, raising over 50 young every year now. The adults are mostly sedentary, but the young range over a wide area of Europe, returning to their home areas in spring.

Red Kite

Laurie Campbell

The birds build their nests high in trees, laying their eggs in April. Incubation takes about 32 days, and fledgling about another 50. During this time the males do most of the hunting. These magnificent birds are very distinctive so keep looking. Sadly they are vulnerable to poisons used to kill rats, and up to a third are killed in this way, as they are very good at finding rodents.

Munlochy Bay and **Udale Bay** are tidal mudflats that are popular with waterfowl and waders especially in migration times and in winter. The best time to view the birds is around high tide when the birds crowd up to the shore or take to the wing in spectacular numbers. In summer breeding waders and ducks as well as Osprey may be seen. There are many locations from which the car is a good hide.

The Dolphin & Seal Visitor Centre on the A9 just after the bridge has a hydrophone system which allows visitors to listen to the sounds the dolphins make as well as information on studies on the marine mammals in the Moray Firth area. The Visitor Information Centre is also situated here.

The Black Isle Wildlife & Country Park at Drumsmittal is an ideal family visit. It has friendly ducks, geese and swans on its ponds. There are goats, rabbits and pot-bellied pigs as well as rare breeds of cattle and sheep. There is also a picnic and play area, a shop and a tearoom.

Common Seals are often seen on the Cromarty Firth

Oystercatcher

Sanderling flock on migration

Lapwing

Redshank

WESTER ROSS

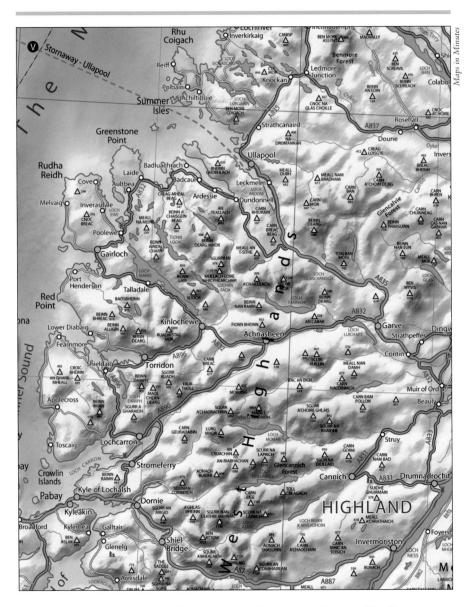

WESTER ROSS stretches from Kintail in the south to Inverpolly in the north and extends from the western watershed of Ross and Cromarty. The Atlantic coastline extends to over 300 miles (500km) and is heavily indented with sea lochs.

This is an area of ancient mountains, tranquil coastal settlements, single track roads and few inhabitants. It has some of the most stunning scenery of anywhere in the UK, a huge variety of wildlife and a very changeable climate.

Geology The diverse scenery of Wester Ross is due to the complex geology of the area. The base rock, Lewisian Gneiss, is overlain by a succession of sedimentary strata - Torridonian Sandstone, Cambrian Quartzite and Limestone.

Eilean Donan Castle on Loch Duich is an iconic Scottish scene

In Wester Ross the **Moine Thrust** runs from Glenelg in the south west to Knockan Crag in the north, adding to the geological confusion. Erosion over many millions of years has produced the spectacular scenery of today.

Settlements in Wester Ross are sparse. Apart from the main centres such as Ullapool, Gairloch or Lochcarron the villages are very small. Much of the landscape is unpopulated and frequently it is possible to walk all day without seeing another soul.

In this book Wester Ross is taken to begin at Shiel Bridge in the south and to include Lochalsh and Kintail, since anyone approaching from the south will pass this way. Whichever way one enters this area, the pace of life suddenly becomes slower.

Even some of the main roads are windy single tracks. There are spectacular views round every corner which vary with the season, weather and time of day.

Beinn Eighe is a National Nature Reserve

Big Sand Beach at Gairloch

Loch Broom with Ullapool in the distance

267

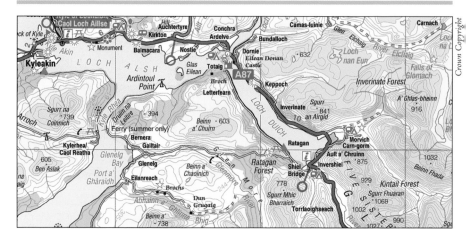

Loch Duich and the Five Sisters from Bealach Ratagan on the road to Glenelg

KINTAIL (G *Ceann t-saile*, Head of the Salt Water) in the southeast provides a dramatic entrance to Wester Ross. The A87 passes though Glen Shiel with 1,000m mountains on both sides of the road, including the lovely Five Sisters of Kintail, before descending to Shiel Bridge at the head of Loch Duich.

The Five Sisters of Kintail dominate the east end of Loch Duich. The highest of the five peaks is Sgurr Fuaran (1068m) from the summit of which there is a superb panoramic view on a clear day. This is a classic ridge walk, with an arduous 550m climb at the start, which makes for a long and satisfying day.

The **Falls of Glomach** (G *Glom*, chasm, NG977222) at 113m, are arguably the most spectacular, though not the highest in UK. They can be reached by a 4 mile hike up a good path from the Forestry Commission car park at Strath Coe, off the A87 and inland from Morvich. Though the falls themselves

Loch Duich and the Five Sisters from Bealach Ratagan on the road to Glenelg

Ptarmigan

are more spectacular after rain, the walk itself is better in clear weather.

Glenelg An unmissable detour is the side road which runs to Glenelg. The view from **Bealach Ratagan** (339m) over Loch Duich and the Five Sisters is spectacular. There are also fine views across to Skye further along the road.

The **Bernera Barracks** at Glenelg were built in 1723 after the 1715 Jacobite uprising, but were abandoned by the 1790s. A small ferry runs from here across fast flowing Kyle Rhea to Skye.

Brochs In Gleann Beag, Dun Telve broch still stands 10m high, while nearby Dun Troddan is about 7m (NG829172). These two brochs are the best preserved on the Scottish mainland, and clearly show how they were constructed and how imposing they must have been.

Near **Totaig** another broch overlooks Loch Alsh and Loch Long (NG867251). Its walls are still 5m high in places and it has a massive triangular lin-

Totaig Broch,   *Dun Troddan intramural stairway*

Glenelg

Bernera Barracks, Glenelg

Dun Telve Broch, Glenelg   *Dun Telve Broch, Glenelg*

Eilean Donan Castle floodlit

1932 by Lt Colonel John Macrae-Gilstrap, who bought the island in 1911. With his Clerk of Works, Farquar Macrae, he used old plans to create this replica.

The first castle was built here in the 13th century, but its strategic position suggests that it was the site of much earlier defence works. The island is probably named after St Donan, who came over from Ireland about 580AD. There was possibly an early monastic settlement here.

During the first Jacobite rebellion, the castle was bombarded for several days by three Royal Navy frigates in 1719 when it was being held by a troupe of 46 Spanish soldiers. The castle walls stood up well to the cannons, but the Spanish were outnumbered and soon surrendered.

They had over 300 barrels of gunpowder but no cannon to shoot back with. The Navy then used this to demolish the castle which had valiantly resisted so many cannonballs. It remained ruinous for over 200 years.

tel. From here a steep climb to the ridge above the trees opens a good vista.

Loch Duich (G *Loch Dubhthaich*, Black Loch) stretches from Shiel Bridge to Dornie, where it is joined by Loch Long before meeting Loch Alsh. There are fine views over the loch from Bealach Ratagan on the road to Glenelg and from the old road which runs above the A87 from north of Inverinate to Dornie.

Selkie Legend Allegedly, three brothers were fishing on the loch one evening when they encountered three beautiful maidens, who were in fact seals who had cast off their coats to lure the young men. The brothers stored their skins so as to enable them to take the seal maidens as their wives.

The youngest brother felt sorry for his maiden, who was very distressed and so gave her back her skin. Her father allowed him to visit her every ninth night in return. One of the other seal maidens found her skin and escaped, while the other was burnt while the eldest brother tried to burn her skin.

Eilean Donan Castle, one of Scotland's iconic landmarks, sits on a tidal island in Loch Duich. The Castle was reconstructed between 1911 and

Eilean Donan Castle reflected in the waters of Loch Duich at high tide

Today Eilean Donan Castle is open to the public, except in winter. The Visitor Centre has an interesting gift shop, coffee shop and tourist information on the area. Readers of *Scotland* magazine voted it the Best Castle in Scotland in the *Icons of Scotland* 2007 awards.

Skye Bridge was opened in 1995 after three years of construction work, and replaced the ferries which ran from Kyle of Lochalsh to Kyleakin on Skye. After a long campaign the bridge tolls were abolished in 2004.

Kyle of Lochalsh is much quieter than it was, but remains a pleasant place to stop or to stay. Boat trips are run on Loch Alsh from here. Ploc of Kyle, west of the village offers a fine vista of the Skye Bridge. The station is the terminus of the Kyle Line from Inverness.

Routes The road continues to Kyle of Lochalsh and Skye, with further viewpoints along the way. The A890 runs north to Stromeferry on Loch Carron, but a much prettier minor road winds slowly across the moor to Plockton.

Dornie is a pretty little village where Loch Long meets Loch Duich

Skye Bridge from Ploc of Kyle

Eilean Donan Castle in 1821 by William Daniell

Kyle of Lochalsh Railway Museum is in the station

Kyle of Lochalsh railway station

271

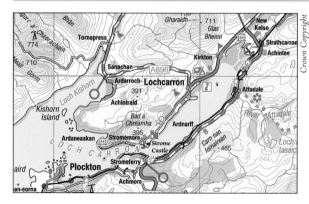

Applecross. A ferry ran across the narrows here for hundreds of years, but in 1970 it was replaced by a new road around Loch Carron. The best viewpoints are at Fernaig on the road to Plockton and from the hill above the village, Am Meallan.

Loch Carron (P *Kars*, stone, rough) and Loch Kishorn (N *Keis Ord*, Big Headland) are sheltered by Applecross to the northwest and Skye to the west. Several laybys offer panoramic views over the loch. Glen Carron leads to Achnasheen and on to Dingwall or Gairloch.

Plockton from the south end of the village

The saltmarshes at the head of both lochs are very colourful with wild flowers in summer, and the combination of sheltered inlets, rocky shores, mudflats, rivers and lochs is great for Otters, waders and waterfowl.

Plockton (G *am Ploc*, The Lump) is an impossibly picturesque little village which nestles in a sheltered bay at the mouth of Loch Carron. The National Trust has been successful in preserving its charm, without turning it into a museum. It was built as a planned fishing village in the early 19th century.

Britain's Prettiest Village is popular with artists, yachtsmen and people who come to enjoy its quiet charm. There is a fine viewpoint at Creag nan Garadh above the village, and the little coves and beaches are well worth exploring.

Stromeferry offers fine views over Loch Carron and

Attadale Gardens are just south of Strathcarron. The house was first built in 1755 therefore the gardens of today have been cultivated for over 250 years. The mild climate

Plockton panoramic from the south with Loch Carron in the background and Applecross in the distance on the left

has allowed a variety of themes. These include Water, Japanese, Sunken, Shade, Woodland and Kitchen Gardens as well as Rhododendron and Woodland Walks.

Strathcarron from near Attadale

Strathcarron is a good place to stop and observe the salt-marshes or to take one of several paths along the River Carron. There are many patches of deciduous and conifer woodland to explore. The River Carron with its small lochs and marshes is good habitat for wetland wild flowers.

Loch Carron from above Stromeferry looking northeast

Lochcarron is an attractive village, strung out along the northwest side of the loch. After 1813, when the Parliamentary Road reached here, the settlement grew considerably. This vibrant little village offers many facilities to visitors, including shops, a wide range of accommodation, cafes and restaurants, a good campsite, fuel, and a garage.

Lochcarron from the south

Strome Castle is now a ruin, but from Norse times or earli-

Stromemore and jetty

Strome Castle was blown up in 1602

Kishorn from Beallach na Ba

er it was an important strategic site. The present building dates from the 15ᵗʰ century, when it was most likely a fortified tower house. It was fought over many times by the MacKenzies and the MacDonalds.

In 1602 the Lord of Kintail, Kenneth MacKenzie, laid siege to the castle. He was on the point of leaving when he heard that some of the women of the castle had been drawing water from the well and by accident tipped it into the gunpowder cask, instead of the water one.

The MacDonalds surrendered, allowing the MacKenzies to gain possession, who promptly blew up the castle, leaving the gaunt ruins seen today.

Ardaneaskan It is worthwhile exploring further west to Ardaneaskan, if only for its fine views over Loch Carron to Plockton and west to Applecross. A track goes to nearby Loch Reraig and its wooded burn.

Kishorn is an area of scattered houses around the east side of the Loch. A minor road goes to an arc of pretty cottages and a jetty. The views across Loch Kishorn to Applecross are spectacular.

Loch Kishorn is very deep and was selected as a North Sea Oil yard. In 1975 a large drydock and construction site was opened here by Howard Doris to build oil platforms. In 1977 over 3,000 were employed on the site and were accommodated on two old liners anchored in the loch.

At 600,000, tonnes the Ninian Central Platform was floated out in 1978. It remains the largest floating and moveable structure so far created. By 1984 demand for huge oil platforms had dwindled and the site closed in 1987. The dry dock was used to build the footings for the Skye Bridge in 1992, but it is now derelict.

Rassal Ashwood NNR

Weathered limestone at Rassal

Kishorn Seafood Bar offers a wonderful menu after a day trekking and exploring. "*The emphasis is very much on local shellfish; with Oysters; Prawns and Squat Lobster from Loch Kishorn; Mussels and Queen Scallops from Lochcarron and Crab, King Scallops, Lobster, Smoked Salmon and Fresh Salmon also obtained locally. These are all simply cooked and served along Spanish lines.* "

Saltmarsh at the Head of Loch Kishorn

Rassal Ashwood NNR on the A896 north of Kishorn, is the most northerly in Scotland. The limestone outcrop here results in fertile soil. This supports a wide range of wild flowers. Apart from the Ash trees and their amazing lichens, there are Hazel, Rowan and Willows.

Vivienne Rollo , proprietor of Kishorn Seafood Bar

The area has been used as grazing for centuries and many of the trees have been coppiced. In former times crops were grown within small walled enclosures. The A896 continues north to Torridon. The best time to visit is probably from April to July.

Oysters

Garlic Scallops

Sunset over Loch Kishorn and Sgurr a Ghaoracha

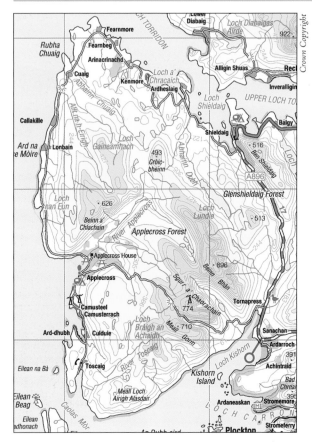

Glacially carved boulder

Bealach na Ba (G Pass of the Cattle) which reaches a maximum height of 626m takes a very steep and windy route from Loch Kishorn. It climbs through the spectacular corrie of Coire na Ba between the crags of Meall Gorm (710m) and Sgurr a'Chaorachain (792m) to a viewpoint at Carn Glas (NG774426).

On a clear day there are panoramic views across the Inner Sound to Raasay, the Cullins, Northern Skye and to the Western Isles. A track leads up to a radio mast (776m) and by skirting the crags and climbing a ridge to the east another viewpoint can be reached (792m). From here there is a panoramic view of the pass, Loch Kishorn and Loch Carron.

APPLECROSS (P *Aber Crossan*, Mouth of the Crossan) is a large mountainous peninsula composed of Torridonian Sandstone between Loch Kishorn and Loch Torridon.

Though not unique in the Highlands for its remote situation, Applecross remains a thriving community. It can only be reached by two long narrow roads or by sea.

Loch Kishorn from below Bealach na Ba

The Parliamentary Road over Bealach na Ba was completed in 1822, but it was not until the 1950s that it received a bitumen covering. Even today the pass can be blocked in winter for long periods and is unsuitable for caravans, coaches and large vehicles. There are plenty of places to pull over to admire the view.

Bealach na Ba with Sgurr a Ghaorachain on left, Kishorn in the distance and Meall Gorm on the right

Coast Road It took until 1976 for the coast road to Shieldaig to be completed. The first section was opened by Princess Margaret on 11th May 1970, over 90 years after the Napier Report of 1884 recommended its construction. This was to serve a military development at Sand.

The road south of Applecross village passes through, the unspoilt crofting townships of Camusteel with its tiny beach at Camusterrach. It ends at Toscaig Pier.

Bealach na Ba from above Loch Kishorn

Skye from Carn Glas viewpoint

Applecross Village has a shop, campsite and hotel. There is a ruined broch next to the campsite. Applecross house dates from the 1730s, while nearby are two Top Barns which originally had heather thatched roofs. They were used to store hay and unthreshed oats.

277

Cross-slab in the graveyard

A'Chomraich In c.673AD the Irish monk St Maelrubha founded a monastery here. He was born in Londonderry c642. The surrounding land was declared a Sanctuary (G, *A'Chomraich*) and the name still survives in Gaelic. No trace remains today of this early Christian settlement, or of most of the Pictish cross-slabs which are said to have been broken up and buried by over zealous 19th century masons.

Next to the entrance of the graveyard a large cross-slab may commemorate Abbot Mor MacAogan, who died in 801AD at Bangor. The Vikings are said to have attacked the abbey around this time. Sadly no major archaeology has been done here yet to investigate this important early Christian site.

Apart from the impressive cross-slab there are a number of other ancient grave markers, some of which are inscribed. Most are either very weathered or obviously broken. The small chapel east of the church is 15th century while the present church was built in 1817, most likely on the site of a much earlier one.

The **Heritage Centre** near the church has displays describing the archaeology and history of the area. Artifacts, archive and old photographs can be seen here. It also has three parts of a broken carved cross which was found in recent times.

Mesolithic Age At the beautiful sandy beach of Sand

(NG682488) on the coast road north of Applecross Bay, a mound in front of a rock shelter has yielded evidence of Mesolithic occupation around 6000BC. Shells (mostly Limpets), fish bones, bone and stone tools were found. Some of the stone tools were of bloodstone from Rum, others from Skye.

Loch Torridon North of Sand the road offers fine views over Inner Sound. From Fearnmore eastwards it winds over the rocky terrain and offers many fine views over Loch Torridon and Loch Shieldaig with the Torridon Mountains in the background.

Allt Beag above Applecross Bay

Ancient carved headstone

Applecross Bay from near the church

Applecross Bay with the Skye Cuillins in the background

Walking and Wildlife This remote peninsula is a great place for walking or cycling, whether gentle or extreme. Many paths lead into the interior and along the coast. Sea kayaking is available and there are guided walks led by Highland Council Rangers.

Mature Sots Pine

Golden and White-tailed Eagles, Red Deer and Otters are present here. The stands of mature Scots Pine around Applecross Bay are home to Pine Marten as well as many species of birds and plants. Common Seals regularly haul out on the shore, while Porpoises are often seen. Minke Whales and Dolphins are occasionally present.

Inner Sound from north of Sand

Torridon from the new north road to Applecross

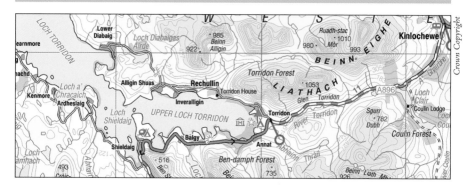

TORRIDON (ON Thorfinn's Township, or G Place of Transference) is full of scenic grandeur, its ancient mountains rising steeply and dramatically from sea level to over 1,000m. They loom majestically over Upper Loch Torridon, the little villages of Torridon or Fasag, Inver Alligin, Alligin Shuas and Diabaig at their foot.

Shieldaig (ON *Sild Vik*, Herring Bay), a planned fishing village, built to encourage the development of fishing, is in a very sheltered position on Loch Shieldaig, a branch of Loch Torridon. The idea was to increase the supply of seamen for the Royal Navy, and building work commenced in 1810, followed by the church in 1825.

Finance was provided for fishing boats, but as is often the case with such military-inspired things, the threat was long gone before any sailors were ready to fight. A new road was built to Kishorn, fish prices were guaranteed and salt provided duty-free. Prawns are still landed here, and Mussels farmed, but nowadays tourism has largely replaced fishing.

Shieldaig Island is covered with mature Scots Pine, planted in the 19th century to provide timber and spars for boats and fishing. It is home to Grey Herons, Black Guillemots, Long-eared Owls and Kestrels. Seals and Otters frequent these quiet shores.

Shieldaig from the west

Shieldaig island and a Spanish Armada cannon

Shieldaig Village nestles along the shore

Upper Loch Torridon and Liathach from the southwest

Upper Loch Torridon Approaching from the south, the A896 offers several panoramic views over Torridon. This link was only completed in the 1960s, previously a trip of over 60 miles was needed. By taking a walk over the moorland from one of several viewpoints, the whole vista opens up.

A path also leads from the Torridon Hotel through woods along the shore to Dubh-aird, from where the whole expanse of loch and

Red Deer Museum

mountains can be seen. The loch is shallow with a muddy bottom, an ideal habitat for prawns. They are caught in special creels which do not damage the seabed.

Shieldaig Mussels

Deer Museum The National Trust Countryside Centre has displays, information on the area, its wildlife and current events as well as a small shop. The nearby Deer Museum

Liathach dwarfs Torridon Village

Upper Loch Torridon and Ben-Damph Forest from Bealach na Gaoithe

Mountains Beinn Alligin (G The Jewel, (985m), Liathach (G The Grey One, 1054m) and Beinn Eighe (G File Mountain, 1010m) form one of the most spectacular skylines in Scotland. Their cliffs, buttresses, corries and peaks look splendid from below and they offer some of the best hillwalking and climbing in the country.

explains the life cycle and management of Red Deer, a number of which can be seen in a nearby fenced enclosure.

Diabaig A minor road along the north side of the loch leads to Diabaig, a charming little harbour and village. It passes Inveralligin before reaching the steep Bealach na Gaoithe, from where there are further dramatic views over Loch Torridon to Ben-Damph Forest to the south and Beinn Alligin to the east.

Glen Torridon The road to Kinlochewe offers spectacular views of Liathach and Beinn Eighe. The scene changes constantly depending on the light and weather so that sometimes the mountains are shrouded in mist and at other times they are revealed in all their lofty splendour.

There is a fine view from above Lochan an Iasgair, which can be reached via a bridge and a path just east of the Glen Torridon car park below Liathach (NG958569). Perhaps best of all is that over Loch Clair, which is accessible on foot via the road to Coulin Lodge.

Beinn Alligin from Bealach na Gaoithe

Diabaig is a pretty bay and settlement

Coire Dubh Mor (G Big Black Corrie) runs northwest between the crags of Liathach and Beinn Eighe. A signposted 4 mile long path from the car park goes through Coire Dubh Mor to Coire Mhic Fhearchair on the northwest side of Beinn Eighe.

This spectacular corrie with its triple buttresses of red Torridonian Sandstone topped by Quartzite which glitters in

Liathach (1064m) from the southeast above the Glen Torridon car park

the sun is well worth the effort needed to reach it. The lochan in the foreground completes an idyllic scene on a clear day.

Geology The red Torridonian Sandstones were laid down about 900-750 million years ago (Ma) on top of much older (c.2,000Ma) Lewisian Gneiss. Many of the mountains are capped with Cambrian Quartzite from c.200Ma later, which glints in the sun, especially if wet.

Hummocky moraine

River Torridon looking east towards Sgurr Dubh (782m)

Spectacular cliffs rise up vertically from the valley bottoms to 900m in several places. These hard rocks erode slowly and do not produce fertile soils, thereby giving the landscape a somewhat savage beauty. Here, you will find, nature has an uncompromising splendour.

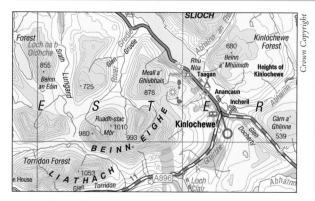

Crown Copyright

Laurie Campbell

Pine Marten

DANGER
HIDDEN CREVASSES
THE PUBLIC ARE ADVISED
NOT TO LEAVE CAR PARK

BEINN EIGHE and Slioch to the north stand sentinel over Loch Maree. In 1951 the first National Nature Reserve was created here, consisting of 230ha of relict Caledonian Forest (G *Coille na Glas Leitre*, Wood of the Grey Slope) and over 4,000ha of mountain and moorland.

Woodland Trail This type of woodland is known as temperate rainforest, where the flora and fauna are adapted to the cool, wet climate. In the last 50 years much has been done to regenerate these woodlands. The Woodland Trail is about a mile long and winds through the Scots Pinewoods which have existed here since after the end of the last Ice Age.

Birch, Bird Cherry, Rowan, Willow, Holly and Alder also grow here and large areas have been fenced off to keep out Red Deer and allow the regeneration of woodlands over a total of about 1,100ha.

The Pinewoods are ideal territory for Pine Martens, whose droppings are often seen.

Otters may be seen at the lochside or near streams and the Wildcat hunts here, but is rarely seen. Of particular interest are the 13 species of Dragonflies which like the more open marshy places. Many species of lichen, liverworts, mosses and ferns live on the trees and rocks in these woods.

Mountain Trail This climbs to 550m and covers about 4 miles, passing through several climatic zones on the way. Climbing through the Pinewoods, there are many ancient trees which could be up to 400 years old, as well as younger, straighter ones. Scottish Crossbills may be seen or heard here.

From the cairn at the top of the trail (550m) there are views over Loch Maree and Slioch to the north, to Ben Wyvis in the east and Kintail in the south, but the jagged ridge of Beinn Eighe to the southwest is the most impressive. Here only plants which are adapted to harsh conditions can grow. These include

Beinn Eighe from the top of the Mountain Trail

Juniper, Alpine Bearberry, and Mountain Azalea as well as sedges and clubmosses.

Red Deer and Mountain Hares may be seen, as well as Golden Eagles and Ravens. Ptarmigan and Red Grouse are also present. Lower down the wooded Allt na h-Airidhe Gorge attracts woodland birds. Dippers hunt in the stream for insects and Great Spotted Woodpeckers may be seen or at least heard.

Visitor Centre The Reserve Visitor Centre near Kinlochewe has displays covering Beinn Eighe and Loch Maree, as well as an interesting bookshop and helpful staff. It also has an outside picnic area.

Iain Sarjeant

The triple buttresses of Coire Mhic Fhearchair, Beinn Eighe

Dipper

Laurie Campbell

Scottish Crossbill

Laurie Campbell

Crested Tit

Wildcat

Mature Scots Pine

Dwarf Cornel

Laurie Campbell

Laurie Campbell

285

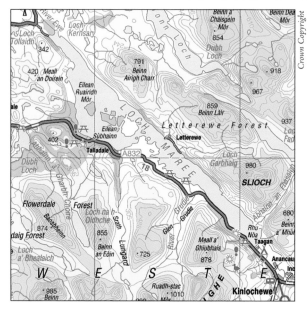

LOCH MAREE (G *Loch ma-Ruibh*, St Maelrubha's Loch) is one of the largest and most beautiful lochs in Scotland.

Kinlochewe is an ideal place to start any of several fine walks. A track goes up the valley of Abhainn Bruachaig to narrow sided Gleann Muice. Another follows the Kinlochewe River to the end of Loch Maree, past Oakwoods to Gleann Bianasdail and eventually to Loch Fada. One route up **Slioch** (G Spear, 980m) goes from this path.

Anancaun (G Ford of the Heads) is on the Kinlochewe River. After a battle between Clans MacKenzie and MacLeod the heads of the latter were tossed into the river, and became stuck in the ford.

Slattadale Forest has a car park and forest walks. There is a fine view back down the loch over the islands from a clearing north of the car park. The nearby Victoria Falls are named after the 1877 visit of the Queen.

Loch Maree Islands NNR includes the three large and about forty small islands in the loch. They hold ancient Scots Pine and mature Juniper, which have been protected from grazing.

Black-throated Divers nest on these islands. They can be heard frequently as they fly in with fish for their young. This is probably the best place in Scotland to observe them. They can be seen from the Loch Maree Hotel hide as well as places along the loch.

Ironworking using bog iron and wood charcoal has been carried out around Loch Maree since at least Pictish times. There were plentiful supplies of the raw materials in the area, which encouraged Sir George Hay to set up furnaces at Letterewe in 1607.

Wrought and cast iron were made here, and later at the Red Smiddy, Poolewe, in vast quantities until the trees in the vicinity had all been consumed. Iron ore was shipped in from England and it seems English workers were employed. The operations lasted for about 60 years.

Black-throated Divers nest on the islands

Old Scots Pine overlooking Loch Maree and Slioch

Tollie viewpoint At the north end of the loch, there are fine views from the A832 at Tollie. Nearby Tollie Bay is very picturesque with its deciduous woods.

The east side of Loch Maree can be accessed by a track which goes from Poolewe to Kernsary then eventually all the way to Kinlochewe via Letterewe and its old ironworks.

Tollie viewpoint near Poolewe

Osprey sometimes fish here

AIR CRASH

On 13th March 1951 a Lancaster bomber from RAF Kinloss crashed into the Triple Buttresses of Beinn Eighe in bad weather with the loss of all the crew. Because of the weather and location, it was several weeks until the bodies were retrieved.

As a result the RAF Mountain Rescue Unit was formed. The aircraft was blown up but not recovered and substantial pieces are scattered down the gully on the south side of the buttresses, including its Merlin engines, undercarriage and wing parts.

The fuselage section remains stuck near the top. It is inappropriate to remove any of this wreckage, which is a memorial to those who died here.

Laurie Campbell

Golden Eagles are regularly seen soaring while they search for prey around Loch Maree

ISLE MAREE, or Innis Maree, in contrast to the other islands, is wooded with ancient Oaks as well as Holly, Chestnut and other deciduous trees, suggesting that it is a pre-Christian religious site. The Wishing Tree, now dead, and studded with coins and nails driven into it for good luck, stands inside a small walled enclosure.

St Maelrubha is said to have built a chapel or cell on Isle Maree in the late 7th century, which was occupied by hermits for many years thereafter. Remains of the chapel and graveyard are inside this enclosure. It is here that the Viking prince and princess of the tragic tale are buried. Their graveslabs lie end to end at the centre of the island, one marked with an angular cross, the other with a rounded one.

The holy well is now dry but is still in existence near the shore. The waters were reputed to cure mental illness. The cure also involved rowing round the island three times in a clockwise direction and repeated immersion in the loch. Tradition does not record whether this worked.

Sacrifice of Bulls The sacrifice of bulls continued here until 1678, latterly in support of curing the insane. This tradition seems to be ancient and probably long pre-dates Christianity. In the Highlands cattle were, for thousands of years, the basis of the economy.

The sacrifice of a prime bull to their god would have been a highly symbolic offering. Early Christians were adept at taking over existing customs and superstitions, and perhaps Maelrubha did just this, except that henceforth the benefits of the sacrifice would work through the Christian God.

The Highlanders had a rite termed *taghairm*, where a seer or clairvoyant would don the hide of a newly sacrificed bull so that he might communicate with spirits to devine the future. This seems to have continued in some places into the 18th century. Doubtless the Church was very strongly opposed to such practices.

The Muc-sheilch is a monster which is said to live in Loch Maree (G *Muc*, pig; ON *selkie*, seal). Another such beast is said to live in Loch-na-Beiste (G Loch of the Beast) near Aultbea. An 1850 attempt to drain this loch was an expensive failure for a Mr Banks from Letterewe. There have been no recent reports of these elusive beasts.

White-tailed Eagles can be seen fishing here

Laurie Campbell

THE TRAGEDY OF ISLE MAREE

Olaf, a young Norse Prince, had a restless and ungovernable temper and if all did not go his way he lost all self control. He lived with his fighting men on his longship except during the winter, when they encamped on one of the islands of Loch Ewe.

It was natural for one so impulsive to fall head over heels in love - "We need not try to imagine the story of Olaf's love; it was no common attachment; the flame burned in his breast with an intensity becoming his fiery spirit." So that Prince Olaf might be near his bride a tower was built on the Isle of Maree for the lovers.

The crew kept sending messages to return to the ship but he could not tear himself away. Eventually an expedition was ready to start, so with a heavy heart he told the Princess he would have to leave. She was very upset, thinking he might be killed, while he was concerned something may cause her death.

Thus a plan was devised: "When the Prince should return, a white flag would be flown from his barge if all were well; if otherwise, a black one. The Princess was to leave the island in her barge whenever his boat should come into sight, and she was to display a white or black flag to denote her safety or the reverse."

The Prince set off, all ended well and the victorious galley

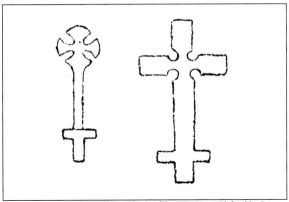

Graveslabs said to be of the Norse Prince Olaf and his Princess

returned to Poolewe. Half crazy with excitement he got on to his boat on Loch Maree and raised his white banner of success. During his absence the Princess had been extremely anxious.

Various doubts had passed through her head since his departure, not least, was he still alive? Did her Prince prefer the excitement of warfare to being at home with her? Did he still really love her? Had he ever loved her? Jealousy began to absorb the Princess completely and she devised a plan to test the Prince's love for her should he ever return.

At last Olaf's barge hove in sight with the white flag. Everything had been arranged to carry out her strange plan. The barge set sail on the Loch and the black flag was raised. The Princess lay on a bier and feigned death, with all her maidens pretending to be grieving around her.

Prince Olaf eventually caught

sight of the Princess's barge. Could he be mistaken? Was that the black flag of death, which waved above it? The Prince was frantic with despair. "His agony increased each moment; his manly face became like a maniac's; his words and gestures were those of a man possessed."

Before the vessels touched the Prince leapt aboard the barge. He saw the shroud; he raised it; he gazed a moment on the still, pale face of his bride; he gave one agonised cry; then he plunged his dirk into his own breast, and in a moment that storm-crazed heart ceased to beat! The Princess leapt up from the bier, convinced too late of her husband's passionate love; there he lay dead.

She drew the dirk from Olaf's heart and plunged it into her own. The bodies of the tragic pair were buried on the island; they were laid with their feet towards each other, and smooth stones with outlines of medieval crosses were placed over their graves.

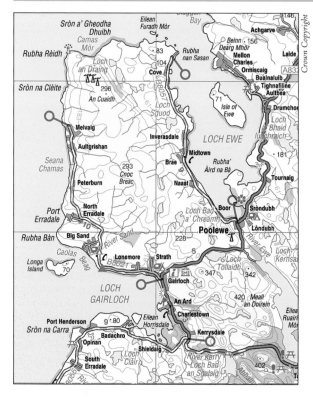

the area. In former times Cod and Haddock fishing was the main industry here. The fish were split, salted and dried for export to France and Spain.

The scenic A832 road from Slattadale to Gairloch follows the River Kerry and offers fine views to the Torridon mountains to the south. In Gairloch a viewpoint next to the golf course gives access to fine sandy beaches.

Gairloch Heritage Museum is in an old farm steading and tells the story of the area from the first people to the present. It has Neolithic and Bronze Age artifacts, as well as a broken Pictish symbol stone with a fish and part of an eagle inscribed on it.

Life on the croft, the school room, the village shop and an illicit whisky still are all illustrated. Also on display is the old lens from Rubha Reidh lighthouse, one of the largest in Scotland. Outside, old wooden fishing boats can be seen. The Museum has a small shop and a cafe.

GAIRLOCH (G *Gearr Loch*, Short Loch) until recent times looked to the sea for access to the external world. It offers much of what the West Highlands visitor expects and is an excellent base from which to explore the area.

The village consists of a series of little settlements nestling round the shore of the loch. Charlestown is the first to be reached by the road from Loch Maree, and the site of the harbour, which was once the main route in and out of

Gairloch from Lonemore with the Torridon Mountains in the background

Sunset over Big Sand with the Western Isles in the distance

The Harbour still has fishing boats which land prawns, crabs, and lobsters which may be available in local establishments. There are also boat trips in summer to see whales, dolphins, seals, and seabirds.

The Village offers a wide range of accommodation, places to eat and to shop. However, undoubtedly, its biggest asset is its location and its wonderful scenery. The interplay of changing light on the sea, sky and landscape around Gairloch is truly captivating.

Gairloch Beach with An Dun broch in the background

Gairloch's history includes Neolithic, Bronze Age and Iron Age people, as well as Picts, Vikings and Scots. All probably came originally by sea, attracted by the sheltered harbour, good fishing and fertile land on the sand dunes.

Big Sand is a wide sandy beach, backed by extensive dunes and links. It is sheltered

Gairloch Heritage Museum

Old bridge at Charlestown and the Old Inn in 1821 by William Daniell

291

The street above Strath Bay

Fishing boat unloading its catch of prawns

The harbour at Charlestown

Badachro

from the west by Longa Island, and is the site of an expansive and very fine campsite.

Rubha Reidh The road continues north from here to Melvaig and ultimately Rubha Reidh lighthouse. A path follows the cliffs from the lighthouse to the remote and enchanting beach at Camas Mor. The lighthouse was first lit in 1912, after a lengthy campaign dating back to 1853. The station was automated in 1986.

All along this road there are panoramic views to Skye and the Western Isles. About a mile before the lighthouse, a road leading to a radiomast offers an extra 275m of height at Maol Breac.

Kerrysdale to Redpoint Just south of Gairloch the B8056 crosses the River Kerry, eventually reaching Redpoint. This winding single track road is very scenic and offers fine views. It passes a series of lovely little bays, sheltered by small islands and lined with woods.

Badachro is perhaps the prettiest bay. In former times Cod was dried on the shingle beaches. The local inn is a great place to stop for a meal and to watch the boating activities in the bay.

Redpoint The road continues though a suddenly fertile crofting landscape with fields

Redpoint

Victorian postbox, Redpoint

of cattle and small farms. Dramatic vistas open up to the west at Opinan, where there is a fine sandy beach. The road ends at Redpoint car park, from where a path leads to a beach of red sand, backed by extensive dunes.

Redpoint itself hides another lovely south facing beach with an old fishing station. A path leads along the coast via a remote Youth Hostel at Craig, to Lower Diabaig in Torridon. There are fine views to Beinn Alligin and across Loch Torridon to the mountains beyond.

The relatively fertile soils and red sand here are derived from the Torridonian sandstone. Copious quantities of seaweed get washed up in the winter and have been used to fertilise the fields for millennia.

Just north of the car park at An Tarbh (64m) there are stunning views across to Skye and on a clear day across the Minch to the Western Isles.

Skye from near Redpoint

Gairloch from the viewpoint on the road to Poolewe

Rubha Reidh lighthouse was first lit in 1912

293

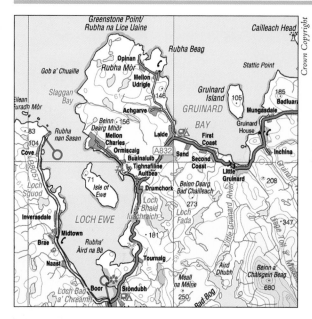

Poolewe Pictish Stone

until 1952 when she gifted them to the National Trust for Scotland in 1952, who maintain and continue to develop this enchanting place.

POOLEWE (ON *Bolstadir*, farm, Farm of Ewe) sits at the head of Loch Ewe where the short River Ewe enters the sea from Loch Maree. The name *Ewe* is ancient, but could refer to Yew trees, which have always been regarded as holy or, the Tree of Life.

Pictish Stone There is a Pictish symbol in the old graveyard near a ruined chapel. It is surrounded by iron railings. In contrast to Easter Ross, very few such stones have so far been found

in the west. There are several other interesting stones here, including a knocking stone, an unusual graveslab with uprights at each end and three military graves.

Inverewe Gardens were created by Osgood MacKenzie, who purchased the estate of Kernsary with help from his mother in 1862. From then until his death in 1922, he transformed a barren hillside into spectacular gardens and woodlands. His daughter, Mairi, continued his work

The mild climate and sheltered position have allowed the creation of a hugely diverse collection of plants from New Zealand, South America, China, Tasmania South Africa and the Himalayas. MacKenzie is said to have had Irish soil shipped in and doubtless used seaweed and sand from the bay.

He planted over 100 acres of woodland for shelter, mostly Scots Pine, but also including many other species, local and exotic. A network of paths leads through an amazing selection of garden themes, from the original kitchen garden to the many imported flowers, trees and shrubs.

A visit is worthwhile in any season, while May, June and July are perhaps the best months. There is a visitor centre and restaurant.

Poolewe Cemetery - hand quern

Poolewe Cemetery unusual gravestone

Camas Allt Eoin Thomais is a lovely little beach south of Cove

Cove Road The B8057 follows the west side of Loch Ewe to Cove. It passes through a crofting landscape and offers fine views across the loch to the mountains behind. There is a fine sandy beach, backed by dunes and machair at Firemore. Camas Allt Eoin Thomais a little further on is more intimate and sheltered.

Gille Dubh, according to folklore, was a fairy who dressed in leaves and moss and lived in the Birchwoods near Gairloch. Apparently this benevolent little creature was said to help people who were lost to find their way home, but he has not been encountered recently.

Firemore Beach on the road to Cove

Inverewe Gardens from Poolewe

Inverewe Gardens

Inverewe Gardens

295

WWII 6-inch coastal battery and Russian Convoy memorial

WWII anti-aircraft battery

LOCH EWE North from Inverewe there are fine views to the west and to the Isle of Ewe. **Aultbea** and **Mellon Charles** are pretty villages with small harbours and **Laide** has an ancient chapel said to date from the 6th century. Further north, **Mellon Udrigle** has very fine beach, Camas a'Charaig with white sands, impossibly green-blue sea sheltered by rocky headlands on both sides are backed by dunes. This is perhaps the most attractive seaside feature in Wester Ross.

Loch Ewe in WWII In 1939 the east coast ports of Rosyth and Invergordon were too vulnerable to air attack and Scapa Flow was not yet secure either. Loch Ewe and Loch Eriboll were thus selected as alternative anchorages. Extensive defences, including anti-aircraft, coastal batteries, a minefield and an anti-submarine boom were all eventually installed. The lack of preparation was underlined when *HMS Nelson* was severely damaged by a magnetic mine in December 1939.

Russian Convoys The main wartime use of Loch Ewe was as a refuelling base for escorts and as a rendezvous for ships taking part in the Arctic Convoys to Russia. The first of 19 left on 6 February 1942 and the last on 30 December 1944. Of 489 merchant ships that sailed from here only 16 were sunk, along with 5 escort vessels. Altogether over 100 merchant ships and nearly 60 naval vessels were lost on both sides. A NATO refuelling base is still operational near Aultbea.

USS William H Walsh was an American Liberty Ship which went aground on February 26 1944 south of Eilean Furaidh Mor. It was a total loss and only 12 survived out of a crew of 74. That this was the only such accident says much for the skills of the seamen. Two battered steel lifeboats can still be seen at Black Bay. But for the prompt action of local people no one would have survived.

Loch Ewe from above the NATO refuelling station, with Mellon Charles and Aultbea in the background

Gruinard Bay from the west

Gruinard Bay (ON *Grunna Fjordur*, Shallow Bay) runs in a wide sweep from Mellon Udrigle to Little Loch Broom. At its head a large area of sand is exposed at low tide. To the west the shore is shingly and is backed by a prominent raised beach. At the viewpoint above Little Gruinard a scramble to the top of the rise gives a much better view. Paths follow the Rivers Little Gruinard, Inverianvie and, Gruinard inland through forest and onto the moorland behind.

Gruinard Island was the site of one of the most bizarre and irresponsible military operations ever conducted. Fears that the Nazis or Japanese might use chemical or biological weapons led to the British research and trials.

In 1941 a canister of Anthrax spores was exploded on the island near a group of sheep which were secured in wooden frames. All died in a few days and they were dumped over a cliff and covered in rocks, but one drifted ashore and infected other sheep nearby.

For many years signs saying *Landing is Prohibited* were displayed but finally the MOD was shamed into action. In 1987 £0.5m was paid to decontaminate the ground with 280 tonnes of formaldehyde and to remove topsoil. Anthrax spores are extremely hardy and can survive for many years. Sheep seem to be able live on the island now, but it remains an object lesson in the arrogance of the military.

The head of Gruinard Bay from the east

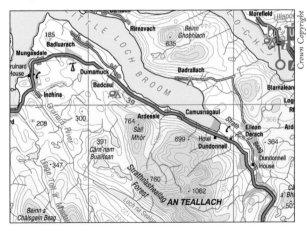

Crown Copyright

LITTLE LOCH BROOM is a long, narrow inlet north of Gruinard Bay. The road goes through wild and lonely country. The little community of Scoraig can only be reached by boat from Badluarach or by walking in from Badrallach.

Ardessie Falls can be reached from the Ardessie car park (NH053897) by a steep path which follows the Allt Airdeasaidh for about 1,500m. There are several small falls and interesting pools before the main water-fall. There are fine views down Little Loch Broom, while Sail Mhor (767m) looms to the southwest.

Dundonnell, at the head of the loch, has a large area of salt marsh which is ablaze with colourful flowers in May and June. The side road leading to Badrallach has fine views over the loch, An Teallach and over to Ullapool.

The Dundonnell River winds over Strath Beag and then further up it cascades down a narrow valley. From a viewpoint at 279m there are fine vistas down the valley and over to An Teallach. The mixed woodlands, meadows and riversides are also full of wild flowers in summer.

The Dundonnell Yew may be the second oldest tree in Scotland, perhaps 2,000 years old. This tree is in Dundonnell House gardens which are occasionally open to the public and has been cut back so that it is less irregular than most Yews. The gardens are very much worth visiting.

Birds The varied habitat makes this a satisfying place for birdwatchers. Golden Eagles and Buzzards quarter the moors, while Peregrines are often seen hunting small birds. The saltmarsh attracts many waders which may be observed from the road. The mixed woodland areas and the garden attract many species of passerine, as well as owls and, perhaps, a Merlin.

Little Loch Broom from the A832 above Durnamuck

Ardessie Falls with Sail Mhor in the background

Iain Sargeant

Looking southeast from Bidean a'Ghlas Thuill towards the Fannichs

Adam Ward

AN TEALLACH (G The Forge) is perhaps named for its mists rising like smoke from its heights. This ridge of high peaks, corries, buttresses and craigs dominates Little Loch Broom, but to appreciate its real splendour one needs to do some hiking as the spectacular main corrie is not visible from the road.

The mountain has nine peaks over 950m, the highest two being Sgurr Fiona (The Fair Peak) and Bidean a'Glas Thuill (G The Sharp Peak of the Hollow). An Teallach is composed of Torridonian Sandstone with a cap of Quartzite. Its ascent is outside the scope of this book.

Loch Toll an Lochain below the huge Corrie Toll is easily reached without any climbing experience. Paths go from Corrie Hallie and Dundonnell Village. The loch is situated at about 520m. The best time of day to go is early morning when the sun illuminates the corrie.

Glas Mheall Mor from Bidean a'Ghlas Thuill

Adam Ward

Sgurr Fiona from Toll an Lochain

Adam Ward

The Falls of Measach in Corrieshalloch Gorge

LOCH BROOM (G *bhraion*, Place of Rain Showers) is a long, narrow sea loch formed during the Ice Age. After the bleak moorland of the roads from Dundonnell or Garve suddenly the landscape suddenly becomes softer and greener with trees and some farms.

View down Loch Broom from the A832

Corrieshalloch (G *Coire Shalach*, Ugly Corry) has a fine waterfall, *Eisan na Miasaich*, (G Fall of the Place of Platters) or the Falls of Measach. This 61m deep box canyon is situated just south of Braemore, 12 miles east of Ullapool. The car park and access is off the A832 just after the junction with the

A835. The River Droma cascades 46m over these falls, which are most impressive after heavy rain or when snow is melting.

Well made footpaths allow walkers to explore this interesting site at will. The falls and gorge can be seen from a small suspension bridge which is situated directly over the waterfall. A path leads to a platform which juts out over the cliffs to give a dramatic view back up the gorge to the long narrow falls.

River Broom flows through the flat alluvial valley of Strath More. Its estuary has mudflats and a saltmarsh which are best viewed by taking the side road on the west side of the loch to Letters. This road passes several small settlements before ending at Blarnalearoch. There are fine views over Ullapool and Loch Broom from here.

Dun an Ruigh Ruaidh (NH149901) is built prominently against a cliff above Rhiroy. This C-shaped structure has been described as a proto-broch and dates from the 3rd or 2nd century BC. There is a central hearth and an upper floor which rested on the scarcement stones.

Dun an Ruigh Ruaidh is an unusual broch with one side straight

Much of the broch has been used to build a now abandoned sheep wash, but the remains of an intramural stairway and the characteristic double wall construction can be seen. The front wall must have been straight rather than round, but has completely gone.

Dun an Ruigh Ruaidh - part of the wall survives to nearly 2m

Dun Lagaidh (NH142914) is about a mile further on overlooking Loch Broom and Ullapool and can be reached via a track. In the Bronze Age a timber laced hillfort stood here. This was burnt c.700BC as shown by the vitrified stones.

Dun Lagaidh with Loch Broom and Ullapool in the background

Around the 1st century BC a round dun was built on the eastern end of the fort. Later, in the 12th century, the dun was used to make a small castle and bailey. Lime mortar was used to strengthen the structure.

Dun Lagaidh is in a very good defensive site above Loch Broom

Loch Broom from Ardcharnich with Ullapool in the background

Leckmelm Arboretum (G *Leac Mailm*, Gravestone of Mailm) is a Victorian Arboretum planted in the 1870s, 3 miles southeast of Ullapool. After being abandoned for many years it is now being tended again. The Victorians collected trees and shrubs from temperate zones all around the world. This garden has a good selection of such plants. It is best visited in early summer for foliage and flowers and in autumn for colours. The garden has many very large mature trees and flowering shrubs with paths winding through. The place has a romantic, fairytale feeling.

Battle of Leckmelm In the 1580s clan warfare was frequent and brutal. In 1586 the Gunns defeated the MacKays at the Battle of Allt Camhna near Auldgown in Caithness. It was said that the Clan Gunn killed 1,400 Caithnessmen, including Captain Henry Sinclair, and that only nightfall saved the rest. Soon afterwards the Gunns took their revenge. This time the Sutherlands and Mackays triumphed.

"The Sutherland-men, under command of William Sutherland, grandson of Alexander the heir, were joined by Niel MacKay and his clan, together with James Macleod, chieftain of the Slight-ean-Voir and the MacLeods of his tribe. The Gunns took the alarm, and fled towards the Western Isles; but as they were on their journey thither, James Mack-Rory (Macleod) and Niel Mack-ean-Mack-William, rencountered with them at Lochbroom, at a place called Leckmelm, where after a sharp skirmish, the Clan Gunn were overthrown, and most of their company slain."

Leckmelm Arboretum is a tranquil place

Hector was an old Dutch cargo or *Boot* ship of about 200 tons and 110ft in length. This old 3 masted ship was pressed into service and used to take emigrants to Nova Scotia. A Scottish minister, John Witherspoon and his partner, John Pagan, bought 200,000 acres of land at Pictou from the Philadelphia Land Grant Company.

A notice in *The Edinburgh Advertiser* offering free land, provisions for a year and passage resulted in great interest in the prospect of a new life in the New World. In July 1773 she sailed from Loch Broom for Pictou in Nova Scotia with 207 people on board. Sadly, during the 11 week voyage, 18 passengers, mostly children, died of smallpox.

Loch Broom on a peaceful summer day from south of Leckmelm

After a stormy voyage the Hector arrived at Pictou Harbour on 15th September. The food and accommodation on board were not good, but the emigrants soon found their new lives much better than at home. This was the start of mass emigration from the Highlands and Islands of Scotland.

Loch Broom in 1821 by William Daniell

Loch Broom from the Stornoway ferry

A replica of the *Hector*, which was launched in 2000, is the centrepiece of *The Hector Heritage Quay Experience*. An Interpretative Centre working blacksmith shop, rigger's shop, carpentry shop, resident artist's studio and, The Ship Hector Company Store complete Pictou's waterfront visitor attraction.

Ullapool from Braes

ULLAPOOL (N *Ulli Bolstadir*, Ulli's Stead) is situated on a sheltered headland near the mouth of Loch Broom. The approach from the east on the A835 gives fine views of the village, with the white washed houses of Shore Street curving round the bay.

This attractive spot has probably been inhabited for thousands of years. Perhaps the oldest building is the roofless Catholic Chapel in the graveyard which may have associations with St Maelrubha. Ullapool is marked on a 1596 map, while a 1775 plan shows over 20 buildings, roads and a mill, but no pier.

The village was planned by the British Fisheries Society, which built the infrastructure needed for the Herring fishing and laid out the grid pattern of the streets. Buildings included the pier and the Customs House (to store salt). Houses were then built on plots by the villagers themselves.

Ullapool is the main centre in the northwest. The harbour is the centre of activity, with fishing boats, the Stornoway ferry, tour boats and yachts coming and going. In summer this is a busy little town, yet it never loses its charm despite the crowds. Out of season, especially on a fine autumn day, it is especially appealing.

Ullapool Museum is based in a former Parliamentary Church designed by Thomas Telford and built in 1829. It *"tells the story of Lochbroom - the land and its people, through a blend of traditional and multimedia displays."*

There are displays on wildlife, the emigrants on the *Hector*, Ullapool's bicentenary and a special old-fashioned schoolroom. A large archive of documents and photographs is available to be consulted including much of interest to genealogists.

Herring Fishing Loch Broom was famous for the abundance of Herring, which

Shore Street, Ullapool from the Stornoway ferry

were so numerous that they were used to fertilize the land. In 1698 Sir George MacKenzie of Tarbat set up a small fishing station on the Loch to process and export salt Herring.

However, it was to be nearly 100 years before the west coast fishery really got underway. The British Fisheries Society developed Ullapool, Tobermory on Mull and Lochbay on Skye to encourage the development of a west coast fishery. The eventual result was over exploitation and a collapse in catches.

In WWII many east coast boats fished from here. Later, in the 1960s, Norwegian klondykers arrived every year to buy Herring to process for export. In the 1970s and 80s Eastern European factory ships came in substantial numbers to buy and process Herring and Mackerel.

Although the klondykers no longer come, local fishing boats catch prawns with creels. Lobsters, crabs and

Shore Street reflections from Braes

Scallops are also landed. All may found be on local menus. Fish is still landed at Lochinver and Kinlochbervie in Sutherland, but nowadays it is Scrabster in Caithness that is the biggest northern fishing port.

Boat Trips to the Summer Isles are run from the pier during the season. Seals, Dolphins, Porpoises, Minke Whales and many species of seabirds may be seen. A visit to Tanera Mor, which is still inhabited, is the climax of the cruise.

Boats are often pulled up on the shingly shore

The Town Clock

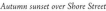

Autumn sunset over Shore Street

The Old Custom House and Shore Street

Ullapool from Morefield to the west of the village

views of the village.

Rhue and Ardmair Park at the sign for Rhue and head down the road to the lighthouse at Rubha Cadail. There are fine views over the Minch and Coigach from Meall Mhor (165m). Cul a Bhogha at Ardmair is a lovely shingly beach with some sand. Round the sheltering spit is the anchorage of Loch Kanaird.

Loch Achall A track runs up the Ullapool River from the bridge at Morefield. This follows the river to Loch Achall. Suddenly Ullapool seems many miles away. For a longer walk keep on the track to East Rhidorroch Lodge, then follow a path through Strath Nimhe which reaches the main road near Leckmelm.

Isle Martin lies just off Ardmair. It is unknown who Martin was, but an ancient graveslab, marked with a triple cross stands in the graveyard and is said to be his. In 1775 John Woodhouse from Liverpool set up a Herring curing station here. The fishing was very good but had collapsed by 1813. Today the island is owned by the Isle

Martin Trust and it is unpopulated, except by birds and seals. In summer a small ferry runs to the island from Ardmair.

Walks The Ullapool area offers many fine walks, some of which are signposted from the village. The Braes of Ullapool have several paths from which there are fine

Cula Bhogha beach. Ardmair

Summer sunset over Ullapool and Loch Broom from Braes

Loch Kanaird at Ardmair

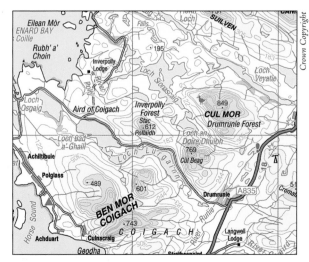

Polly just to the north. Its summit is only 500m above the car park via a very clear path. The views from the top more than repay the effort.

Inverpolly Special Area of Conservation is spread out before you. It covers the ground west of the A835, the Coigach lochs and ends at the Sutherland border. Loch Sionascaig is 3 miles long, but has a coastline of 17 miles.

Ben Mor Coigach (743m) is most easily climbed from Culnacraig, at the end of the Achiltibuie road. The route is steep and rocky and leads to a long summit ridge with dramatic northern cliffs.

Walks Before the road to Achiltibuie was built, access was by sea from Ullapool, or by taking the path from Strath Kanaird to Culnacraig. This 5-mile coastal route makes a fine walk, but is extremely rough in places. The postman used to do this every day!

COIGACH (G *na Coig Achaidhean*, The Five Ach's), the mountainous peninsula north of Loch Broom was divided into Coig's, or fifths. It is accessed by a single track road that winds its way to Achiltibuie, or north to Lochinver. The road follows Lochs Lurgainn, Bad a'Ghaill and Osgaig, and offers many fine views of Cul Beag (769m), Stac Pollaidh (613m) and the huge mass of Ben Mor Coigach (743m).

None of these mountains are very high, but all are individually impressive. This is a quite inspir-ing and magnificent landscape. Though now all clothed in grass, the valleys and lower slopes were formerly covered in Pine and Oak woods.

Geology Coigach consists of Torridonian Sandstone, which overlies much more ancient, hummocky Lewisian Gneiss. Only Cul Mor has a cap of Cambrian Quartzite. The mountains overlook a landscape of rocks, bogs and lochs, big and small.

Stac Pollaidh (613m) may take its name from the River

Former Times Today, apart from Achiltibuie, Coigach is almost devoid of people, but

Stac Pollaidh (613m) from the road

Suilven (731m) and Cul Mor (849m) from Stac Pollaidh (613m)

in 1841 4,500 people lived here. Most emigrated to the New World after the clearances.

For many centuries this area was famous for its black cattle, but today the lush grassland lies ungrazed except by a few Red Deer or sheep. The former Coigach Forest has also gone, its last remnant allegedly burnt by Hanoverian thugs in 1747.

Wildlife Ravens, Ring Ouzels, Red Grouse and Ptarmigan nest in the hills.

Loch Lurgainn looking west from below Stac Pollaidh

Buzzards, Golden and White-tailed Eagles soar overhead and the lochs are the haunt of Black-throated Divers. Corncrakes are still sometimes heard in the croft meadows of Achiltibuie. The high tops are home to many Alpine plant species.

Cul Beag from Stac Pollaidh

Stac Pollaidh from the northwest

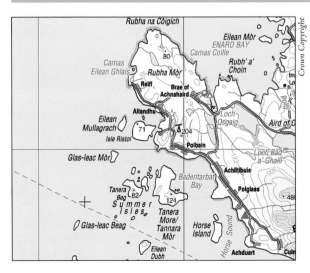

Crown Copyright

The **Hydroponicum** was set up in the 1980s to supply fresh vegetables to the nearby hotel. A wide selection of plants are grown in water without soil. There is a shop selling hydroponics equipment and information as well as a cafe. A variety of solar panels, chargers and solar-powered toys are on sale.

Beaches Achnahaird Bay is long and narrow, with a vast expanse of reddish sand at low tide. It is backed by dunes and machair, with extensive salt-marsh at its head. **Garvie Bay** is a lovely isolated cove, while **Reiff** faces southwest and is more rocky.

ACHILTIBUIE is a remote crofting and fishing township on the west side of Coigach peninsula. *"There is a marvellous amount of nothing to do in Achiltibuie"*, says the brochure of the Summer Isles Hotel.

This is a place to be savoured by those who appreciate how the west of Scotland used to be. It offers much to those who appreciate outdoor pursuits, whether energetic or more leisurely.

Archaeology Polglass Broch NC029069 is on a small rise just above the shore. The walls are still about 2m high but it has been used as a quarry for the ruined cottages built into it. In former times the nearby marshland was a loch.

Walks and Views The low coastline and tranquil coastline here offers many pleasant walks. The area also has several trails for more serious hikers. There are fine views from many places. These

The Summer Isles from above Ardmair

Tomatoes growing in the Hydroponicum

Polglass broch

View south over Tanera Mor and Loch Broom to An Teallach and Torridon

include south over the Summer Isles and Loch Broom to An Teallach and the Torridon Mountains, or north over Inverpolly to Suilven and Cul Mor.

Summer Isles Smokehouse is well worth a visit to observe the process of Salmon curing and smoking as well as to purchase some of their wide range of produce.

Summer Isles (G *Samhraidh*, Summer) This group of small islands is just off the coast of Achiltibuie. **Tanera Mor** (ON *Hafna-ey*, Harbour Isle) is inhabited with a cafe and issues its own stamps. There are holiday lets and a sailing school on the island. Boat trips are run to these magical islands in the summer.

The island was the site of a Herring station in the late 18th and early 19th centuries, The naturalist Frank Fraser Darling lived here 1939-1943 and it is the location for his book *Island Years*.

Sunset over Tanera Mor

Achnahaird Bay

Suilven from near Altandhu

Debby Snook

Crown Copyright

Colourful lichens abound

KNOCKAN CRAG (G *Creag a' Chnocain*, Crag of the Small Hill), is 13 miles north of Ullapool on the A835. This site is famous for its geology as it formed part of the scientific debate about what is now called the **Moine Thrust**, where older rocks are thrust horizontally over newer ones.

A combination of rock art, rock trails and a rock room, as well as extracts from poems by Norman McCaig give an alternative narrative of Scotland's geological past. The rock art pieces and poetry stones give an alternative view of the site.

The Rock Room is open-sided and explains the landscape by means of hands on models, touch screen computers, comic strips and a rock show. Although aimed at children, adults will find that it is in fact very informative.

Rock Trails Three Rock Trails allow visitors to explore the Crag. The short and easy Quarry Trail takes only 20 minutes and involves no climbing. The Thrust Trail takes about half an hour. It shows how older rocks overly younger strata in the Moine Thrust.

The Crag Top Trail continues from here to the top of Knockan Crag (386m) from where there are excellent views north to Assynt and west over Lochan an Ais to Cul Mor and Stac Pollaidh in Coigach. The path continues along the ridge, with fine views over Loch Broom and south to Torridon before returning to the car park. This takes at least an hour, more if the vistas are to be savoured.

Rocks Knockan Crag illustrates the succession of rocks

Knockan Crag is a cross section of the Moine Thrust

Suilven and Ben More Assynt from the top of Knockan Crag

Lochan an Ais, Cul Beag, Stac Pollaidh and Cul Mor from the top of the Crag

discussed by geologists. It is a section cut through the underlying younger Cambrian limestone strata up into the older rocks of the Moine Thrust. From the bottom first is Pipe Rock, followed by Fucoid Beds, Salterella and then Durness Limestone, overlain by much older Moine Schist.

The interface of the Thrust itself is very sharply defined, although the rocks above and below it were heavily shattered by shearing forces as the Moine Schist was pushed northwestwards over younger rocks.

The Moine Thrust showing Moine Schist on top of Cambrian Limestone

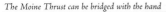

The Moine Thrust can be bridged with the hand

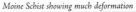

Moine Schist showing much deformation

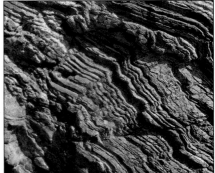

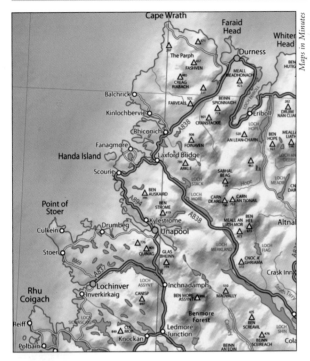

Maps in Minutes

The west coast of Sutherland runs from Loch Kirkaig to Cape Wrath. These *Lonely Lands* have some of the most spectacular scenery in the whole of Britain. Although the mountains here are not as high as those further south, their individual splendour is striking.

This is a starkly beautiful landscape of ancient rocks, lochs, sea lochs and islands lovely on a fine day, but dour when the weather is bad. Most of the roads are single track and require care, but they also force you to slow down and afford a new vista around every turn.

Geology Most of the area has been designated as the North West Highlands Geopark, whose eastern boundary roughly follows the Moine Thrust from east of Loch Eriboll south to Ben More Assynt. Coigach and the Summer Isles, to the south, are also included.

Much of the landscape is composed of ancient Lewisian Gneiss, but this is overlain by Torridonian Sandstone in several places. The mountains of Suilven, Canisp and Quinag are examples, as is the Stoer Peninsula, Handa Island and much of the Parph Peninsula.

Outcrops of limestone at Durness, Inchnadamph and Elphin are lush in comparison to most of the area. Many of the mountains are capped with Cambrian Quartzite,

Shona McMillan

Sandwood Bay is reputed to be the home of a mermaid

Loch Borralan with Suilven (731m) and Canisp (846m)

which gleams in the sunshine, especially when wet.

This complex geology combined with the relatively mild climate leads to a hugely diverse range of habitats, making it a compelling place for naturalists to visit. There are many localities where one can spend the entire day without seeing anyone, or any sign of human habitation.

The changeability of the weather creates enchanting and variable light at all times of year. To see the wild flowers and breeding birds the best time to visit is early summer. Snow rarely lingers long near the coast, but when it falls the landscape is transformed.

Shona McMillan

Suilven (731m) is an imposing lump of Torridonian Sandstone

Loch Assynt

Kylesku Bridge

Handa Island has 120m sandstone cliffs

Puffins can be seen on Handa Island

Laurie Campbell

317

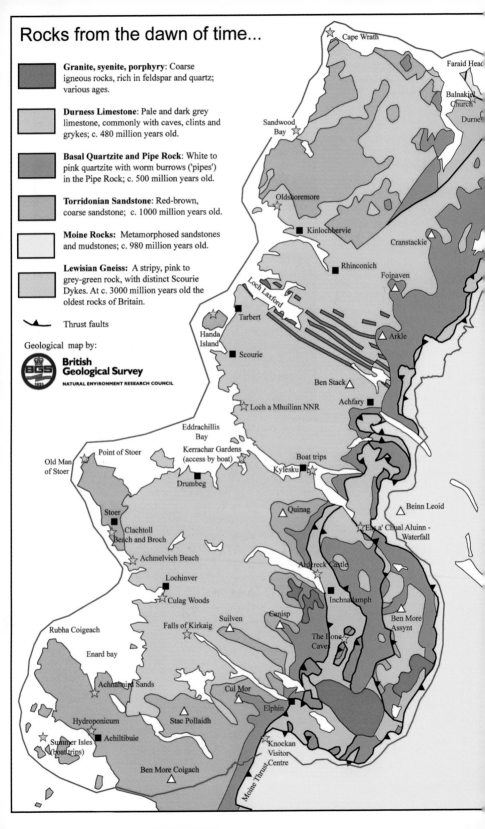

Rocks from the dawn of time...

Granite, syenite, porphyry: Coarse igneous rocks, rich in feldspar and quartz; various ages.

Durness Limestone: Pale and dark grey limestone, commonly with caves, clints and grykes; c. 480 million years old.

Basal Quartzite and Pipe Rock: White to pink quartzite with worm burrows ('pipes') in the Pipe Rock; c. 500 million years old.

Torridonian Sandstone: Red-brown, coarse sandstone; c. 1000 million years old.

Moine Rocks: Metamorphosed sandstones and mudstones; c. 980 million years old.

Lewisian Gneiss: A stripy, pink to grey-green rock, with distinct Scourie Dykes. At c. 3000 million years old the oldest rocks of Britain.

Thrust faults

Geological map by:

British Geological Survey
NATURAL ENVIRONMENT RESEARCH COUNCIL

Cape Wrath
Faraid Head
Balnakiel Church
Durness
Sandwood Bay
Oldshoremore
Kinlochbervie
Cranstackie
Rhiconich
Foinaven
Loch Laxford
Tarbert
Handa Island
Scourie
Arkle
Ben Stack
Achfary
Loch a Mhuilinn NNR
Eddrachillis Bay
Kerrachar Gardens (access by boat)
Boat trips
Point of Stoer
Kylesku
Old Man of Stoer
Drumbeg
Quinag
Beinn Leod
Stoer
Eas a' Chual Aluinn - Waterfall
Clachtoll Beach and Broch
Ardvreck Castle
Achmelvich Beach
Lochinver
Culag Woods
Inchnadamph
Ben More Assynt
Suilven
Canisp
Rubha Coigeach
Falls of Kirkaig
The Bone Caves
Enard bay
Achnahaird Sands
Cul Mor
Hydroponicum
Elphin
Achiltibuie
Stac Pollaidh
Summer Isles (boat trips)
Knockan Visitor Centre
Ben More Coigach
Moine Thrust

North West Highlands GEOPARK

Iar-Thuath na Gàidhealtachd

We hope you enjoyed your visit

Mar sin Leibh, an dòchas gun do chòrd ur turas ribh

"A Moving Story - Landscapes like these mark the memory and that is due to the difference that geology makes. Over billions of years the continents have drifted around the earth. 500 million years ago Scotland was separated from England and Wales by the ancient Iapetus Ocean. For most of the last billion years, Scotland was joined to America and Greenland. They only became separate a mere 60 million years ago when the North Atlantic began to form.

Over billions of years' the rocks that now make up the North West Highlands have seen many climates - hot deserts, tropical humidity and several Ice Ages. About 430 million years ago two ancient continents collided creating the British Isles as we know it today - give or take the impact of a few million years of Ice Age. This was the great crunch which created many of the distinctive Scottish mountains.

During this time huge sheets of rock were pushed up to 100km to the west, creating the Moine Thrust. This feature confused Victorian geologists who expected to find younger rocks on top of older ones . Instead they found the opposite.

This story can be read in the landscape around you. In the Geopark there is information and interpretation to help you recognize this geological legacy which can be seen in the mountains, from the roadsides, down at the beach, out fishing, in the townships and - at all times - under your feet.

A Geopark is a place where you will experience the incredible legacy left by an extraordinary geological past. Our mountains and coasts, our flora and fauna, our communities and culture - all owe a great deal to the difference which this geology makes. Our Geopark is one of 32 partners in the European Geopark Network. Globally there are 55 Geoparks - all endorsed by UNESCO.

Like ours they are all driven by local communities seeking to celebrate their geological heritage and achieve sustainable development. The North West Highlands Geopark has beautiful scenery, strong communities and world-class geology. We hope that you enjoy all that our Geopark has to offer.

North West Highlands Geopark became Scotland's first Geopark in 2004."

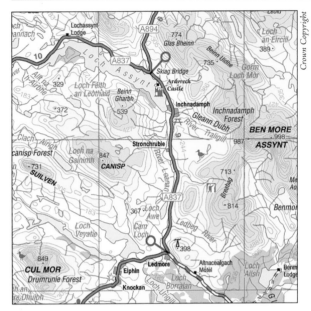

Loch Assynt is 16 miles long, and 80m deep. It is overlooked by the brooding masses of Quinag, Glas Beinn and Ben More Assynt, while Suilven and Canisp dominate the southern horizon. The surrounding moorland is mostly bare and rocky, but in former times it was heavily forested. The small islands on the loch show what protection from grazing can do.

Ardvreck Castle stands at the south end of Loch Assynt. Now a gaunt ruin, it dates from the late 15th century, and was the seat of the MacLeods of Assynt. It was a tower house, at least three storeys high. The circular, corbelled section enclosed the staircase while the vaulted basement probably held the kitchen, storerooms and dungeons.

Neil MacLeod gained notoriety for the kidnap and imprisonment (by his wife, Christine) of the Marquis of Montrose after the Battle of Carbisdale in 1650. Montrose was one of the more colourful characters in Scottish history and a staunch Royalist. MacLeod received £20,000 and 400 bolls of sour meal from the government.

Montrose was lashed backwards to his horse and taken to Edinburgh where he was found guilty of treason. Before being executed in the Grassmarket, he made a most eloquent speech, which ended in *"God have mercy on this afflicted land!"*

ASSYNT (ON *Ass*, big rocky ridge) stretches from Elphin in the south to Kylesku in the north. It is a somewhat severe landscape of rolling rocky moorland with many lochs, all dominated by several unique mountains. In contrast, the Limestone at Elphin and Inchnadamph creates a softer, greener landscape. The coast is mostly low and rocky, with many big sea lochs, but also several fine sandy beaches.

Elphin and Cam Loch
Elphin is a sudden patch of verdant grass, caused by the outcrop of Limestone. A chambered cairn attests to ancient inhabitants. Crofts, animals and modern houses dot the landscape. Further on there are classic views of Suilven and Canisp over the Cam Loch. There are two more prominent cairns at Ledmore and Ledbeg.

Elphin - an oasis of green due to the underlying Limestone rocks

Loch Assynt from near Calda House, with Ardvreck Castle and Quinag in the background

There were constant disputes within Clan MacLeod and with Clan MacKenzie from Wester Ross. After a siege in 1672 the castle was abandoned, and the MacKenzies ousted the MacLeods by buying up their debts. The last inhabitants were a pair of Ospreys in the 19th century.

Ardvreck Castle - site of the kidnap of Montrose in 1650

Calda House was built in 1726 and burnt down 11 years later

Calda House was built in 1726, using stone from the castle by the MacKenzies, and must have been very impressive in its time. It had 14 rooms, each with a fireplace, and a huge central chimney, which collapsed a few years ago. During clan fighting the house was burnt down in 1737 and never rebuilt. The MacKenzie estates were made bankrupt in 1739 and in 1757 the Sutherland Estate finally succeeded in ousting them by buying up their lands.

Adam Ward

Looking north from Conival to Na Tuadhan and Coire na Mhadaidh

Ben More Assynt (998m) and **Conival** (987m) are the highest peaks in the district. Only the great western bulk of Conival is visible from the road. Both are capped by Cambrian Quartzite, grey on a dull day but bright in the sun. The ascent is normally made from Inchnadamph Hotel, but it is a serious expedition of 11 miles and 1,750m of ascent.

Suilven (ON *Sula*, Pillar Rock G *Bheinn*, mountain, 731m) is perhaps Scotland's most iconic mountain, though far from its highest. It towers over its surrounding moorland and lochs, yet is a relatively easy climb, either from Inverkirkaig or from the north via Glencanisp Lodge near Lochinver. Both routes involve long walks.

Canisp (ON White Mountain, 846m) is to the northeast of Suilven and stands isolated 691m above its surrounding wilderness. The view from the top is regarded as being one of the best in Scotland, and which repays the long trek in from the Cam Loch, Loch Awe or Lochinver.

Inchnadamph NNR is something of a paradise for geologists and botanists. The former come to study the complex rock formations of the Moine Thrust, while the latter are attracted by the amazing diversity of plants which grow on the limestone outcrops in this area. Even people with little knowledge of geology or botany cannot fail to notice the landforms and diversity of plant life.

Many alpine species grow here at low altitudes, including Mountain Avens, Purple Saxifrage, Yellow Saxifrage, Moss Campion and Alpine Meadow-rue. Several rare sedges, ferns, mosses and bryophytes are also present.

Suilven and the Cam Loch

RAF wreckage Ben More Assynt

Adam Ward

Adam Ward

Suilven from Stac Pollaidh, Loch Sionascaig and Inverpolly in foreground

Elphin graveyard

Geologists The Victorian geologists, Peach and Horne, based themselves at the Inchnadamph Hotel when they were surveying the area. They worked together for 40 years. Their meticulous field mapping was to lead to the then spectacular explanation of the Moine Thrust, which led eventually to an understanding of plate tectonics.

Mountain Avens

Yellow Saxifrage

Roadside Geology Roadside cuttings on the A837 between Inchnadamph and Lochinver offer good exposures of the various rock types. At NC213251 Torridonian Sandstone lies on top of Lewisian Gneiss. The former is 800 million years old and the latter at least 2,000Ma, an unconformity of at least 2,000 million years.

At least 600m of Torridonian Sandstone stretches nearly to the southern summit of Quinag from here, but the top is of white Cambrian Quartzite, another unconformity representing a 250 million year long gap.

Loch Assynt from Glas Beinn

Adam Ward

Quinag from the A894

SUTHERLAND - THE FAR NORTHWEST

Loch Assynt from the A837 with Quinag in the background

Quartzite outcrops in several places near Skiag Bridge. The road cuttings at NC232246 and NC232246 expose light coloured Quartzite filled with vertical fossil worm burrows - known as Pipe Rock. In a cutting near Ardvreck Castle this rock is overlain by Fucoid Beds, which in turn lie below Salterella Grit.

Durness Limestone overlies all of these. The crags at Stronchrubie on the roadside at Inchnadamph expose strata which span many millions of years. To the west lies the unaltered foreland, while to the east these rocks are jumbled up by the various thrusts, which took place around 430 million years ago.

Inchnadamph Bone Caves
The four Bone Caves near Inchnadamph face north from the foot of the limestone Creag nan Uamh overlooking Allt nan Uamh burn (NC268171). Excavations revealed many animal and some human bones. The remains of four people date to about 2600BC.

Many bits of Reindeer antler were found which date from 8,000 to 47,000 years ago. Bones from at least 22 other species were also present, including arctic species such as Polar Bear from 18,000 years ago, Arctic Fox, Brown Bear, Wolf, rodents and Lynx.

The bones may have been washed there by glacial meltwater or taken there by ani-

The Bone Caves are half way up a steep hillside

The Bone Caves are quite large inside

The entrance to one of the Bone Caves

Neolithic chambered cairns, absent from Wester Ross, occur in a cluster in Assynt. At least a dozen are strung out near the road between Elphin and Skiag Bridge. There is a further cluster near the head of Glen Oykel near Loch Ailsh and next to Loch Borralan.

These cairns are all ruinous and none are formally present-ed for public viewing. Their presence suggests a substantial population in Neolithic times. Doubtless this is due to the limestone outcrops in this part of Assynt which give rise to fertile soils and rich grassland. So far there is very little other evidence from these times. Perhaps the abundance of timber meant that most structures were wooden.

mals, or both. There is no evidence of human habitation. Reindeer formerly gathered to calf on the slopes of Breabag. Reindeer Cave and Bone Cave are connected by a narrow passage which children can crawl through.

The caves are a little over 1 mile along a track from a signposted car park itself about 4 miles north of Ledmore Junction. Great care should be taken on the paths leading up to the caves.

Along the burn there is much of botanical interest, including an intriguing spring about half way. Dippers and Grey Wagtail frequent the burn, while Buzzards and Golden Eagles can often be seen soaring above the crags.

The cave system here has been extensively explored from a large sink hole on the northeast shoulder of Beinn an Fhuarain. A path goes from the caves to the site. It is dangerous to enter such cave systems without suitable knowledge, experience and equipment.

Ledbeg chambered cairn

Ledmore chambered cairn

Loch Assynt road cutting - be aware of fast traffic and remember to park safely

Loch Assynt islands and Canisp from the A837

Crown Copyright

Adam Ward

View northeast from Quinag showing the Moine Thrust

QUINAG (G *Chuineag,* milking pail) is a large mountain (808m), which dominates the landscape all around it. Perhaps the most striking view is from the road north of the Kylesku Bridge. The mountain is composed of Torridonian Sandstone and the high peaks are topped by Cambrian Quartzite.

Loch Glencoul The flanks of Ben Aird da Loch on the north side of Loch Glencoul very clearly show where older rocks were thrust over newer ones in the Moine and Glencoul Thrusts. There are several good view points along the road south of Kylesku.

Kylesku Bridge is an elegant curved structure which crosses the Caolas Cumhann. It is of pre-stressed box girder construction with a span of 275m and a height of 24m and was opened in 1984. It replaced a small ferry and greatly improved access to the far northwest.

Eas a' Chual Aluinn (200m) and Eas an't Strutha Ghil (290m) are the highest waterfalls in Britain. They cascade into Loch Beag at the head of Loch Glencoul and are at their best after there has been a lot of rain. Boat trips run in summer from Kylesku. It can also be reached on foot from south

of Loch na Gainmhich, about 3 miles south of Kylesku.

Kylesku is an attractive little village just off the main road, south of the bridge. It has a pier from which boat trips are run in the summer to the Kerrachar Gardens and to the waterfalls. These afford a good chance to see wildlife such as seals, Otters or Golden Eagles.

Maryck Memories of Childhood has an exhibition of dolls, teddies, dolls houses and other toys dating from 1880 to the present. There is also a play corner for children, tea room, and crafts.

Quinag from Kylestrome in 1821 by William Daniell

Waterfall on Glendhu

Maryck Memories, Kylesku

Adam Ward

Sunset from the top of Quinag

The hotel is very popular due to its excellent food and extensive menu serving much local seafood. The area immediately next to Kylesku offers short strolls with fine views of the bridge which crosses the Caolas Cumhann Narrows and over Glencoul to the Moine Thrust planes.

Adam Ward

Quinag

Kylestrome, just north of the bridge, is an attractive place and explore. Otters are often seen in the gloaming along this shore. A two mile path leads to the waterfalls at the Maldie Burn, not so high as the more famous ones, but much easier to reach and to view. There are good views of the Moine Thrust from here.

Moine Thrust planes on Ben Aird da Loch

Loch Glendhu from Kylesku

X-craft Memorial The XIIth Submarine Flotilla operated out of Lochs Glendhu and Glencoul from 1943. X-craft miniature submarine crews trained here before going to Norway where they succeeded in disabling the German battleship *Tirpitz*. The memorial north of the bridge honours the 39 men who died as well as the local people *"who knew so much and talked so little."*

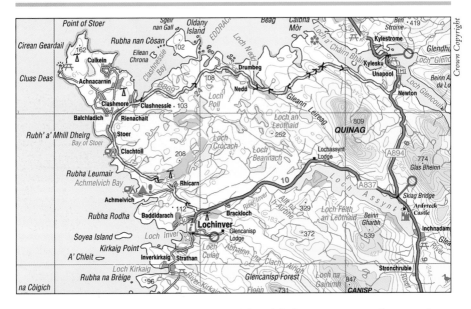

Lochinver is the only large village in Assynt, and owes its prosperity to its excellent harbour. Fishing boats land their catches of whitefish and shellfish here for shipment south. The imposing sugar loaf of Suilven, and neighbouring Canisp, provide a magnificent backdrop to the village.

Perhaps the best views are from the side road going west from the bridge at the north end of the street. A rocky knoll near the pottery is a good place from which to admire the scene.

Lochinver from above the kirkyard

Inverkirkaig

Lochinver offers a wide range of services including accommodation, eating out, fuel and shops. The Assynt Visitor Centre has displays on the area, tourist information and books for sale. It is also the base for the Highland Council Ranger Service in Assynt, which organises walks and events all year. There is also a reference library for information on wildlife, geology and local history.

Lochinver Larder is a culinary delight, offering delicious pies, with savoury, vegetarian

Falls of Kirkaig

Lochinver and Suilven in 1821 by William Daniell

and dessert fillings. Additionally a full menu is available.

Michael Winner enthused after a visit here, "*I had steak and ale pie and a chicken, cheese and potato one. Both absolutely tiptop. We eat in a large room overlooking the loch, an old church, wonderful scenery. Then I chose a chocolate fudge cake and a vanilla fudge cake. Totally, absolutely, incredibly historic.*"

Culag Woods cover the headland on the south side of Lochinver. It is a mixture of native and planted trees covering 36ha. Paths are laid out through the woods and there is a woodland play area for children. Strange wooden sculptures lurk in among trees. The marshy area is attractive to dragonflies.

Live pictures can be seen during the breeding season at the Assynt Visitor Centre of the 30 or more pairs of Herons which nest in the trees. Pictures from other nests such as Tawny Owl, Blue Tit and House Sparrow may also be on display.

Over 100 species of wild flowers grow here, along with a wide variety of lichens and mosses, which thrive in the moist, clean air. In the early morning or late evening an Otter or Pine Marten might be glimpsed.

Kirkaig (ON *Kirkju-Vagr*, Church Bay) is about 2 miles south of Lochinver on the single track road that goes to Aird of Coigach. The River Kirkaig reaches the sea through a pleasant wooded valley at Inverkirkaig, where there is a fine pebbly, sandy beach. There is also a double surprise for book lovers here, Achins Bookshop, where one can enjoy browsing the interesting books, and indulging in some nice coffee.

Lochinver from Baddidarach with Canisp and Suilven in the background

On the path to the Falls of Kirkaig

Falls of Kirkaig A path follows the river eastwards from here to the Falls of Kirkaig (about 2 miles) through a woodland of Rowan, Hazel and Aspen. The falls themselves are only 18m high, but after rain, they can be quite dramatic. In spring and early summer Salmon may be seen attempting to leap the falls, but they cannot pass here.

This walk may afford views of Dippers and Grey Wagtails on the river, while Pine Marten live in the woods. The path leads on to the Fionn Loch for wonderful views of Suilven. By continuing round the north side of the loch for another 3 miles, the southern approach to the mountain is reached. Waders such as Dunlin, Redshank and

Greenshank breed on the moors and loch sides. Red and Black-throated Divers breed on the lochs and may be seen flying in with fish to feed their young. Particularly during the breeding season, the adults may be heard calling.

Achmelvich is about 3 miles along the very twisty B869, north of Lochinver. This collection of wonderful sandy beaches backed by dunes and machair has some of the most enchanting sands in the north of Scotland. In early summer the machair becomes a riot of colour with wild flowers.

This is a good area for walking, with paths over the moors back to Lochinver, north along the coast and northeast into the lochan dotted moorland. The camping and caravan site vies with Durness and Big Sand for the most enticing location on the coast.

Clachtoll is about 4 miles further west and also has a fine sandy beach as well as exposures of interesting rocks. An abandoned Salmon fishing station bothy and ice house have been restored and have displays relating to the fishery.

On the south side of the Bay of Stoer, Clachtoll Broch still stands 2m high. The entrance has a massive triangular lintel and there are remains of an intramural staircase. On the east side a wall enclosed an area which may have been a settlement.

Achmelvich

Achmelvich

Debby Snook

Suilven from above Achmelvich

Ranger Huts at Clachtoll and Achmelvich have information and displays relating to the wildlife. An annual Sand Sculpture competition is held at Clachtoll by the Rangers.

Point of Stoer A minor road continues for about 4 miles to Stoer lighthouse, first lit in 1870 and another Stevenson design. It was automated in

Highland calf near Drumbeg

1978 and the former keepers' accommodation is now let out by the National Trust as holiday flats. There are stunning views to the south and east taking in Canisp, Suilven and the Coigach mountains. The Western Isles can be seen on the western horizon.

Old Man of Stoer From the lighthouse it is a two mile walk across moorland and past low cliffs to the Old Man of Stoer, a 61m high stack. There is a fine view from Sidhean Mor (G Big Fairy Hill, 161m), the nearby hill with a radio mast.

Clashmore, Stoer

Stoer Lighthouse

This headland is a good place to look out for cetaceans, especially between July and September. Porpoises are often seen, but Minke Whales, White-sided Dolphins and Killer Whales may also be spotted, especially if shoals of Mackerel or Herring are about. Basking Sharks may also be present.

Culkein is another former Salmon fishing station. An unusual design of ice house sits near the ruined pier. There is a fine small sandy beach, sheltered from every direction but northeast. The nearby headland of Rubh'an Dunain has a ruined dun, a natural arch and caves.

Clashnessie (G *Cleas an easidh*, Glen of the Waterfall) has a pretty little waterfall on the burn about 800m inland.

Panoramic view east and south from the Point of Stoer to Canisp, Suilven, Cul Mor, Stac Pollaidh and the Coigach

Numerous lochans drain into this stream. Red and Black-throated Divers may be seen or heard as they fly in from fishing at sea. It also has a fine little north facing beach.

Drumbeg The B869 continues west through wild country via Drumbeg and Nedd to the A894 south of Kylesku. This road offers some of the best views in the northwest on a clear day. There are many good viewpoints as it winds over rocky moorland and patches of woodland, one of the best being from the west end of Drumbeg.

Ardvar Woods in Glen Ardvar is a remnant of the forests that once covered much of the North Highlands. These old sessile Oakwoods are dominated by Birch but also have Rowan, Hazel, Wych Elm and Oak. A large variety of mosses and lichens grow here.

Kerrachar Gardens are situated in a sheltered spot near the entrance to Loch a Chairn Bhain about 4 miles west of Kylesku. There is no road or path, instead a small ferry runs from the pier next to the Kylesku Hotel.

The gardens have been developed since 1995 on abandoned croftland. They have featured in gardening magazines and, in 2006, *The Independent* included Kerrachar in a list of 10 Best Gardens to Visit in Summer.

Loch Ardbhair and Eddrachillies Bay

SUTHERLAND - THE FAR NORTHWEST

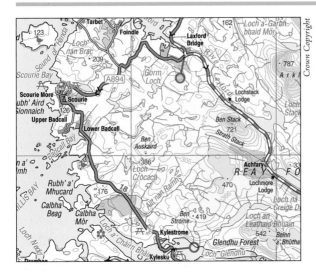

Badcall Bay is one of the most enchanting of the many fine bays on this coast. It is strewn with small islands and a summer evening stroll can be very romantic, just so long as the midgies are not out! A Salmon fishing station formerly operated here. The old fishing station and jetty date from about 1840 and a Salmon farm now occupies the site. The nearby old manse is now the highly rated Eddrachillies Hotel.

Scourie (G *Scobh Airigh*, Shieling by the Little Wood) is a small village situated at the head of Scourie Bay. A small sandy beach is backed by an area of machair. Now bypassed by the A894, the village is a good place to stop and also a fine base from which to explore the far northwest. Most of the cottages date from the 19th century.

Loch a'Mhuilinn NNR is situated on the coast south of Badcall Bay. It is the most northerly patch of native Oak woodland in UK. Dominated by Birch, it has Rowan, Hazel, Aspen and Willow trees as well as a large flora of lichens and mosses. It is a peaceful and pleasant place to stop.

All around there are dramatic exposures of twisted and convoluted Lewisian Gneiss, with later Scourian Dykes, where molten rock has infiltrated cracks. The low rocky shores offer fine walking as well as

Loch a'Mhuilinn NNR

Duartmore between Scourie and Kylestrome

Badcall Bay has many small islands

lovely views to Handa and over Eddrachillies Bay.

Tarbat and Fanagmore are reached by a small side road north of Scourie which crosses rocky moorland and many lochans on the way. Divers breed on these lochans and waders in the marshy areas.

Loch Laxford (ON *Lax*, Salmon) is larger than Badcall Bay, but also strikingly beautiful, with its many islands and rocky headlands. The River Laxford is fed by Loch Stack and both are famed for their Salmon angling. Road cuttings on Laxford Braes show interesting patterns in the Lewisian Gneiss rocks.

Near Laxford Bridge, mudflats, sandy areas and saltmarsh attract many waders. Grey and Common Seals are often present and this is prime Otter territory. The many small patches of woodland attract small birds.

Loch Stack and Arkle There are fine views of Arkle (ON *Ark Fjell*, Flat-Topped Hill, 787m) from the A838 around Loch Stack. The mountain is made of Cambrian Quartzite from whose glistening appearance it gets its name. Black-throated Divers nest around the lochs here, Greenshanks may be heard calling and Dippers may be seen by the river. Several other waders breed here.

Scourie from the south

Arkle and Loch Stack

Shona McMillan

335

Puffins

Laurie Campbell

The Great Stack of Handa

Birds In summer the island is home to over 180,000 nesting seabirds. The high cliffs (120m) and the Great Stack hold thousands of Guillemots, Razorbills, Puffins, Shags, Kittiwakes and Fulmars, while Great Skuas, Arctic Skuas and gulls nest on the hill. Handa is easily the best place in the area to see breeding seabirds in large numbers.

HANDA (ON, *Sand-ey*, Sandy Isle) is a small island near Scourie famous for its birds and wild flowers, taking its name from its beaches. It is composed of Torridonian Sandstone which gives it a totally different character to much of the nearby mainland, and which weathers to make the ledges so liked by birds.

Although it is now uninhabited, over 60 people lived here until 1847, when they all emigrated to Nova Scotia. They were not cleared, but left as they had become over reliant on potatoes, and blight caused their crop to fail. This seems unlikely to be the entire reason as there is a wealth of birds and fish as well as fertile land to grow other crops.

Wild Flowers The combination of sandstone rock, lots of bird droppings and low grazing pressure means that Handa has a very interesting selection of wild flowers. Probably they are at their best in late June when Thrift, Spring Squill, Grass of Parnassus, Sea Plantain and many others give a wonderful display of colour.

Razorbills

Great Skua (Bonxie)

Visit A small ferry runs from Tarbet during the summer on demand and depending on the weather. Tarbet is about 5 miles north of Scourie. Handa is a somewhat romantic place with its ancient graveyard and ruined settlement near the landing.

A path leads across the hill to the spectacular northwest cliffs and the Great Stack. In early summer the ledges are occupied by thousands of breeding Guillemots and Razorbills. Puffins nest in burrows on top of the stack, but there are also some on Handa itself.

The path follows the high cliffs before it drops to a rocky shoreline and then back to the old settlement. There are spectacular views north to Cape Wrath, east to the mountains of Assynt and south to the Stoer Peninsula and Coigach.

Handa was undoubtedly used by the Vikings because of its sheltered landing and ease of access from the Minch. This would have been one of the better places to pull up a longship on this hard and inhos-

Laurie Campbell

Handa has a fine little beach

pitable coast. There is an ancient ruined chapel in the graveyard, where traditionally people from the nearby mainland were buried so that they were not dug up by wolves. The ruined settlement has an

ancient and slightly mysterious feeling about it, especially on a misty day. According to folklore the ancient inhabitants had their own queen, the eldest widow, and a parliament which met to decide on daily chores.

Guillemots

Arctic Skua

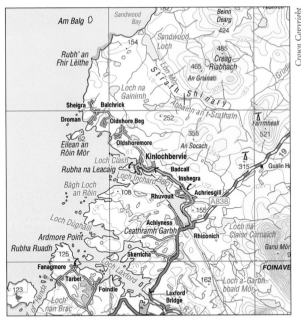

Loch Inchard (G *Innis Ard*, Pasture Head) is the last sheltered inlet before Cape Wrath. In former times this area was famous for its yellow cattle and was heavily forested. Parts of the landscape remain very green today and there is evidence of ancient settlement.

Kinlochbervie is now a major landing port for white fish trawlers and the fish market makes an interesting visit during an auction. The flurry of activity as the catch is landed, sorted, sold and despatched on trucks is in great contrast to the relaxed atmosphere which pervades most of the time.

Apart from a number of inshore boats which catch shellfish, most of the trawlers are from the northeast and base themselves here to save fuel, the crews returning home at the weekends. Sadly the Fishermen's Mission is now closed.

Oldshoremore beach from the east in winter

Oldshoremore beach

Before the roads were built in the 1830s, all access was by sea. In 1936 a new pier was built for the MacBrayne's steamer, which called regularly with supplies. After WWII road improvements meant that this service stopped and the Glasgow steamer was no more. Harbour developments have continued over the years as have road improvements which have sustained Kinlochbervie's port status.

Loch Inchard

Oldshoremore The road west of Kinlochbervie passes the crofting townships of Oldshoremore, Oldshore Beg, Balchrick and Sheigra. Each has an attractive beach, backed by dunes and machair. They are different in character, but all have lovely sands, sheltered on each side by rocky headlands.

Perhaps the finest is the one

Kinlochbervie Fishselling Co truck

Achlyness, Loch Inchard

Magnus with Cotton Grass

Sandwood Bay from the south

at Polin. There are very interesting rock exposures especially in the low cliffs of Oldshoremore. In summer the machair is covered by a colourful carpet of over 200 species of wild flowers.

Sandwood Bay (ON *Sand Vik*, Sandy Bay) is a four mile hike across the moorland from a car park near Blairmore. This beach is nearly 2 miles long and is said to be the home of a mermaid, who lures seamen with her hauntingly beautiful songs. Many ships were certainly wrecked here in the days of sail and sometimes people have a feeling of a slight shiver down their back, an unease that makes them eager to leave. Certainly the house is said to be haunted.

The stack, **Am Buchaille** (G The Shepherd), stands to the south, while Cape Wrath is 8 miles of hard trekking to the north. The beach is backed by

a large area of sand dunes and machair best in early summer for rare wild flowers. Recently a large expanse around Allt Briste has been fenced off to exclude deer and sheep. It has been planted with thousands of native trees to regenerate some of the forest that formerly stood here.

Sandwood Bay and Am Buchaille

Building sandcastles at Polin

Shona McMillan

Foinaven reflected

Foinaven (G *Fion Bheinn*, White Mountain) The peaks of Ben Stack (721m), Arkle (787m), Foinaven (908m) and Carnstackie (800m) dominate the eastern horizon. Ben Stack is composed of Lewisian Gneiss while the others are all composed of Cambrian Quartzite which gleams in the sun, especially after rain. These mountains may not be very high but they present spectacular views along the A838 on the road to Durness.

They have steep scree covered slopes, and great corries, where frost shattered quartzite has tumbled downwards, but also gentler slopes allowing access to walkers. All but Ben Stack involve long treks over rough ground.

Srath Dionard runs southeast between Carnstackie and Foinaven. A track follows the river up the valley, from which there are dramatic views of the eastern corries of Foinaven and the screes of Conamheall (482m). The lonely A838 continues north through a bleak landscape which suddenly becomes green and lush near the Kyle of Durness when the outcrop of limestone at Durness is reached.

Foinaven in winter

Srath Dionard

Shona McMillan

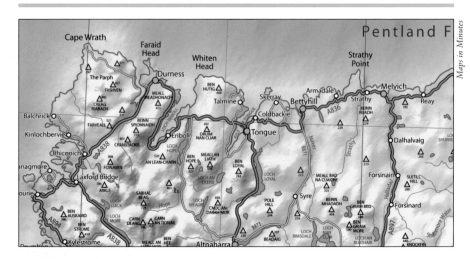

Maps in Minutes

Cape Wrath lighthouse

The north coast of Sutherland stretches from Cape Wrath in the west to Strathy Point and Melvich in the east. It is a gentler coast than that of the west, with three large indentations, the Kyle of Durness, Loch Eriboll and the Kyle of Tongue. Apart from Ben Hope (927m) and Ben Loyal (764m) in the west, much of the hinterland is relatively low lying with blanket peat bog.

The landscape is dotted with many lochs, large and small. Strath More, Strathnaver and Strath Halladale were all formerly inhabited. Evidence can be seen of this in the form of chambered cairns, brochs and more recent ruined farmsteads and settlements.

Most of this area made up the former Pictish and Norse province of Strathnaver. It

Midsummer sunrise at Sango Sands, Durness

The Kyle of Tongue and Ben Loyal

was MacKay or Reay country and was for centuries the scene of disputes between the MacKays and their neighbours, the Sinclairs, Sutherlands, MacLeods, and MacKenzies. Eventually it was nearly all bought up by the Sutherland Estate, which introduced large scale sheep farming in the 19th century.

The north of Sutherland is an ideal place for nature lovers, its varied habitats harbouring many interesting species of birds, mammals, insects and plants. Perhaps the diversity of wild flowers is the most remarkable feature of this landscape.

Primula scotica

Looking west from Strathy Point

Strath Halladale and the Flow Country

Pine Marten

Laurie Campbell

345

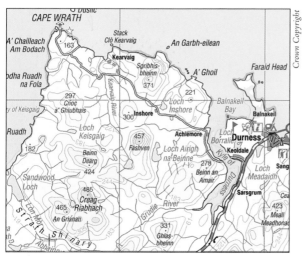

Durness itself is located on a large outcrop of Limestone, making for fertile soils and thus attractive for settlement. There are also outcrops of Limestone on the east side of Loch Eriboll.

East of the Moine Thrust the rocks are Moine Schists, which are very hard and result in a vast area of peat bog with a few hills and mountains. Ben Hope is the highest and rises to 927m. It is the most northerly Munro (mountain over 3,000ft).

DURNESS is the most remote and least populated parish in the UK, with only 2.4 people per square mile. Despite this it has a vibrant community and a long history. Most of the coastline is cliffs, reaching 190m at Clo Mor. The major inlets of the Kyle of Durness and Loch Eriboll are different in character. The former is shallow and sandy, while the latter is much larger and very deep.

Geology To the west, the plateau of The Parph is composed of Lewisian Gneiss overlain in places with Torridonian Sandstone. It is mostly peaty moorland with rolling hills. Between the Kyle and Eriboll a range of Quartzite hills stretches from Foinaven (908m) to Beinn Ceannabeinne (383m). The Moine Thrust follows the east slopes of Loch Eriboll and onward in a southeasterly direction.

Archaeology Most of the ancient sites visible today are concentrated on Limestone areas. These include several Neolithic chambered cairns, Bronze Age cist burials, Iron Age houses, souterrains, brochs and duns. Apart from a Norse burial at Balnakeil, there is no physical evidence of the Vikings. However there is an abundance of Old Norse placenames, which attest to settlement.

The Kyle of Durness

Sango Bay with Faraid Head in the background

The Military In WWII a radar station was established here in 1940 and involved hundreds of personnel. Many ruinous buildings remain from this time. A new radar station was planned after the war, but was abandoned in 1954 before it became operational. Since 1932 Garvie Island, the adjacent coast and sea have been used as a live firing range by warships. Aircraft practice dropping live bombs, firing guns and missiles, as well as low level attacks. Access to Cape Wrath is curtailed at times.

Chambered cairn above the Kyle of Durness

Ceannabeinne Beach east of Durness

Shona McMillan

DURNESS
Origin of the name

In the Sagas and old manuscripts the parish is always referred to as *Dyrnes* (ON *Dyr Nes*, Deer Headland). Until 1724 the parish extended from Kylesku to the Water of Borgie. Now it encompasses Durness itself, the Parph district to the west and the Moine, including Eriboll to the east. Many of the placenames are of Norse origin, suggesting that this area was well settled by the Vikings. However some are undoubtedly pre-Norse, including Parph, Moine and Loyal. The names may be Pictish or even handed down from the original settlers.

Smoo Cave in 1821 by William Daniell

Wildlife The landscape is largely devoid of trees, partly due to exposure and partly because excessive grazing by sheep and deer prevents any regeneration of saplings. However, the Limestone areas support an extremely diverse range of over 500 species of plants. Alpine plants grow at sea level here. The clifftops support maritime heath, with *Primula scotica* and other rare plants.

Smoo Cave (ON *Smuggja*, rocky cleft) has the biggest entrance of any sea cave in the UK. It is about 15m high, while the main chamber is 60m by 40m. Allt Smoo plunges 25m down a sink hole into an inner cave. The waterfall can be observed from a platform. Further caves can only be reached by means of boat tours.

Geodha Smoo and the caves can be accessed by paths and steps from a nearby car park. After heavy rain Allt Smoo swells and flows into the underground pool with a mighty roar.

John Lennon had a cousin in Durness and, as a child, used to come here for summer holidays. In 2002 an area next to the village hall was landscaped, part of which was dedicated to the memory of Lennon. He was last here in 1989 with Yoko Ono, Julian and Kyoko.

Walks The Durness Path Network booklet describes a number of interesting walks in the area. These cover most of the places of interest. Many are coastal, but others follow peat roads into the moorland.

Puffins breed on Faraid Head, Divers are present on many of the lochs and Corncrakes are still heard calling here in summer. Durness can also be a good location to seek rare species during migration times.

Badgers, Otters, Foxes and Wild Cats live in the area. Grey Seals haul out to have their young on shingle beaches below Whiten Head, the largest such colony on the Mainland.

John Lennon, Yoko Ono and family at Durness in 1969

John Lennon Memorial Garden

Mather's shop in 1982

Smoo Cave waterfall in the inner cave

Mather's shop in 2006

Smoo Cave is the biggest sea cave in the UK

Geodha Smoo

Balnakeil Bay

Balnakeil Bay (G Township of the Chapel) is a beautiful 1.5-mile arc of sand north of Durness. It is backed by sand dunes and machair which is a sea of colour with wild flowers in summer. To the north **Faraid Head** (G, *am Faire Aite*, the Watch Place, 100m) has an MOD radar station which controls the nearby firing range.

Balnakeil Craft Village is housed in an abandoned 1950s military site. A wide range of businesses occupy these concrete buildings.

They range from a bookshop and cafe to a chocolate factory and a whole variety of other creative outlets. On no account let the stark military architecture put you off.

Fossils The shoreline below the Golf Course has many exposures of stromatolites. These fossil cyanobacteria, or blue-green algae, are some of the earliest forms of life on Earth. Here they date from 480 million years ago, and were responsible for producing our oxygen rich atmosphere.

Balnakeil Kirkyard is the site of a very early Culdean Christian settlement. A ruined chapel here may be on the site of one established by St Maelrubha in the 7th century. The now roofless church was built around 1619 on the site of a much earlier one. There was a monastery here in former times which was rich enough to contribute funds to the Third Crusade in 1190.

There are a number of interesting tombstones, including that of Donald MacMurdo, a local villain who died in 1623,

Marsh Orchid

Stromatolites at Balnakeil Bay

and Rob Donn, who was a bard and composer of Gaelic songs, who died in 1828.

Shinty at New Year In former times Shinty was played on the sands of Balnakeil on Old Christmas and Old New Year's Day. Up to 100 players took part on each side, cheered on by their womenfolk and older men. The game continued until dark and often took to the sea. It was occasionally violent but, as in other traditional events, animosity ended with the game.

Balnakeil House is built on the site of a 7th century monastery. The Bishop of Caithness had a residence here in the 12th century but by the 16th century the house belonged to the chief of Clan MacKay, later Lord Reay.

In 1744 the house was rebuilt in Georgian style. It incorporates the remains of the original towerhouse and remains substantially unchanged today. The farm steading was built in 1801 but destroyed by fire in 1995. The ruinous mill is also 19th century.

The author being photographed at Balnakeil Bay

Thorfinn at Balnakeil Bay

DURNESS GOLF CLUB
Most Northerly
on British Mainland
CLUB CAR PARK

Durness Golf Club sign

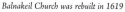

Balnakeil Church was rebuilt in 1619

Frog Orchid

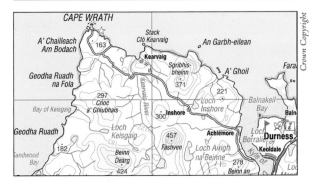

Passing ships radioed details of their cargoes, destinations and estimated time of arrival.

Kearvaig is a beautiful sandy bay about 3 miles east of the Cape. There is a lovely walk from the lighthouse along the clifftops to this enchanting bay. The Vikings are said to have pulled up their boats here.

CAPE WRATH (ON *Hvarf*, Turning Point) is the most northwesterly point of the Scottish mainland.

Lighthouse The engineer in charge of building Cape Wrath lighthouse was Robert Stevenson. It was first lit in 1828, and has an elevation of 122m. Stone for the tower and dwelling houses was quarried at nearby Clais Charnach, near the jetty and landing place used for supplies. The road from the Kyle of Durness also dates from 1828.

The gaunt building on the hill above the lighthouse is Lloyd's Signal Station which operated from about 1903 until 1932.

The rock at the east end of the bay is nicknamed *The Cathedral* on account of its twin spires. The beach has fine white sand with shingle at the top. Another mile to the east the dramatic Torridonian Sandstone cliffs of Clo Mor are the highest on the UK mainland at nearly 200m.

Kyle of Durness The sandbanks and channels in the Kyle change from year to year. There are stunning views from the road between Ferry House and Daill, which change with the tides, weather and light.

Getting there A small passenger ferry runs in summer from the jetty at Keoldale to another jetty on the Cape side.

Cape Wrath lighthouse

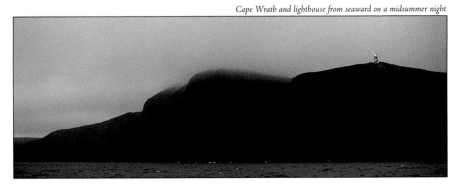

Cape Wrath and lighthouse from seaward on a midsummer night

The Kyle of Durness has many sandbanks - Faraid Head is in the distance

Dulsic Rock is a major hazard off Cape Wrath

Cliffs east of Clo Mor between Kearvaig and Cape Wrath

From there minibuses take visitors the 12 miles to the lighthouse. If the weather is fine there is a spectacular walk back along the cliffs.

Military exercises take place regularly on the Cape Wrath Range. Live firing of munitions by warships, and by the Army of artillery, mortars, and

missiles is carried out on the Range. Aircraft practise bombing and test fully armed bombs, missiles, and cannons on Garvie Island.

Access to Cape Wrath and adjacent areas may be restricted during these exercises, which are necessary, *"to maintain the skills our armed forces*

need to carry out the tasks which they may be called upon to perform."

CAPE WRATH
Origin of the name

The name Cape Wrath is a map-maker's invention. The Sagas refer to it as *Hvarf*. Ptolemy's map has a *Torvedunum* which may be this prominent headland. It is interesting that the hill behind the lighthouse is called Dunan. Parph and Dunan may well be ancient pre-Celtic names, perhaps also meaning turning point, thus giving the name Ptolemy quotes.

Kearvaig from the west

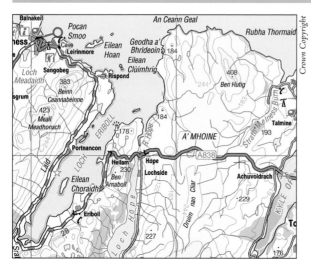

King Haakon and his fleet anchored here on their return from their unsuccessful mission south in October 1263. In 1937 *HMS Hood* anchored here for 9 days, during which the crew left its name on the hillside. During May 1945 the loch was the site of the surrender of over 30 German U-boats. The servicemen of WWII called it *Lock 'Orrible* due to the lack of shore facilities.

Rispond has the only harbour in the area. It was developed in the 1780s by Peterhead merchants trading in fish and kelp. Until the roads were built in the 1830s it was the landing place for supplies, most of which came from Orkney.

Loch Eriboll (ON *Eyrr Bolstadir*, Ayre Farm, from the tombolo at Ard Neakie, is about 10 miles long, with a depth of 30m to 120m, and has, for a long time, been used as a safe anchorage by ships, including the Royal Navy. A tradition developed when crew members were given leave to go ashore. They set out the names of their ships in stones on the hillside.

Ard Neakie is joined to the east shore of the loch by an ayre. In the 1870s the Reay Estate opened a quarry and built limekilns on the island to supply fertiliser for its land reclamation projects.

Loch Eriboll and Ben Hope

Ard Neakie and Loch Eriboll from the northeast

Whiten Head, at the east entrance to Loch Eriboll, rises to over 170m. The Quartzite cliffs gleam white in the sun and have many caves. The largest mainland colony of Grey Seals in the UK comes ashore to pup here each autumn. There is no path to Whiten Head, which is a 5 mile hike along the cliffs north of the road.

Strath Beag is an attractive little valley at the south end of the loch. It runs inland for about 2 miles. A path goes up the eastern side, then follows the river to deciduous woodland. Pine Martens live in the woods and Otters may be seen here. Dippers and Wagtails feed on the river, and Golden Eagles frequently quarter the ground. Red and Black-throated Divers breed on the high lochans.

A'Mhoine (G Peaty Ground) is a rather monotonous area of rolling hills, lochans and peat bog between Loch Eriboll and Tongue. The rocks are hard Moine Schist, derived from sandstones and mudstones which were metamorphosed before being once more thrust to the surface.

The Moine Thrust takes its name from the a'Moine area. From Whiten Head to Strath Beag there are exposures all along the eastern slopes of Loch Eriboll of features of these massive earth movements, where older rocks were thrust over younger strata. The Arnaboll thrust subsequently carried Lewisian Gneiss over this already complex sequence.

Whiten Head in 1921 by William Daniell

Whiten Head from Ceannabeinne east of Durness

Herding sheep on Loch Eriboll

A'Mhoine landscape, looking southwest over Clar-loch Mor to Ben Loyal

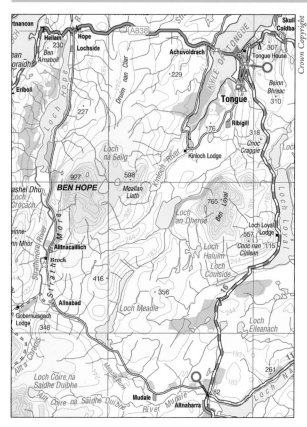

Ben Hope (ON *Hjop*, Bay, 927m) is the highest mountain in the north. Its northern and western aspects are dramatic and craggy. It can be climbed from Alltnacaillich (NC459457) by following a well marked, but steep and rocky path for about 3.5 miles. The panoramas from the summit are worth the climb. Many alpine wild flowers grow on the mountain.

Loch Hope is over 5 miles long, and drains to Loch Eriboll by the short River Hope. It is famous for its Sea Trout and Salmon angling and it is the most highly reharded of all Scottish lochs. The road passes good farmland with grazing cattle as well as abundant evidence of ancient human occupation.

Dun Dornaigil (NC457450) is a well preserved broch, still rising to 6.7m. It has an impressively large triangular lintel stone, and is well situated to guard the fertile valley of Strath More. In the 19th century the interior was filled with stones to stop it falling down, so it is obscured.

STRATH MORE The main road from Eriboll to Tongue passes through the plateau of a'Mhoine. It offers fine views of Ben Hope, Ben Loyal and the Kyle of Tongue, often with pretty lochans in the foreground. A much more scenic route is the narrow side road down the east side of Loch Hope to Altnaharra, passing the west flank of Ben Hope on the way to remote Altnaharra.

Strath More continues south of the broch over lonely moorland. There are particularly fine views over Loch Meadie to the southwestern flanks of Ben Loyal. The road passes several isolated farms and follows the River Mudale to Loch Naver. This narrow single track road is remote and offers an opportunity to see Red Deer and Golden Eagles.

Ben Hope from the A'Mhoine road

Fishermen on Loch Hope

Laurie Campbell

Golden Eagle

Altnaharra (G *Allt* N *Herra*, Stream of the Parish) is one of the remotest villages in the UK. It holds the record for the lowest temperature, of minus 27.2°C in December 1995. It is a popular base for anglers, deer stalkers, climbers and, hill walkers. From here the A836 goes north to Tongue and south to Lairg. The B873 follows Loch Naver and then lonely Strathnaver to Bettyhill. At Syre the B871 heads east to Kinbrace.

River Mudale at Altnaharra

Loch Loyal The road north to Tongue passes Loch Loyal and the eastern ramparts of Ben Loyal. The many lochs here are the haunt of Red and Black-throated Divers, while Greenshank, Golden Plovers and Dunlin also breed.

Ben Loyal from the southeast

Dun Dornaigil in Strath More below Ben Hope

Purple Saxifrage

Laurie Campbell

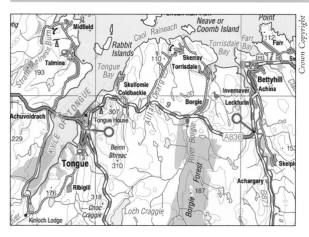

TONGUE (ON *Tonga*, Tongue) is a sheltered village on the east side of the Kyle of Tongue. For long this was Reay territory, which stretched from Kylesku to Bighouse, but by 1830 all this land belonged to the Sutherland Estate.

Kyle of Tongue A causeway and bridge across the Kyle was opened in 1971 as part of road improvements to the far northwest. This means that visitors no longer have to negotiate the winding 10 miles around the head of the Kyle. However those who wish to explore this quiet road will find chambered cairns,

cup-marked stones and a broch. There are also wonderful views over Ben Loyal.

Varrich Castle stands on a promontory above the Rhian Burn. It is most likely of Norse origin and may be the *Beruvik* of the *Orkneyinga Saga*. Later it was a MacKay stronghold. A path leads up to it from the village. There are fine views down the Kyle from here, and even better from An Garbh Chnoc (124m) to the south.

Cnoc Fhreiceadain (G Watch Hill, 307m) above Coldbackie offers fine views across the Kyle and the Pentland Firth.

This little hill is notable for its rounded top. Nearby Ben Tongue (300m) has good vistas to the west.

Ben Loyal (perhaps pre-Celtic, 764m) is a Syenite volcanic intrusion with four summits. Its most spectacular aspect is probably from the north from the car park on the Kyle of Tongue causeway. Another fine viewpoint is over Lochan Hakel on the old road round the Kyle. The normal ascent route follows a track from Ribigill Farm about 2 miles south of Tongue.

Kinloch chambered cairn (NC594587) is ruined but its original form can just be made out from the surviving upright stones. No other Neolithic structures exist here, but clearly people were present 5,000 years ago. A large shell midden near the west end of the Kyle bridge is further settlement evidence.

Dun na Maig (NC553530) is a ruined Iron Age broch at the head of the Kyle. The walls are still 3m high, with an intramural staircase, entrance passage with guard cell and

The Kyle of Tongue from the causeway

Varrich Castle and Ben Hope from Tongue

ramparts. There are fine views down the Kyle from here.

Iron Age Dun Loch Hakel has a dun at its south end, called Grianan (NC559527). This is most likely an Iron Age roundhouse. On the south shore two large boulders have cupmarks and rings carved on them, probably dating from the Bronze Age. There are over 30 cups about 8cm in diameter, many of which have rings up to 18cm in diameter

around them. Further along the road towards Kinloch another stone also has cup marks carved into it.

Scrabster, off the side road going round the Kyle, is a small settlement cleared of people in 1821. The ruins include 12 longhouses, with outbuildings and a kiln for drying grain. This ancient village is surrounded by a boundary dyke to keep livestock off the infields. It has a

feeling of desolation and sadness.

Tongue House stands a mile north of the village overlooking the Kyle. It is the ancient seat of Clan Mackay and dates from the 1670s. The previous house was burnt in reprisal for Lord Reay's support of the Royalists in the Civil War. This was the first of a series of financial disasters and eventually everything was sold to the Sutherland Estate.

The bridge and causeway across the Kyle of Tongue

Kyle of Tongue Cnoc an Fhreiceadain and Ben Tongue from Melness

Clan Mackay has an illustrious military past, during the 30 Years War, in 1715 and 1745 on the government side, in the Crimean War and at Waterloo, where the lone piper was a Mackay.

1746 Jacobite Rebellion In early 1746 the ship *Prince Charles* was chased into the Kyle by the Royal Navy frigate *HMS Sheerness*. The Jacobite ship was in fact the commandeered Royal Navy ship, *HMS Hazard* and was carrying £13,000 in French gold to pay the rebels as well as supplies bound for Inverness.

After a three hour gun battle, the rebel ship was disabled and was grounded on a sandbank off Melness. The crew got off with the gold in the dark but were stopped near Loch Hakel. The MacKays did not support the Jacobites and soon rounded up the crew and the ship's valuable cargo. Meanwhile a force of 1,500 men was sent north by Bonnie Prince Charlie, only to be apprehended en route by the MacKenzies. It has been said that the outcome at Culloden may have been different if the men in Inverness had been paid and stores had arrived.

Melness (ON *Melr Nes*, Sand Headland) The single track road which heads north around the Kyle passes a number of crofting townships including Melness, Midtown, Skinnet, Talmine, Portvasgo and Midfield. Many of these crofts were created in the 19th century for displaced tenants.

There are several fine beaches and a small harbour, which the road winds through. With fine views over the Kyle and many good places for walks this tranquil area is well worth visiting.

Talmine, Melness

Varrich Castle

Old boat ashore at Talmine, Melness

Tongue from the west

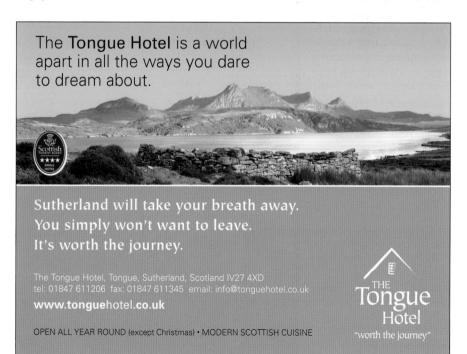

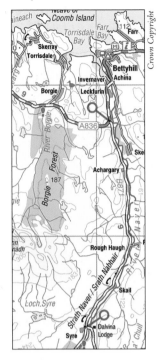

Bettyhill is said to take its name from the Countess of Sutherland who created the village to accommodate evicted tenants. It occupies the peninsula between the estuary of the River Naver and Farr Bay. For many years there was a large Salmon netting fishery at Navermouth. Today only an icehouse, pier, and ruined buildings remain.

Strathnaver Museum is housed in the Old Parish Kirk of St Columba, built in the 1700s. It has many interesting displays related to the clearances, the archaeology, and the history of the area. The Clan McKay Room is upstairs. It has information and exhibits which tell the story of the clan.

Farr Stone before cleaning

STRATHNAVER The Province of Strathnaver originally stretched from Kylesku to Caithness. There is evidence of long settlement here from ancient times with Neolithic chambered cairns, stone circles, Bronze Age cist burials and Iron Age brochs. A mixture of Gaelic and Norse placenames as well as many ruined farmsteads and settlements evoke more recent times.

The Strathnaver Trail runs 26 miles from Farr Old Parish Kirk to Loch Naver. There are 29 marked sites along the way which take in over 5,000 years of settlement in this lovely valley. The river, moorland and lochs are home to many birds and plants.

Bettyhill and Farr Bay

Strathnaver Museum

The Farr Stone dates from the 8th century or so. It stands on the west side of the kirkyard. Unfortunately it was misguidedly cleaned of its centuries of lichens which has greatly diminished its splendour. It has a large wheeled cross with many symbols. There are three other Pictish inscribed stones in the Museum.

Torrisdale Bay from the east

Farr Bay to the east of the village is a lovely sandy beach, backed by dunes and machair. In summer there is an abundance of wild flowers which support several species of bumblebees, some of which are rare. The beach is popular with surfers who take advantage of the big swells which often come into the bay.

Debby Snook

Surfers at Farr Bay

Torrisdale Bay is a smaller version of the Kyle of Tongue, with large areas of tidal sandbanks fed by the River Naver. The area between the mouths of the Rivers Naver and Borgie is famous for its diversity of flora, which results from its various habitats and exposed situation. Plants which are normally alpine flourish near sea level here.

Midsummer sunset over Torrisdale Bay

Farr Bay

These include Crowberry, Mountain Avens, Bearberry, Moss Campion and dwarf shrubs. The banks of the River Naver are quite accessible and full of floral interest in summer. The former NNR itself can be accessed on foot from Invernaver or south of Torrisdale.

Loch Rosail near Syre and Rosal Village

Clearances The clearance of Strathnaver, by the Sutherland Estate, to create sheep farms began in 1814.

This was overseen by the Estate factor, one Patrick Sellar, who later faced trial for his actions.

Rosal clearance village south of Syre

Loch Strathnaver from the east

Donald MacLeod of Rosal said, *"The consternation and confusion were extreme. Little or no time was given for the removal of persons or property; the people striving to remove the sick and the helpless before the fire should reach them; next, struggling to save the most valuable of their effects. The cries of the women and children, the roaring of the affrighted cattle, hunted at the same time by the yelling dogs of the shepherds amid the smoke and fire, altogether presented a scene that completely baffles description, it required to be seen to be believed."*

"A dense cloud of smoke enveloped the whole country by day, and even extended far out to sea. At night an awfully grand but terrific scene presented itself - all the houses in an extensive district in flames at once. I myself ascended a height about eleven o'clock in the

evening, and counted two hundred and fifty blazing houses, many of the owners of which I personally knew, but whose present condition - whether in or out of the flames I could not tell. The conflagration lasted six days, till the whole of the dwellings were reduced to ashes or smoking ruins."

The ruins of Achanlochy village overlook Loch Duinte

Sites to visit The minor road to Skelpick has chambered cairns at Achcoillenaborgie (NC716590) and Skelpick (NC722568). Both are ruined but the chambers and outlines are visible. There are also ruined brochs near both sites, as well as a clearance village overlooking Loch Duinte.

Achcoillenaborgie chambered cairn on the road to Skelpick

Dunviden (NC727519) on the B871 about 6 miles north of Syre is another long inhabited site. The standing stones near the broch are the remains of a chambered cairn, perhaps the stones being used to build the now ruined broch. Nearby a cleared village consists of 5 houses with outbuildings, an intact corn kiln and field walls. Bronze Age hut circles and a burnt mound as well as another nearby broch show the longevity of occupation here.

Achcoillenaborgie chambered cairn on the road to Skelpick

Grummore Broch, Loch Naver

Rosal (NC689416) is today a bleak hillside covered in ruined walls in a forest south of Syre on the B873. In 1814 there were 79 people in 15 houses. Homesteads, fields and a corn kiln can be made out under the long grass. An interpretative trail leads around this poignant hillside.

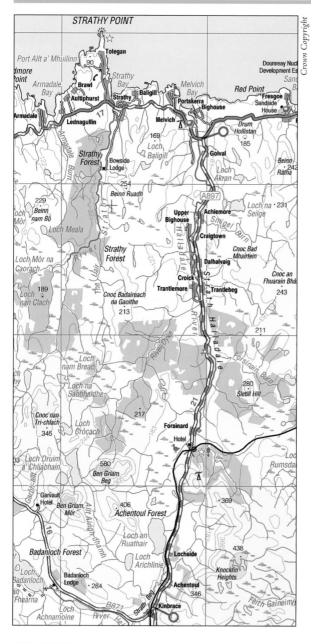

the Highlanders were viewed as anachronistic in the Age of the Enlightenment.

The tenants were relocated in coastal settlements, with small patches of land. Many chose to emigrate to the New World instead. Their former lands were turned into large sheep runs and leased to farmers from the south. Sheep farming on this scale did not last.

Geology Outliers of Old Red Sandstone mean that some of the land here is quite fertile, especially around Strathy itself, Portskerra and eastwards from Bighouse. This explains the sudden appearance of fields in an otherwise barren landscape.

Strathy Point Lighthouse was built in 1958, the last manned one to be built in Scotland and the first to be powered by mains electricity. It was automated in 1997. There are fine views along the coast from here. The clifftop vegetation includes many rare plants including *Primula scotica*. Puffins and other seabirds nest here.

Strathy is a small crofting settlement at the mouth of the River Strathy. Strathy Bay has a fine sheltered, but north facing sandy beach. The coastline of Strathy Point has spectacular low cliffs.

A track follows the River Strathy for about 10 miles into the moorland, passing Strathy Forest and many

STRATHY In 1790 an Edinburgh lawyer by the name of Honeyman bought the Strathy Estate and promptly started the process of clearances and agricultural improvement which were to be so ruthlessly carried out by the Sutherland Estate. The old traditions and culture of

Bighouse Lodge and the estuary of the Halladale River from Melvich

lochans and marshy areas. This is prime territory for a variety of rare birds, including Greenshanks and divers.

Portskerra was created during the clearance of Strath Halladale as a fishing village. There is a small sheltered harbour with a slipway at Portskerra and a modern but rather exposed pier on the west side of Melvich Bay.

A memorial here commemorates the loss of fishermen in three accidents, in 1848, 1890 and 1918, when at least 26 men were lost in total. The coastline to the west is heavily indented and has pretty coves, natural arches, geos and Puffins.

Melvich lies on the west side of the estuary of the Halladale River. This fertile crofting township includes a large area of machair links. In former times Salmon were netted in large numbers with nets set across the rivermouth and in the bay.

Bighouse (ON *Bygdh hus*, Village House) on the east shore dates from the 1760s. It was built and owned by the Mackays until it was sold to the Sutherland Estate in 1830. The main buildings include the Lodge, Barracks, Icehouse and a walled garden.

Old Split Stone On the A 836 a mile east of Melvich, the Old Split Stone marked the boundary with Caithness.

Portskerra

Strathy Point

The Old Split Stone

Looking towards Melvich at the north end of Strath Halladale

coast near Portskerra and Baligill stand sentinel from the past. They were more likely of spiritual than military design. Cairns, brochs and settlement sites confirm that these fertile outliers on the coast have been long inhabited.

STRATH HALLADALE (ON Holy Valley) is a lovely river valley which extends over 15 miles inland from Melvich to Forsinard. It was never completely cleared in the manner of Strathnaver, perhaps because the Sutherland Estate acquired it after the main clearances. The remote A897 passes at least five ruined brochs, many isolated houses and several modern farms. It makes a splendid alternative route south.

The Halladale River is a classic Highland spate river, where the best catches are usually between one and two weeks after heavy rain. The main fish runs are in July and August. Smolts (young Salmon) are released every year from a hatchery to help maintain the Salmon population. The river is short at only 22 miles, but is fed by the vast expanse of the Flow Country and only rarely runs low.

Local folklore says that an old woman was returning from a shopping trip and was chased by the devil. She ran round the stone three times to escape him. The devil became very angry and in frustration, because he could not catch her, he split it in two.

Beaches and Walks There are fine sandy beaches at Armadale, Strathy and Melvich. All three bays have rivers flowing into them and are sheltered by low cliffs to east and west which are interesting to explore. Melvich Bay with its dunes, large area of machair and riverside area is perhaps the best for wild flowers and bumblebees.

Ancient sites "Forts" on the

The Halladale River south of Bighouse

Train passing Loch an Ruathair south of Forsinard

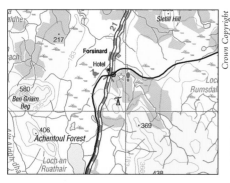

Crown Copyright

Laurie Campbell

Black-throated Diver

RSPB Visitor Centre, Forsinard Railway Station

Sundews are insectivorous

THE FLOW COUNTRY of Caithness and Sutherland is a vast area of blanket peat bog, the largest in the UK and covers about 1,500 square miles. The bogs build up slowly as Sphagnum moss accumulates in areas with poor drainage. The rolling landscape supports a wide range of other plants in pools, on hummocks, ridges and hills.

The Flow Country near Forsinard

Between 1979 and 1987 large areas of the Flow Country were drained and planted with conifers, rich investors taking advantage of tree planting grants and tax breaks. By 1988 it was becoming clear that these activities were destroying this great wilderness and the grants were stopped. The RSPB have created a nature reserve at Forsinard and felled many trees.

Wildlife Birds such as Greenshanks, Dunlins, Golden Plovers, Arctic Skuas, Common Scoters, Red and Black-throated Divers breed on the moors or around the lochans. Hen Harriers, Short-eared Owls and Golden Eagles may also nest here.

Otters are quite common here and many Salmon spawn in the rivers and burns. Red Deer are also seen, especially in winter when they come down from the hills to feed. There are rare Water Beetles and Dragonflies, and the rare freshwater Pearl Mussel survives in a few places. Insectivorous Butterworts and Sundews are common, while some lochans put on a dazzling display of Water Lilies in summer.

Laurie Campbell

Laurie Campbell

Golden Plover

Pale Butterwort

Greenshank

Forsinard RSPB Reserve is open at all times. It has a flagstone trail which winds through the moor past lochans and peat bog. The Visitor Centre in the railway station is open from April to October and has audiovisuals and live nest watch displays. Guided walks are regularly available. There are many roadside viewing sites.

Forsinard to Helmsdale is about 24 miles via Kinbrace and the Strath of Kildonan in East Sutherland. A circular route of Strath Halladale and Strathnaver via Kinbrace makes a very interesting day trip. Helmsdale is about 15 miles to the southeast of Kinbrace via the Strath of Kildonan and Strath Ullie.

Dragonfly

Flybe Embraer 195 at Inverness Airport

GETTING HERE The North Highlands may appear remote from the perspective of southern Britain, Europe or overseas. The reality is that access is easy whether by air, rail, bus, car or ferry.

AIR SERVICES The main airport is at Inverness which has inbound flights from airports in England, Ireland and other parts of Scotland. Several of these are hubs which have inbound flights from a huge number of European and long-haul cities. Inverness Airport is conveniently located to start a tour of the North Highlands and has car hire available on site.

There are onward connections from Inverness to Kirkwall (Orkney), Sumburgh (Shetland), Stornoway (Lewis) and Balivanich (Benbecula). Helicopter charter is also available from here.

Wick airport has more limited services but is a good arrival point for those exploring Caithness and the far north. Taxis meet scheduled flights and car hire is available locally.

TIMETABLE INFORMATION:

TRAVELINE SCOTLAND

For specific routes and transport modes, times or journeys, the company websites listed should be used. Traveline is open 24 hours, 7 days a week. *"We aim to provide accurate, up to date and impartial timetable information to get you to your destination by the quickest public transport mode."*

"On the Plan your Journey page you can select which mode or modes you wish to travel by. When it is needed, full information on connections will be given to make transfers as smooth as possible."
www.travelinescotland.com
Tel 0871 200 22 33

HIGHLAND COUNCIL

Highland Council website has information and links to local transport providers - air, rail, bus, taxis and ferries. Timetables are available at Visitor Information Centres as well as transport terminals.
www.highland.gov.uk/Links/publictransport.
Tel 01463 702695

INVERNESS AIRPORT SCHEDULED FLIGHTS

easyJet to Bristol, Gatwick & Luton
www.easyjet.com
Tel 0871 244 2366

Flybe to Belfast City, Birmingham, Edinburgh, Gatwick, Jersey (seasonal), Kirkwall, Manchester, Southampton, Stornoway & Sumburgh
www.flybe.com
Tel 0871 700 0535

Highland Airways to Stornoway/Benbecula
www.highlandairways.co.uk
Tel 0845 450 2245

Ryanair to East Midlands
www.ryanair.com
Tel 0871 246 0000

WICK AIRPORT SCHEDULED FLIGHTS

Eastern Airways to Aberdeen
www.easternairways.com
Tel 01652 680600

Flybe to Edinburgh
www.flybe.com
Tel 0871 700 0535

TRAIN SERVICES into Inverness Railway Station are operated by First Scotrail. Details of the various lines are listed below along with websites and telephone numbers for enquiries and booking. The two lines which run north and west from Inverness are very scenic and offer an alternative, slow paced introduction to the North Highlands.

"Sprinter" train on the scenic and remote Far North Line

BUS SERVICES The North Highlands is well served by bus services. National carriers offer connections from every part of Britain, while there are local services provided by Stagecoach and a number of smaller companies.

Details of national companies are listed below. The Highland Council website has useful links to all forms of public transport in the area.

SPECIAL DEALS There are many offers available for users of public transport in the Highlands. These change regularly and their availability and restrictions should be checked in advance.

TRAINS TO INVERNESS AND WITHIN THE NORTH HIGHLANDS

First Scotrail runs services on four lines from Inverness Train Station:

From the South via Aviemore and Perth to Edinburgh and Glasgow with onward connections.

From the East via Nairn and Elgin to Aberdeen.

To the West via scenic Kyle Line to Kyle of Lochalsh.

To the North via the Far North Linet to Thurso and Wick
www.firstgroup.com/scotrail
08457 55 00 33

National Rail Enquiries - Find the best-matched trains for your journey. Covers Britain's National Rail network with train operator and timetable information View live departure and arrival information and make bookings.
www.nationalrail.co.uk
Tel 08457 48 49 50

thetrainline.com For further details about UK trains, visit this site for timetables and online booking.
thetrainline.com
Tel 0870 010 1296

BUS SERVICES TO INVERNESS AND WITHIN THE NORTH HIGHLANDS

Megabus is a Stagecoach company and operates budget bus services throughout Britain including from Edinburgh, Glasgow, Dundee, Perth, and Aberdeen to Inverness.
www.megabus.com
Tel 0870 300 6969

Scottish Citylink operate buses between Inverness and destinations all over Scotland. Visit their web site for timetables. You may be able to benefit from the Explorer Pass with offers for unlimited travel between certain dates. Discount tickets (Smart Cards) are available for travellers over 50 and for students aged 16-25.
www.citylink.co.uk
Tel 08705 505050

Stagecoach operates on local routes all over the North Highlands as well as all over Britain. Stagecoach in the Highlands offers a wide range of tickets to help you make the most of travel in your area.
www.stagecoachbus.com
Tel 01463 239292

Scrabster is near Thurso in Caithness

months to places such as Cape Wrath and Handa Island. Cruises are run from various places, including from Ullapool, Gairloch, John o'Groats and a few harbours on the Black Isle. A small two car ferry also runs from Cromarty to Nigg.

ROAD The North Highlands are easily accessible by road from the rest of Britain. The table below gives distances from somes cities and approximate driving times. Lands End to John o'Groats is 833 miles (833 miles (1341km) and will take about 16 hours by car. The

PORTS There are several ports in the North Highlands from which ro-ro ferry services are run by a several of operators. These include passenger and vehicle routes to Orkney and the Western Isles which run all year round. There is also a summer passenger ferry from John o'Groats to Orkney.

A number of small passenger ferries operate in the summer

FERRIES FROM NORTH HIGHLAND PORTS

NorthLink Ferries operate daily Ro-ro services from Scrabster in Caithness to Stromness in Orkney. They also run services from Aberdeen to Orkney and Shetland.
www.northlinkferries.co.uk
Tel 0845 6000 449

Pentland Ferries operate year-round services from St Margaret's Hope to Gills Bay in Caithness.
www.pentlandferries.co.uk
Tel 01856 831226

John o'Groats Ferries operate a summer passenger service between John o' Groats and Burwick in South Ronaldsay in Orkney.
www.jogferry.co.uk
Tel 01955 611353

Calmac operate year-round ro-ro services from Ullapool to Stornoway in Lewis. They also run services from Uig on Skye to Tarbert on Harris and Lochmaddy in North Uist as well as many other islands in the Hebrides.
www.calmac.co.uk
Tel 08000 665 000

DISTANCES AND AVERAGE DRIVING TIMES

Inverness to

London	555 miles (893km)	11h42m
Dover	625 miles (1006km)	12h42m
Hull	421 miles (678km)	8h42m
Edinburgh	155 miles (250kn)	3h34m
Glasgow	170 miles (274km)	3h55m
Aberdeen	104 miles (167km)	3h09m
Fort William	64 miles (103km)	2h25m
Kyle of Lochalsh	78 miles (126km)	2h18m
Ullapool	57 miles (91km)	1h39m
Scrabster	111 miles (178km)	2h48m
John o'Groats	119 miles (192km)	2h50m
Durness	104 miles (167km)	4h25m

Durness to

Kyle of Lochalsh	152 miles(245km)	6h24m
John o'Groats	93 miles (149km)	3h52m

Please note that the distances are by the most direct routes. Driving times may vary depending on traffic, time of day, weather, road works, individual drivers and vehicles. Rest stops are included.

many alternative methods may take considerably longer.

The main routes north from England are the M1/A1 to Edinburgh. From here the M90 goes to Perth followed by the A9 to Inverness. The M6 becomes the M74/A74 near Carlisle. From Glasgow the M73 and M80/M9 lead to the A9 and Perth, all on motorway or dual carriageway.

The A9 from Perth north is a mixture of single and dual carriageways with some three-lane sections. When busy or in poor conditions this combination can be dangerous, drivers may become impatient and frequently pass in risky places.

There are many good places to visit which are bypassed by the A9. These include Pitlochry, Aviemore and other smaller villages as well as visitor attractions and interesting shops. Fuel and refreshment stops can also be found there.

From Fort William the A82 follows a very scenic route via Loch Ness to Inverness. This is a rather slow and windy

Please pull over to allow following traffic to pass - they might be in a hurry unlike you!

road. There are many suitable locations along Loch Ness to stop, take a break from driving and admire the view.

The A96 from Aberdeen can be a very slow road also and is usually busy with cars, trucks and agricultural machines. As with the other approaches to Inverness there are lots of interesting towns, villages and harbours to explore along the way.

Just east of Inverness, Culloden Battlefield is the site of the defeat of Bonnie Prince Charlie and the Jacobites in 1746. The grim tale is told in a fascinating visitor centre.

CYCLING is not recommended on any of these busy main roads, but once in the North Highlands there is a huge choice of excellent quiet roads to explore the countryside at leisure. Bikes can be hired in Inverness as well as in many smaller places. The best place to start is by doing a search on the Internet.

WALKING Suggested walks are mentioned throughout this book. Most are not very long or strenuous, but proper gear should be worn as the terrain can be wet and/or rough. Ordnance Survey maps are recommended and several good books are suggested in the bibliography, including a number specifically about walks.

Kylesku-style Prawns

CAITHNESS

Castle Arms Hotel
Thurso, Caithness
www.castlearms.co.uk
Tel 01847 851244

Forss House Hotel
By Thurso, Caithness
www.forsshousehotel.co.uk
Tel 01847 861201

Mackays Hotel
Wick, Caithness
www.mackayshotel.co.uk
Tel 01955 602323

Northern Sands Hotel
Dunnet, Caithness
www.northernsands.co.uk
Tel 01847 851270

Park Hotel
Thurso, Caithness
www.parkhotelthurso.co.uk
Tel 01847 893251

Pentland Hotel
Thurso, Caithness
www.pentlandhotel.co.uk
Tel 01847 893202

Portland Arms Hotel
Lybster, Caithness
www.portlandarms.co.uk
Tel 01593 721721

Seaview Hotel
John o'Groats, Caithness
www.seaviewjohnogroats.co.uk
Tel 01955 611220

Sinclair Bay Hotel
Keiss, Caithness
www.sinclair-bay-hotel.co.uk
Tel 01955 631233

St Clair Arms Hotel
Castletown, Caithness
www.st-clair-arms-hotel.co.uk
Tel 01847 821656

The Ulbster Arms
Halkirk, Caithness
www.ulbsterarmshotel.co.uk
Tel 01847 831641

The Weigh Inn
Thurso, Caithness
www.weighinn.co.uk
Tel 01847 893722

SUTHERLAND

Ben Loyal Hotel
Tongue, Sutherland
www.benloyal.co.uk
Tel 01847 611216

Queenie Scallops at Portmahomack

Shieldaig Mussels

Bettyhill Hotel
Bettyhill, Sutherland
www.bettyhill.info
Tel 01641 521352

Big House Lodge
Melvich, Sutherland
www.bighouseestate.com
Tel 01641 531207

Borgie Lodge Hotel
Tongue, Sutherland
www.borgielodgehotel.co.uk
Tel 01641 521332

Dornoch Castle Hotel
Dornoch, Sutherland
www.dornochcastlehotel.co.uk
Tel 01862 810216

Drumbeg Hotel
Lochinver, Sutherland
www.drumbeghotel.co.uk
Tel 01571 833236

Eagle Hotel
Dornoch, Sutherland
www.eagledornoch.co.uk
Tel 01862 810008

Golf Links Hotel
Golspie, Sutherland
www.golflinkshotel.co.uk
Tel 01408 633408

Inchnadamph Hotel
Inchnadamph, Sutherland
www.inchnadamphhotel.co.uk
Tel 01571 822202

Kinlochbervie Hotel
By Lairg, Sutherland
www.kinlochberviehotel.com
Tel 01971 521275

Kylesku Hotel
Lairg, Sutherland
www.kyleskuhotel.co.uk
Tel 01971 502231

Mackay's Rooms & Restaurant
Durness, Sutherland
www.visitmackays.com
Tel 01971 511202

Melvich Hotel
by Thurso, Sutherland
www.melvichhotel.co.uk
Tel 01641 531206

Navidale House Hotel
Helmsdale, Sutherland
www.navidalehousehotel.co.uk
Tel 01431 821258

Newton Lodge Hotel
Kylesku, Sutherland
www.newtonlodge.co.uk
Tel 01971 502070

Old School Hotel & Restaurant
Kinlochbervie, Sutherland
www.oldschoolklb.co.uk
Tel 01971 521383

Overscaig House Hotel
Lairg, Sutherland
www.overscaig.com
Tel 01549 431203

Scourie Hotel
Scourie, Sutherland
www.scourie-hotel.co.uk
Tel 01971 502396

Sharvedda
by Thurso, Sutherland
www.sharvedda.co.uk
Tel 01641 541311

Sutherland Arms Hotel
Golspie, Sutherland
www.sutherlandarmshotel.com
Tel 01408 633234

The Albanach Hotel
Lochinver, Sutherland
www.thealbannach.co.uk
Tel 01571 844407

The Bettyhill Hotel
Bettyhill, Sutherland
www.bettyhill.info
Tel 01641 521352

The Nip Inn
Lairg, Sutherland
www.highlands-hotel.co.uk
Tel 01549 402243

The Royal Marine Hotel
Brora, Sutherland
www.royalmarinebrora.com
Tel 01408 621252

Tongue Hotel
Tongue, Sutherland
www.tonguehotel.co.uk
Tel 01847 611206

Morefield Bouillabaisse

The Anderson Scallops

Haddock and Chips at Portmahomack

Plockton Prawns

ROSS-SHIRE

Applecross Inn
Applecross, Ross-shire
www.applecross.uk.com
Tel 01520 744262

Ardvreck House
Ullapool, Ross-Shire
www.smoothhound.co.uk/hotels/ardvreck
Tel 01854 612028

Argyll Hotel
Ullapool, Ross-shire
www.theargyllullapool.com
Tel 01854 612422

Aultbea Hotel
Aultbea, Ross-shire
www.aultbeahotel.co.uk
Tel 01445 731201

Badachro Inn
Gairloch, Ross-shire
www.badachroinn.com
Tel 01445 741255

Ben Damph Inn
Torridon, Ross-shire
www.thetorridon.com
Tel 01445 791242

Caledonian Hotel
Portmahomack, Ross-shire
www.caleyhotel.co.uk
Tel 01862 871345

Dornie Hotel
Dornie, Ross-shire
www.dornie-hotel.co.uk
Tel 01599 555205

The Dower House
Muir of Ord, Ross-shire
www.thedowerhouse.co.uk
Tel 01463 870090

Kincraig House Hotel
Invergordon, Ross-shire
www.kincraig-house-hotel.co.uk
Tel 01349 85258

Kinlochewe Hotel
Kinlochewe, Ross-shire
www.kinlochewehotel.co.uk
Tel 01445 760253

Kintail Lodge Hotel
Shiel Bridge, Ross-shire
www.kintaillodgehotel.co.uk
Tel 01599 511275

Ledgowan Lodge Hotel
Achnasheen, Ross-shire
www.ledgowanlodge.co.uk
Tel 01445 720252

Loch Torridon Country House Hotel
by Achnasheen, Ross-shire
www.lochtorridonhotel.com
Tel 01445 791242

Morefield Motel
Ullapool, Ross-shire
www.morefieldmotel.co.uk
Tel 01854 6121611

Mushrooms at The Anderson

The Anderson Sirloin Steak

Cajun Sirloin Steak at the Anderson

Steak and Chips at Kinlochbervie

North Kessock Hotel
North Kessock, Ross-shire
www.northkessockhotel.com
Tel 01463 731208

Ord House Hotel
Muir of Ord, Ross-shire
www.ord-house.co.uk
Tel 01463 870492

Oystercatcher
Portmahomack, Ross-shire
www.the-oystercatcher.co.uk
Tel 01862 871560

Plockton Hotel
Plockton, Ross-shire
www.plocktonhotel.co.uk
Tel 01599 544274

Plockton Inn
Plockton, Ross-shire
www.plocktoninn.co.uk
Tel 01599 544222

Pool House Hotel
Poolewe, Ross-shire
www.pool-house.co.uk
Tel 01445 781272

Poolewe Hotel
Poolewe, Ross-shire
www.poolewehotel.co.uk
Tel 01445 781241

Royal Hotel
Cromarty, Ross-shire
www.royalcromartyhotel.co.uk
Tel 01381 600217

Shieldaig Lodge Hotel
Gairloch, Ross-shire
www.shieldaiglodge.com
Tel 01445 741250

Summer Isles Hotel
Achiltibuie, Ross-shire
www.summerisleshotel.com
Tel 01854 622282

The Anderson
Fortrose, Ross-shire
www.theanderson.co.uk
Tel 01381 620236

The Ceilidh Place
Ullapool, Ross-shire
www.theceilidhplace.com
Tel 01854 612103

**The Creel Restaurant &
Charleston House**
Gairloch, Ross-shire
www.charlestonhouse.co.uk
Tel 01445 712497

The Haven
Plockton, Ross-shire
www.havenhotelplockton.co.uk
Tel 01599 544223

The Old Inn
Gairloch, Ross-shire
www.theoldinn.net
Tel 01445 712006

Tigh an Eilean Hotel
Loch Torridon, Ross-shire
www.shieldaig.org
Tel 01520 755251

Ullapool Hotel
Ullapool, Ross-shire
www.ullapoolhotel.com
Tel 01854 612181

Dornoch Fillet Steak

Cocoa Mountain - irresistible!

Grilled Oysters at The Anderson

HOTELS

Bighouse Lodge
Melvich, Sutherland
KW17 7YJ
www.bighouseestate.com
Tel 01641 531207
page 369

Mackay's Hotel
Union Street
Wick, Caithness
KW1 5ED
www.mackayshotel.co.uk
Tel 01955 602323
3***, free wifi broadband
inside front cover

Overscaig House Hotel
Loch Shin
Lairg, Sutherland
IV27 4NY
www.overscaig.com
Tel 01549 431203
3***, free wifi broadband
Eat Scotland recommended
page 209

The Castletown Hotel
Castletown
Near Thurso, Caithness
KW14 8TP
www.st-clair-arms-hotel.co.uk
Tel 01847 821656
2**, free wifi broadband
page 141

Smoo Cave Hotel
Durness, Sutherland
IV27 4PZ
www.smoocavehotel.co.uk
Tel 01971 511227
page 349

The Park Hotel
Thurso, Caithness
KW14 8RE
www.parkhotelthurso.co.uk
Tel 01847 893251
3***, free wifi broadband
page 131

Tongue Hotel
Tongue, Sutherland
IV27 4XD
www.tonguehotel.co.uk
Tel 01847 611206
4****, free wifi broadband
page 361

B&B'S AND GUEST HOUSES

The Clachan
13 Randolph Place
Wick, Caithness
KW1 5NJ
www.theclachan.co.uk
Tel 01955 605384
4****, free wifi broadband
Recently upgraded
page 167

Rhian Guest House
Mrs J Anderson
Rhian Cottage
Tongue, Sutherland
IV27 4XJ
www.rhiancottage.co.uk
Tel 01847 611257
3***, wifi broadband
page 361

Curlew Cottage
Mr & Mrs B R MacGregor
Hilliclay Mains, Weydale
Thurso, Caithness
KW14 8YN
www.curlewcottage.com
Tel 01847 895638
4****
page 131

Sharvedda Guest House
Patsy McKaskill
Strathy Point, Sutherland
KW14 7RY
www.sharvedda.co.uk
Tel 01641 541311
4****
page 368

Ardvreck House
Morefield Brae,
North Road
Ullapool, Ross-shire
IV26 2TH
ardvreck@btconnect.com
Tel 01854 612028
4***, free wifi broadband
page 307

SELF-CATERING

Cathair Dhubh Estate
R & S Glover
Lochinver , Sutherland
IV27 4JB
www.cathairdhubh.co.uk
Tel 01571 855277
4****, free wifi broadband
page 331

**The Corner Town House &
Lorne Apartments**
Duncorran House, Bank Row
Wick, Caithness
KW1 5EY
www.visit-wick.co.uk
Tel 01955 651297
4****, free wifi broadband
page 167

Hillhead Caravans
D & M Macleod
Achmelvich
Lochinver , Sutherland
IV27 4JA
www.lochinverholidays.co.uk
Tel 01571 844454
page 331

Kirkwall Self-Catering Apartments
Broad Street Gardens and
Townhouse
Kirkwall, Orkney
KW15 1DH
Tel 01856 873003
kirkwallapartments.co.uk
page 391

RESTAURANTS

The Captains Galley
The Harbour
Scrabster , Caithness
KW14 7UJ
www.captainsgalley.co.uk
Tel 01847 894999
page 135

TRAVEL

Pentland Ferries
St. Margaret's Hope
South Ronaldsay, Orkney
KW17 2SW
www.pentlandferries.co.uk
Tel 01856 831226
page 387

John o'Groats Ferries
The Ferry Office
John o' Groats, Caithness
KW1 4YR
www.jogferry.co.uk
Tel 01955 611353
page 377

NorthLink Ferries Ltd
Kiln Corner,
Ayre Road
Kirkwall, Orkney
KW15 1QX
www.northlinkferries.co.uk
Tel 0845 6000 449
page 385

VISITOR
ATTRACTIONS

Old Pulteney Distillery
Pulteneytown
Wick, Caithness
KW1 5BA
www.oldpulteney.com
Tel 01955 602371
back cover

The Castle & Gardens of Mey
Mey
Caithness
KW14 8XH
www.castleofmey.org.uk
Tel 01847 851473
page 146

Dunbeath Heritage Centre
The Old School
Dunbeath, Caithness
KW6 6ED
www.dunbeath-heritage.org.uk
Tel 01593 731233
page 181

Waterlines Visitor Centre
Lybster, Caithness
KW3 6AH
banniskirk@lybster.freeserve.co.uk
Tel 01593 721520
page 175

Mary Ann's Cottage
Dunnet
Caithness
KW14 8YD
Tel 01847 851765
page 143

RSPB Peatland Visitor Centre
Forsinard Station
Sutherland
KW13 6YT
www.rspb.org.uk/forsinard
Tel 01641 571225
page 371

Caithness Horizons
Town Hall
Thurso, Caithness
KW14 8AJ
www.caithnesshorizons.co.uk
page 133

FOOD AND DRINK

Mey Selections
34a High Street
Wick, Caithness
KW1 4BS
www.mey-selections.com
Tel 0845 838 0488
page 147

BOOKSHOPS

Loch Croispol Bookshop
Balnakeil Craft Village
Durness, Sutherland
IV27 4PT
lochcroispol@btopenworld.com
Tel 01971 511777
page 349

Ullapool Bookshop
Quay Street
Ullapool, Ross-shire
IV26 2UE
ullapoolbookshop@btconnect.com
Tel 01854 612918
page 307

MV "Hamnavoe" passing the Old Man of Hoy

ORKNEY A visit to these islands, which are visible from Caithness and North Sutherland, is suggested as part of a tour of the North Highlands. Two, year round, ro-ro ferries and a summer-only passenger ferry operate from Caithness. Flights are also operated from Inverness to Kirkwall by Flybe.

It has been said about Orkney, *"...scratch the surface and it bleeds archaeology.."* This comment emphasises the rich archaeological heritage of these islands. The soft green and fertile landscape, beautiful beaches, spectacular cliffs, abundant wildlife, and friendly people are equally important in making up Orcadian culture.

The archipelago lies just north of Mainland Scotland at around 59°N and comprises over 70 islands of which 17 or 18 are inhabited, with a population of around 21,000. The first written reference to the islands is by Pytheas the Greek in 325BC, but they have been inhabited for at least 6,000 years. The timeline from pre-history through historical times to the 21st century is continuous, making the division between past and present at times hard to discern.

Orkney is perhaps most famous for its exceptionally well preserved Neolithic monuments, some of which now enjoy World Heritage status. There is a wealth of additional visitor attractions ranging from archaeological sites, museums, the Highland Park Distillery and St Magnus Cathedral, to a diverse array of craft workshops and shops selling attractive local goods.

The underlying Old Red Sandstone rocks produce fertile soils and agricultural land, most of which is used to raise Orkney's renowned beef cattle. The moorland and spectacular coastal fringes, make it a haven for many species of birds in every season, while in spring and summer wild flowers are abundant.

The maritime climate, combined with the relatively warm Atlantic Ocean, is quite equable, with snow and frost rare in winter. Equally, the temperature rarely exceeds 20 degrees in summer. Situated at the meeting point of the North Sea and Atlantic Ocean, the islands are surrounded by waters abundant in fish and shellfish, adding to the wide variety of locally produced quality foods.

Orkney presents a contrast with much of the North Highlands, except for parts of the north and east coasts where